IMAGES
of America

PARK COUNTY

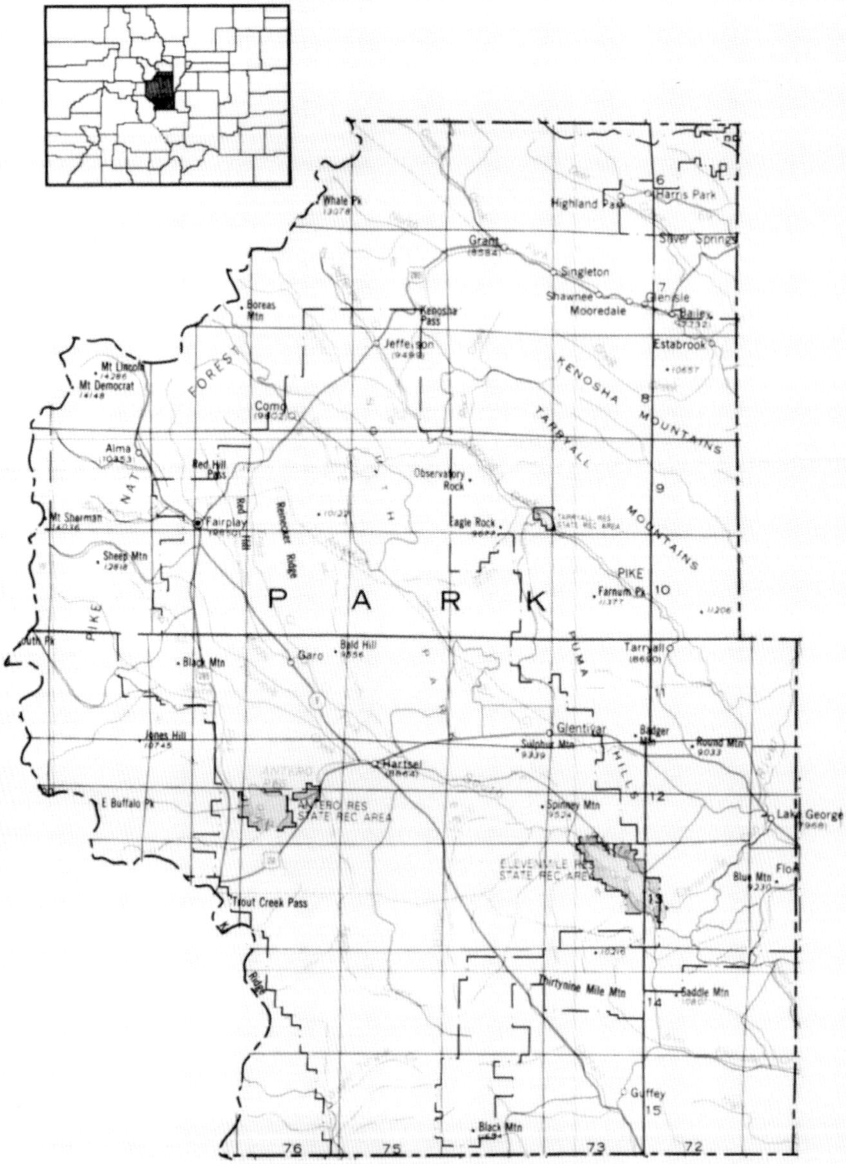

Figure I-1. Park County, Location and General Maps

Park County: Introduction *I-2*

This basic map of Park County depicts major geographical areas, land and water features, and mountain ranges and their respective elevations. (Courtesy of Front Range Research Associates).

On the Cover: The Fairplay Hotel, located in Fairplay, Colorado, was a popular spot for travelers on their way to the gold fields and newcomers needing a place to bunk. This undated photograph, probably taken in the 1880s, shows patrons, both men and women, posing in front of the building. (Courtesy of the Park County Local History Archives.)

IMAGES
of America

PARK COUNTY

Park County Local History Archives

ARCADIA
PUBLISHING

ISBN 978-1-4671-3245-9

Published by Arcadia Publishing
Charleston, South Carolina

Printed in the United States of America

Library of Congress Control Number: 2015937266

For all general information, please contact Arcadia Publishing:
Telephone 843-853-2070
Fax 843-853-0044
E-mail sales@arcadiapublishing.com
For customer service and orders:
Toll-Free 1-888-313-2665

Visit us on the Internet at www.arcadiapublishing.com

To all Park County pioneers, both past and present,
who helped shape the area's history.

Contents

Acknowledgments

The Park County Local History Archives (PCLHA) was founded in 2000 after members of the Park County Historical Society decided there was a need for a separate nonprofit to secure the region's documents and ephemera. Original members included Jerry Davis, Carol Davis, Jane Gilsinger, Michele Kingsford, and Jackie Powell.

Those who participated in this book's project include all board members, Linda Balough, Linda Bjorklund, Jerry Davis, Erica Duvic, Jane Gilsinger, Terry Ketelsen, Gary Minke, Jim Sapp, Bob Schoppe, Amy Under, and Christie Wright, coordinator. A special thanks to Jane Gilsinger, Linda Bjorklund, and Diana Copsey-Adams for their editing prior to publication.

The PCLHA would like to thank all of those who have visited our offices, donated materials, emailed us with questions, interviewed for our oral history project, and showed an interest in the local history. A special thank-you goes to the county commissioners, Mark Dowaliby, Dick Hodges, and Mike Brazell, for providing office space in the historic "old courthouse" for our use. We have truly come home.

Unless otherwise noted, all images appear courtesy of the Park County Local History Archives. Other images in this volume appear courtesy of the Andy Anderson collection, Denver South Park & Pacific Historical Society (AADSP&PHS), and the Denver South Park & Pacific Historical Society (DSP&PHS.)

Introduction

What is now Park County, Colorado, has undergone millions of years of changes, existing as a semitropical inland sea, undergoing volcanic eruptions, and experiencing mighty upheavals of the Ancestral Rockies that were over twice the height of the current Rocky Mountains. Each era played a part in what Park County looks like today. Over 30 million years ago, the eruption of Thirty-nine Mile Mountain closed the southern drainage of the inland sea and turned its outflow through Platte Canyon. Other volcanic activity pushed minerals and molten metals throughout the interior of the mountains, while erosion and glaciers began to grind and tumble the tall Ancestral Rockies into the basin of the inland sea, forming the base and rich soil of the mountain valley today called the South Park. The Rockies of today emerged and reached their present heights, with four peaks topping 14,000 feet above sea level in Park County and many more reaching 13,000 feet.

Archeologists have found evidence that people have occupied the South Park for at least 12,000 years. They used stone, and wood petrified by volcanic ash, to fashion weapons and tools. There is evidence that they established and returned to camps in the area to enjoy the high country's cool, pleasant summers before returning to warmer winter quarters in the lower altitudes. Native peoples such as the Utes, Cheyenne, Arapahoe, Comanche, and, occasionally, other tribes enjoyed abundant summer hunting and comfortable warm-weather living conditions for centuries. In the late 1700s and early 1800s, fur trappers came to the area, which they called Bayou Salado, to collect beaver pelts for trade with merchants back East.

One of those trappers, James Purcell of Kentucky, was captured and jailed by the Spanish, who believed the area was part of their claim to the New World. In the winter of 1806, he told his fellow prisoner, explorer Zebulon Pike, of finding gold three years earlier in the South Park. Other than a record of it in Pike's expedition report to Pres. Thomas Jefferson's administration, neither made much of the gold discovery.

It was not until 1858 that a gold find near Cherry Creek in what is now Denver triggered a rush to collect the precious metals that had lain for millions of years within the Rocky Mountains. Thousands of hopeful prospectors raced to nearly every part of Colorado seeking their fortunes, and many hit "pay dirt" in Park County. Towns and mining camps sprang up nearly overnight in places like Tarryall, Hamilton, and Fair Play Diggings.

Word got out that there was gold in the western portion of the Kansas Territory (which stopped at the Continental Divide). Colorado, which would split off and become its own territory in 1861, had added portions of land west of the divide to complete the boundaries it now has as a state.

Explorers worked their way up through Platte Canyon toward the gold strikes of South Park (the largest of three Colorado "parcs," as the French trappers called the large valley hunting grounds). Numerous wagon trains, small groups, and single adventurers sought lodging and renewed supplies at a number of ranches and farms that had sprung up along the North Fork of the South Platte River. This initiated the first of a continuing tradition of local residents providing lodging and, later, recreation opportunities throughout Park County.

Mining provided the impetus for those from the Eastern United States and Europe to escape the effects of a severe economic depression and seek riches in the Colorado Territory. Others, however, found their livelihood in other pursuits, such as ranching, freight hauling, providing supplies for the new settlers, and timber production. In one case, a settler established one of the first industries in Colorado. The Colorado Salt Works provided salt derived from a natural salt spring in the heart of the South Park. That ranch remains in the same family today.

Towns sprang up, and in many cases, just as quickly disappeared. Gold camps, consisting of hastily built log structures and tent dwellings for the quick influx of miners to the area, sported saloons, mercantile stores, dance halls, banks, and blacksmith shops to support sometimes thousands of people. Then, as the gold "played out" or a richer discovery was found somewhere else, in a few years, only the skeletons of the log buildings remained to mark the previous existence of those "cities." In some cases, the only remnants of once-bustling towns are faded names on old maps at the Park County Local History Archives or worn city plats hanging in the county records office.

But, while many mining workers quickly cleared out at the slightest rumor of another rich strike, others stayed. Unlike the gold rush to California in 1849 that largely consisted of single men set on striking it rich and then bringing their family out later, many of the settlers in the Park County area had already lost the farm or their jobs in the 1857 depression, and so brought their children and extended families with them. They claimed homesteads and began making lives for themselves in the rugged high country where no people had ever before stayed year-round, braving the high winds, cold, and deep snows. These stalwart pioneers became the foundation for the settlement of Park County, one of the first 17 counties of the Colorado Territory. Some towns struggled through the boom and bust of surrounding mines, but they persevered and still exist today.

At first, the county seat jumped from settlement to settlement. Finally, Fairplay became the permanent center of government. Nearby Alma—at 10,578 feet above sea level, the highest incorporated town in North America—also continues to thrive. Other existing towns, while not incorporated now, still enjoy a rich history and sense of community.

Each town or community has its own personality and history. Como was born as a railroad town, established by the Italian railroad workers who arrived with the coming of the Denver, South Park & Pacific Railroad in 1879. Established as stops along the wagon trails into the gold country, Bailey, Shawnee, Grant, Jefferson, and Fairplay also became strong transportation centers for the narrow-gauge Denver, South Park & Pacific Railroad, while Lake George, Garo, and Hartsel served the Colorado Midland Railway's wide-gauge railroad. The trains shipped timber, mining ore, livestock, hay, and ice to the Front Range cities and brought goods, visitors, and sportsmen to the high country.

Businesses grew and schools sprang up as settlers put down roots. Many of the area's historic buildings continue to contribute to the history of the county, as they still house thriving merchants, restaurants, and other businesses. Some ranches still use the massive early hay barns built in the late 1880s, while others have preserved and still occupy the old headquarters buildings. Thousands of acres of Park County have been protected by easements, guaranteeing that the land will remain open for cattle, buffalo, and wild herds of elk, antelope, and other wildlife.

One of the businesses that thrived in the early years of settlement was timbering. Even before the advent of the railroads, huge freight wagons rumbled from the mountain stands of high country timber, coming down through Platte Canyon to the waiting entrepreneurs ready to build their empires of banking, factories, mills, and fine hotels in Denver. The wagons were loaded with massive trees that, in the cold, high country, had formed slowly. These trees had tight, straight trunks—perfect for strong support beams and smooth, beautiful lumber. Nearly every settlement had a sawmill that soon turned hastily built log structures into expanded fine homes that resembled the houses many of the settlers had left back East. Some houses and storefronts still have the original logs as their basic walls. They have been obscured by milled lap siding and interior wood panels covered in wallpaper or other finery.

When the railroads came, the lumber business grew, producing ties for the advancing rail lines. Slash and lesser-quality wood was hauled by train or freight wagon to heat the many smelters in the mining areas that processed the precious metals and other ores. Hillsides and ridges still show the stumps of large cuts that cleared whole areas. However, colonies of ancient trees well over 1,000 years old still stand defiantly braving the winds, snows, and cold high in the Park County mountains.

Even though Park County schools are now consolidated into two school districts, many one-room schoolhouses still dot the landscape, standing as reminders of the importance the early ranchers and miners placed on education. Several schoolhouses are still furnished with the original blackboards, desks, books, and supplies used by hardy high-country kids over 100 years ago.

As Colorado burgeoned at the turn of the 20th century, Platte Canyon became a primary recreation destination for those eager to escape the hot, crowded, dirty cities. Youth and family camps sprang up all along the South Platte River. Popular resorts were built and promoted by the railroad. Denver businessmen invested in Park County and established retreats, including rustic lodges, summer homes, and even cycling parks in the Bailey and Shawnee areas. Pamphlets and brochures extolled the virtues of Park County for its pure air, natural beauty, and bountiful fishing and hunting. Guest ranches were established from the northern edge of the county to the very heart of the South Park to host city people eager for a taste of the "cowboy life." Local celebrations like rodeos and parades were favorites, drawing thousands of attendees from the cities. Events, outdoor recreation, hunting, fishing, and wildlife watching still draw visitors from all over the world to Park County.

While explorers like Zebulon Pike, Kit Carson, and John Fremont met many Native American tribes during their travels in the early to middle 1800s, by the end of the century, the Indians were pushed out of the area and relocated to distant reservations, leaving no tribes remaining in the county. They were replaced by an influx of settlers and workers representing a wide range of nationalities. One list of mining workers at the King Coal Mines near Como included 13 nationalities, ranging from Austrians to, oddly, "Missourians," and there was a fairly large contingency of Chinese workers on the railroads, placer mines, and coal mines. They were reported to have made bricks in the Como area and operated such businesses as laundries in several towns. Some of the most successful ranchers came from England and marketed the excellent hay grown in the South Park to the royalty of Europe. As the ranchers added sheep to their livestock, a number of Hispanic workers came to the area from the San Luis Valley and other locations in Southern Colorado; some sheepherders may have come from the Basque area of Spain. Since modern-day ranchers have concentrated on raising cattle and bison, the Hispanic population has decreased to about 4 percent; 94 percent of current residents are Caucasian.

Water in Colorado has been declared to belong to the people of the state; anyone who wants to use water must declare and be granted a "right to use." Owning land does not mean that one owns either the right to use the water on it or the minerals that might exist below the surface. Each could belong to different owners.

The early miners were quick to establish that the first to declare use for water had the strongest claim and that later arrivals' needs were subordinate to his needs. Miners and ranchers in Park County held some of the oldest established water rights in the state. Soon, the value of the water tumbling from the three headwaters of the South Platte River located in Park County proved to be as valuable as crops, livestock, minerals, or other commodities. As early as the 1880s, the state legislature began looking at ways to set up reservoirs to capture mountain water and distribute it to the growing semidesert Front Range. The very early water rights established in Park County became extremely attractive for purchase by thirsty municipalities.

As more and more cities needed water, and as waves of hard times came and went in the mountains, many of the holders of the oldest water rights gradually began to sell off their rights to use the water that had helped produce some of the richest hay in the country and had processed gold and silver ore. Now, most of the water in the reservoirs in Park County belongs to Denver, Aurora, Colorado Springs, Centennial, and other Front Range cities. With the right to use water to irrigate sold off, once-lush meadows can now only support one cow and calf per 40 acres of land, even with high-protein native grasses. While the landscape has changed from the days of lush wetlands and meadows, it still hosts abundant wildlife, including elk, antelope, deer, and moose; predators like foxes, coyotes, and mountain lions; and plentiful numbers of black bears. The reservoirs are home to large and plentiful fish, much to the delight of anglers from all over the world who come to fish the Gold Medal waters.

One

MINING

"Pikes Peak or Bust!" was the cry from thousands of "Fifty-Niners." The year was 1859, and the Colorado Gold Rush was on. It is estimated that 100,000 people flocked to the gold fields from all over the United States and its territories. Many arrived by wagon train or "headed for the hills" on foot into Park County, then part of Kansas Territory. Others settled in the Denver area and to the north in Central City.

One of the first mining camps established in present-day Park County was Buckskin Joe, located just one mile west of present-day Alma. Gold was discovered there in the summer of 1860, and the first mine was dubbed the Phillips Lode. Over $250,000 was recovered from this claim, according to Charles Henderson's 1926 report, "Mining in Colorado."

The nearby Mosquito Range Mountains fostered a number of other mining districts, such as the Consolidated Montgomery District. The Fairplay "Diggings," seven miles to the west of Buckskin, had its own district, as did the Tarryall region, settled after prospectors trudged into South Park from the Denver area, forming the towns of Hamilton and Tarryall.

The county's mining camps went through the typical cycles of boom and bust. When silver was discovered on Mount Bross in 1868 with the Moose Mine, another rush was on. Silver production rose from $188,000 in 1872 to an astonishing $399,000 just one year later, according to Henderson. Another gold surge in 1933 made the Alma area the "Richest Gold Camp in the World," according to a January 1, 1933, *Denver Post* article.

The town of Como saw the development of its rich coal seams. When the railroad reached into the county in 1879, Como became a local commerce center. Outlying areas of the county, such as Hartsel and Guffey, also experienced gold and silver mining, although not nearly as profitable as in the mountains. Other valuable minerals were mined, including salt and tungsten. Today, some mining is still performed in the Mosquito Range, but not on the scale of what was done in the 19th century.

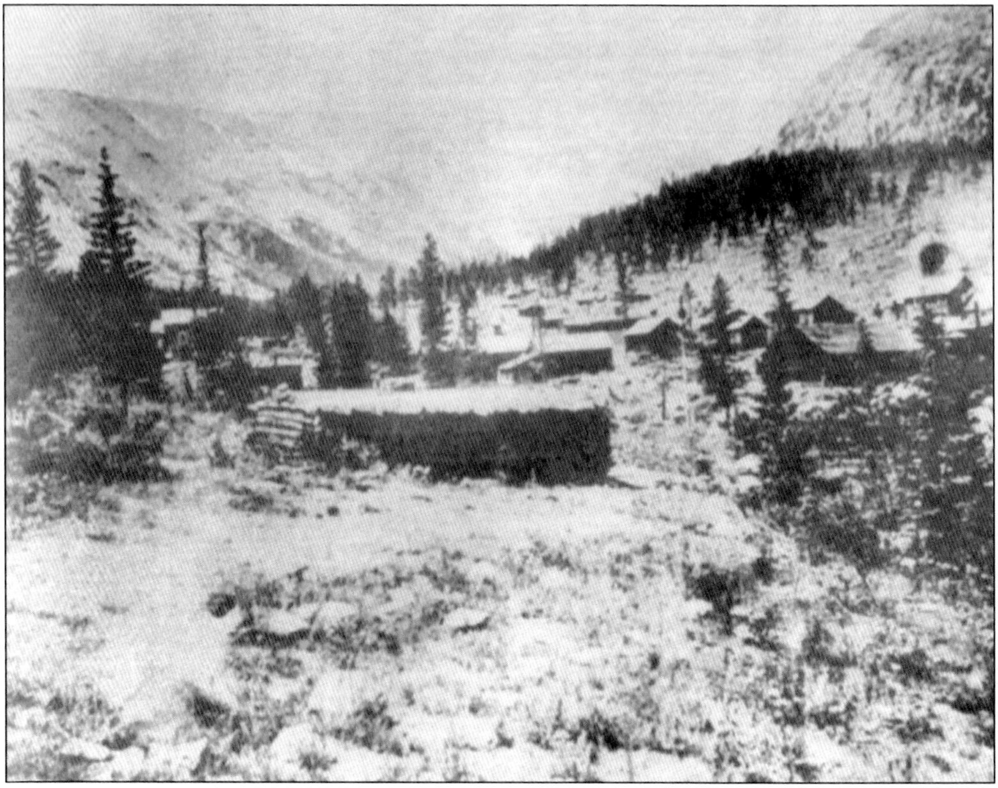

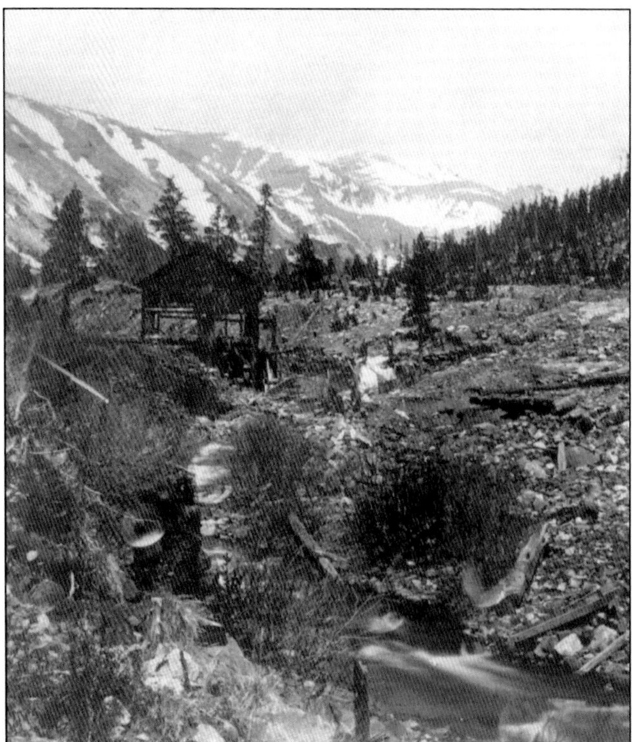

The Buckskin Joe mining camp, seen here in 1864, was one of the earliest mining settlements in Park County. It is located in Buckskin Gulch, accessed by today's Park County Road 8, also called Buckskin Street. Up to 2,000 people lived in the vicinity in search of the nearby mountain's precious gold and silver. There is nothing left of the town today.

The Phillips Group consisted of five adjoining claims in Buckskin Gulch, one mile west of Alma. In 1883, the first edition of the *Colorado Mining Directory* reported that the Phillips had an estimated output of $500,000, with some portions yielding gold-bearing quartz with a milled value of $100 per ton. Shown here is an early mill for the mine on Buckskin Creek.

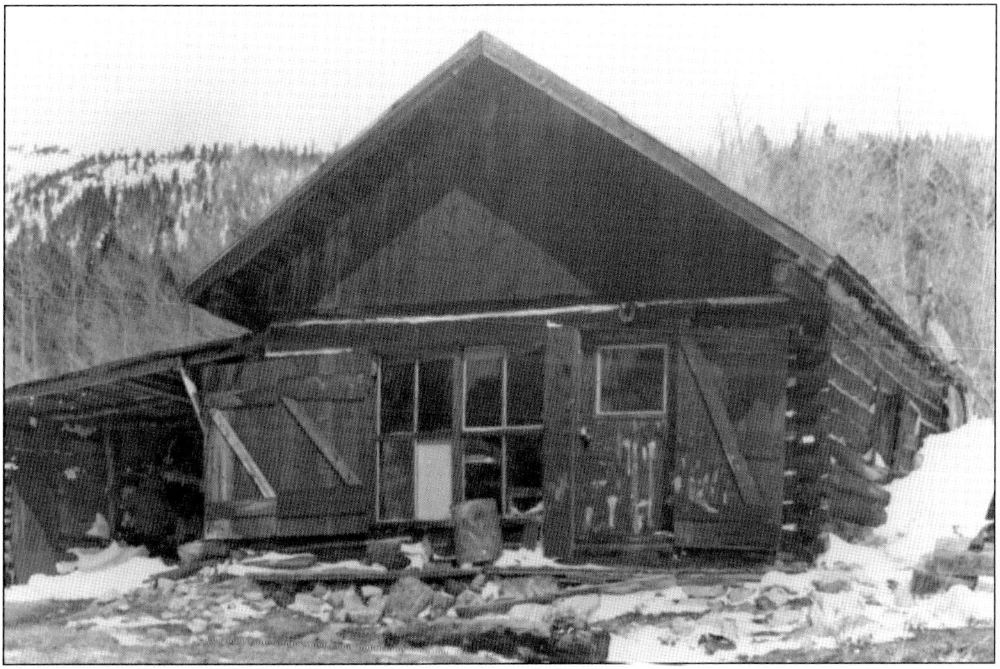

Before Horace Austin Warner "HAW" Tabor became the "Bonanza King of Leadville," he moved to Buckskin Joe with his first wife, Augusta Pierce, and their young son, Nathaniel. In 1957, the Tabor general store and post office were moved to a movie set and theme park called Buckskin Joe Frontier Town & Railway west of Canon City, Colorado. In 2011, the park was sold and disassembled.

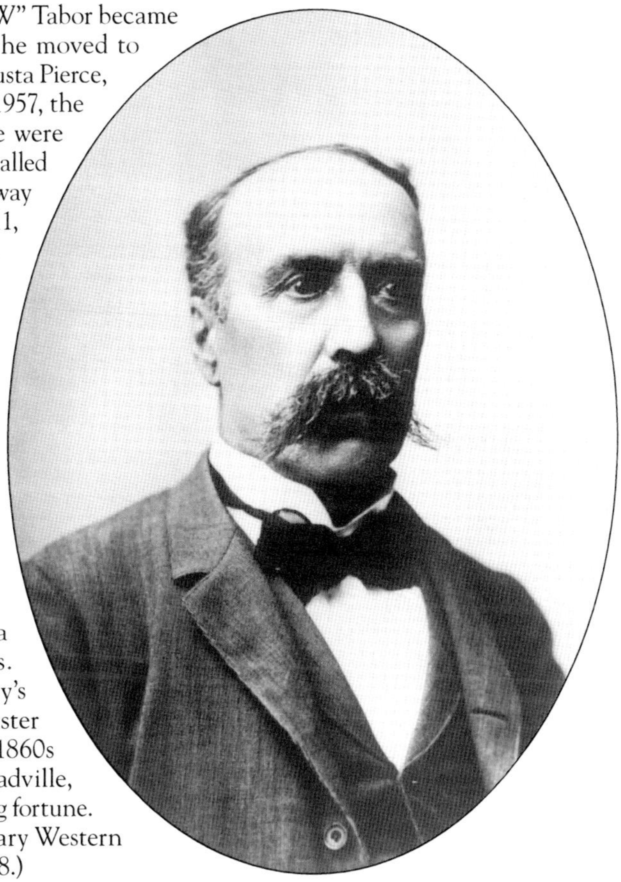

"HAW" Tabor is seen here in a studio portrait from the 1880s. Tabor was involved in Park County's early formation, serving as postmaster and school superintendent in the 1860s before moving his family back to Leadville, Colorado, where he amassed a mining fortune. (Courtesy of the Denver Public Library Western History Collections, call no. X-22028.)

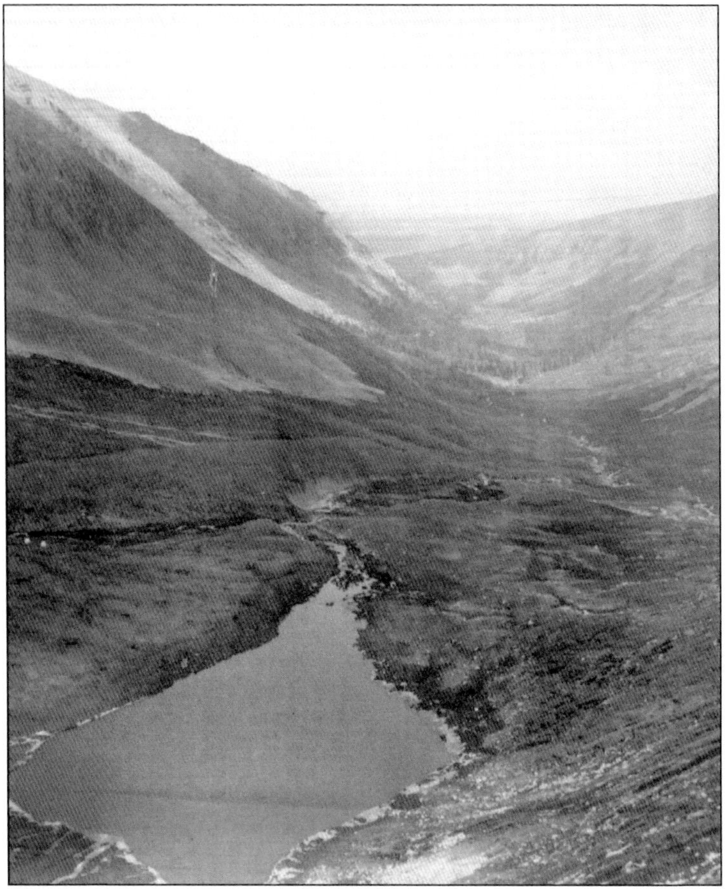

At the head of Buckskin Gulch lies Kite Lake. The shape of this well-named body of water is seen in this 1880s photograph. Mount Democrat, a Colorado "fourteener," towers over the valley below. Today, the lake, located approximately five miles west of Alma on County Road 8, is a popular spot for recreational enthusiasts.

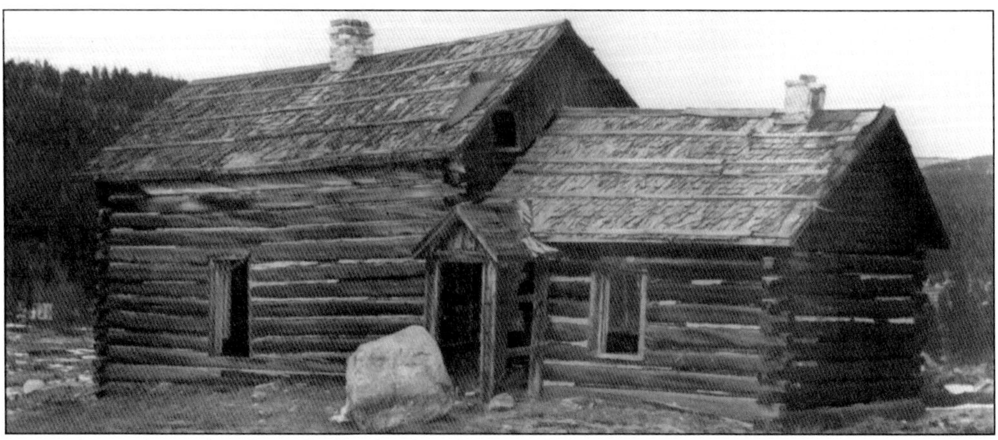

An enduring legend is that of Silverheels, a beautiful dance-hall girl who lived in Buckskin and wore silver shoes when she danced in this log building. After allegedly nursing the miners back to health during a smallpox epidemic, she suddenly left town after contracting the disease.

An angel statue watches silently over the Alma/Buckskin cemetery, one of Colorado's oldest burial grounds. The Silverheels legend includes old stories of her haunting this graveyard, weeping for her deceased miner friends. Her true name remains a mystery to this day. (Courtesy of Sean Brubaker, Evoke Images.)

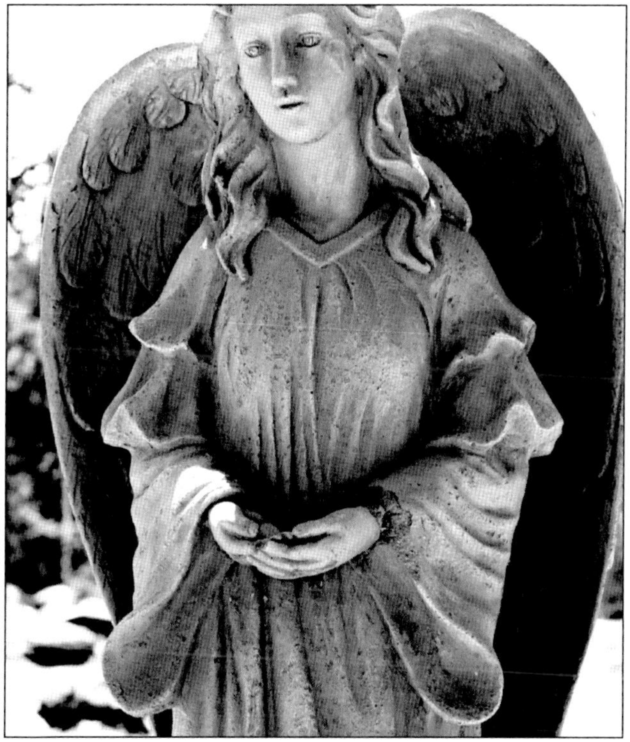

Mount Silverheels, located directly north of the town of Fairplay, is approximately 13,800 feet. It was named in the 1870s to commemorate the mysterious dance-hall girl who disappeared. She is also immortalized in a tapestry that hangs at the Colorado State Capitol. (Courtesy of Christie Wright).

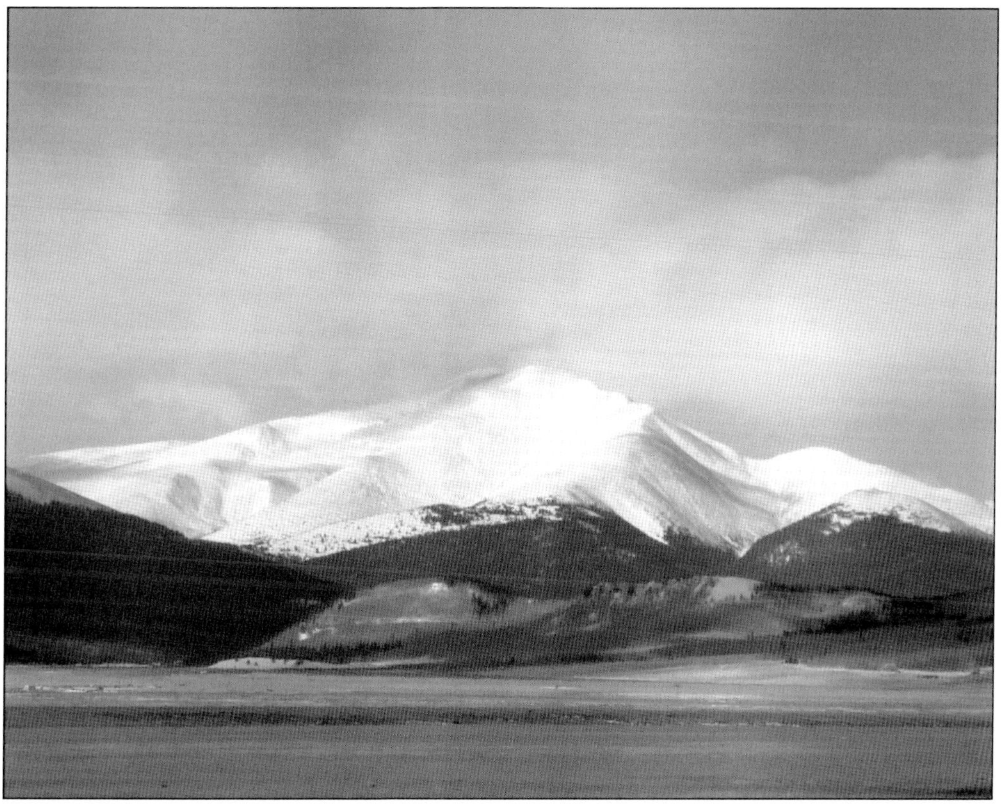

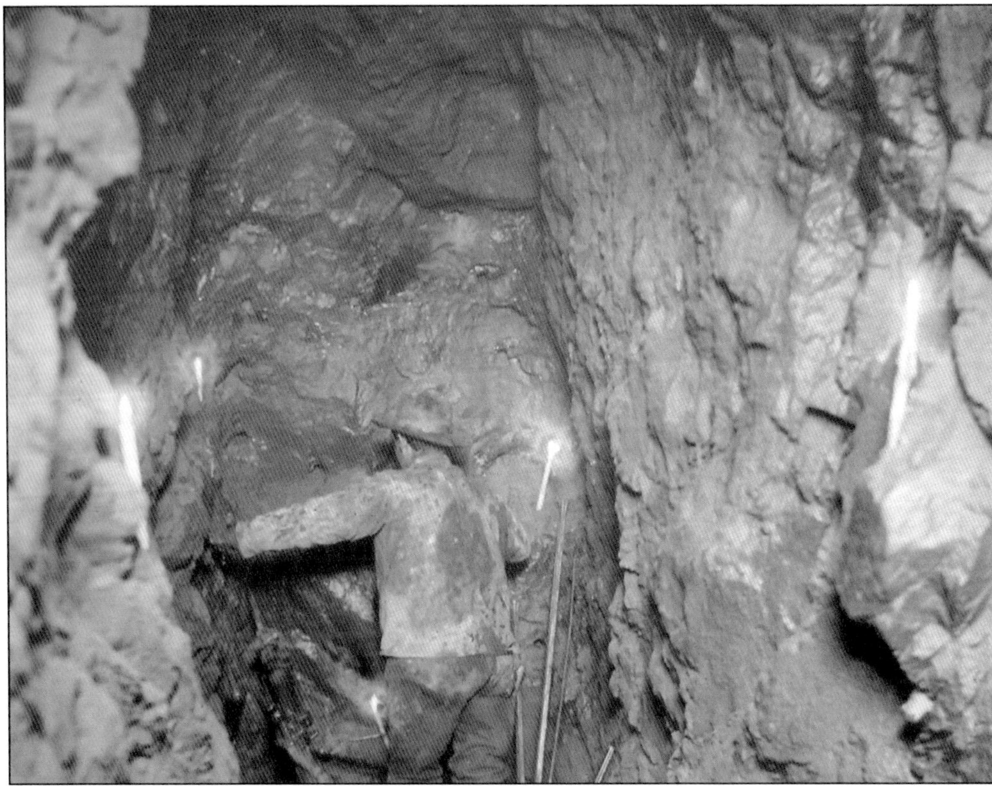

A variety of methods were used to mine gold, silver, and other precious minerals. Hard-rock mining was difficult, dangerous work inside the mountains, paying only $2.50 a day in the 1800s. Metal candlesticks were wedged into the rock's crevices to hold lit candles, providing lighting while blasting dynamite and drilling holes.

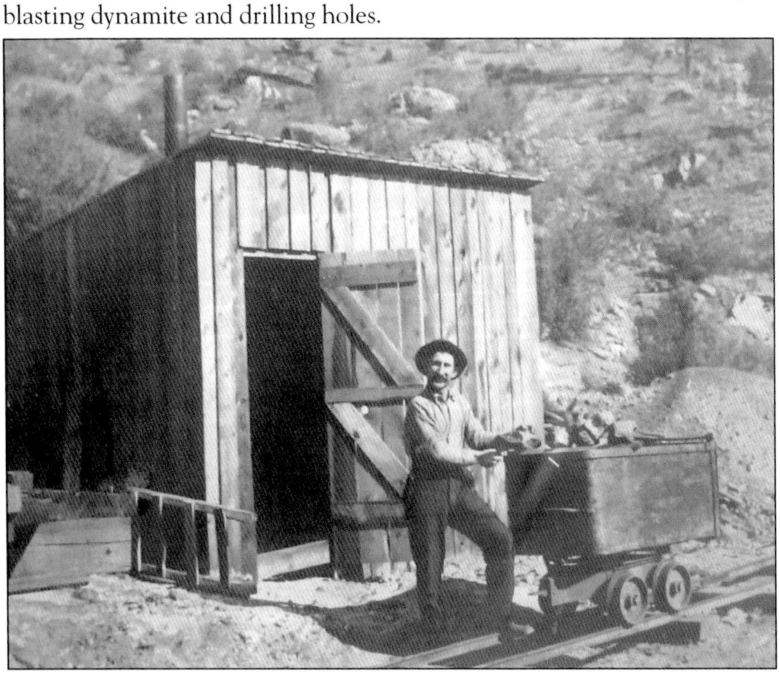

A mine's entrance, or adit, was often covered by a wood structure called a portal. This miner poses with an ore car or cart at the Great Western Mine, located near Lake George, in the early 1900s. The car is ready for transport to a local mill for processing to determine the gold or silver content.

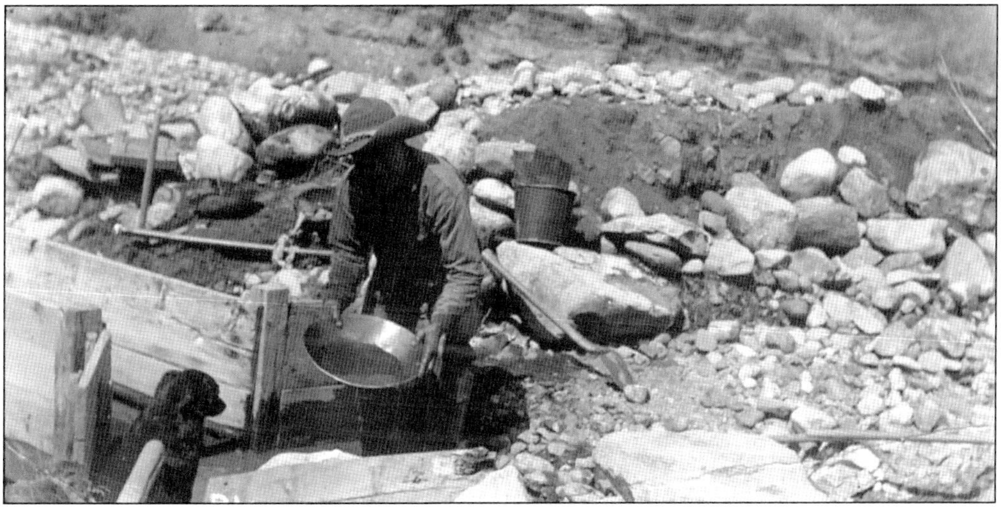

Gold panning or prospecting was the first mineral extraction method used in flowing water. The pan is dipped in the water, and loose gravel is scooped up from the streambed. Raising the pan back up, the prospector swirls the water around, allowing the lightweight pebbles to spill out and leaving the heavier gold in the pan's bottom.

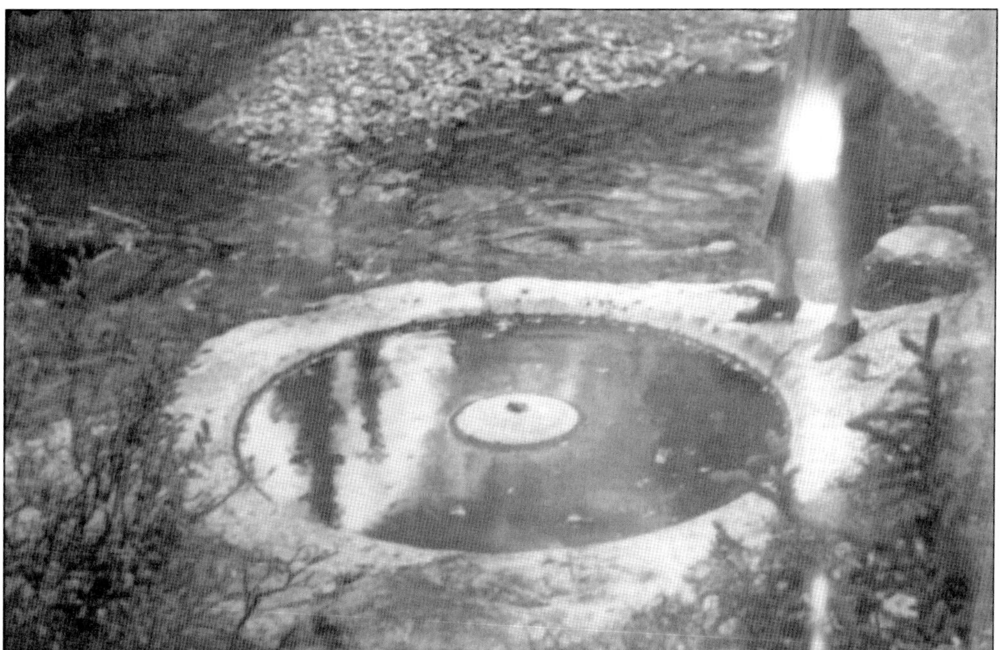

Several different mining processes were employed in the West to extract precious ores. This circular structure in Buckskin Creek is the remains of a primitive arrastra, which utilized flowing stream water to grind up rock. Located in Buckskin Gulch along County Road 8, it is an important remnant of the gold rush era.

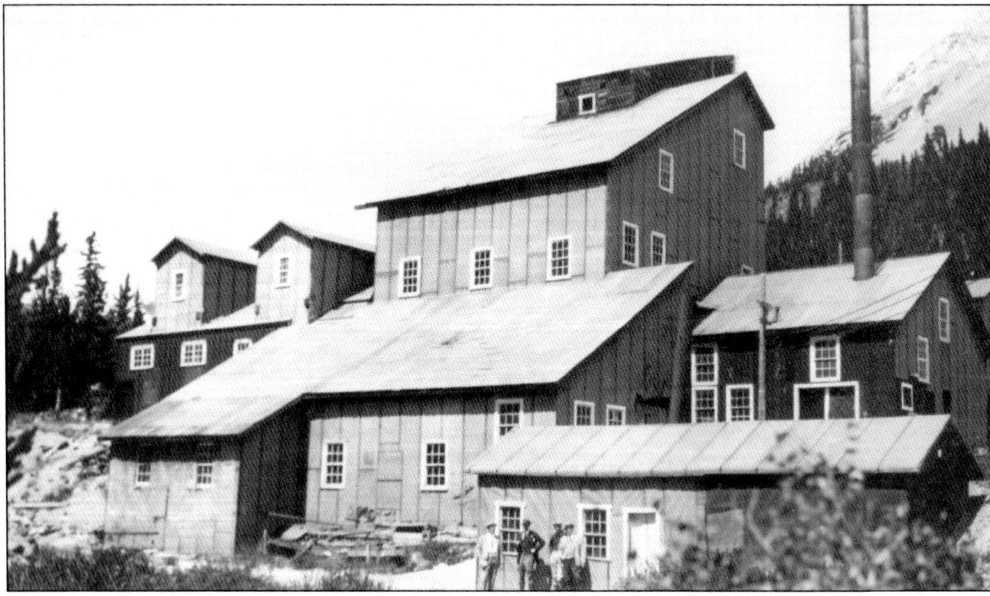

The Paris Mill, completed in 1895, was built to service the Paris Mine, located 750 feet higher on the north cliff. The mill contained a wide variety of machinery for both gold extraction and concentration. Park County owns the structure, which is being rehabilitated. No trespassing is allowed, but guided tours may be arranged as conditions allow.

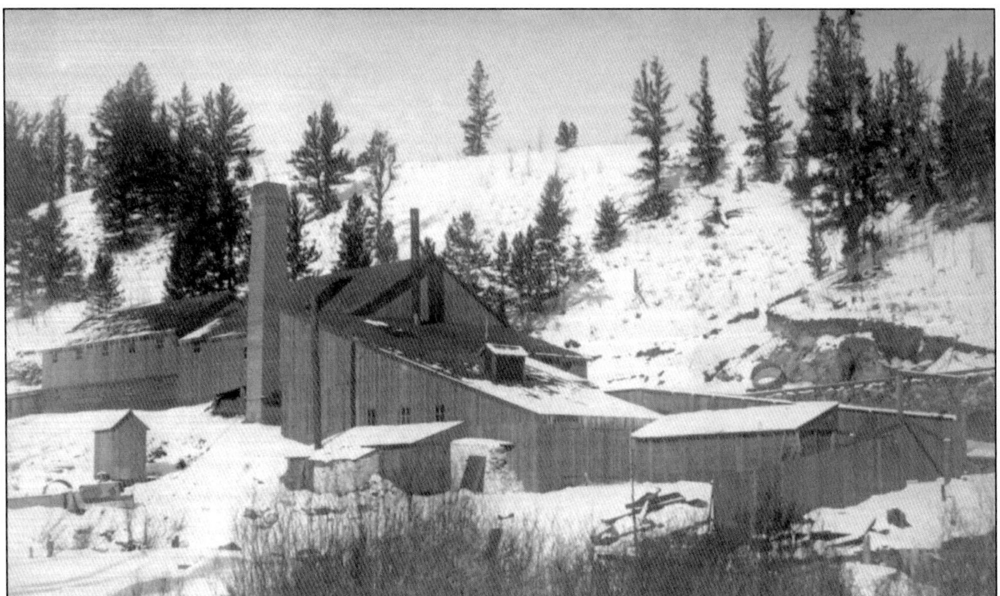

The Alma smelter, shown here in the 1880s, served the local mines. Smelters were used to extract gold and silver from ore rock, where it was frequently found high on the mountainsides. Through various crushing, heating, and refining processes, the gold was coaxed out and then measured or assayed. This building no longer stands.

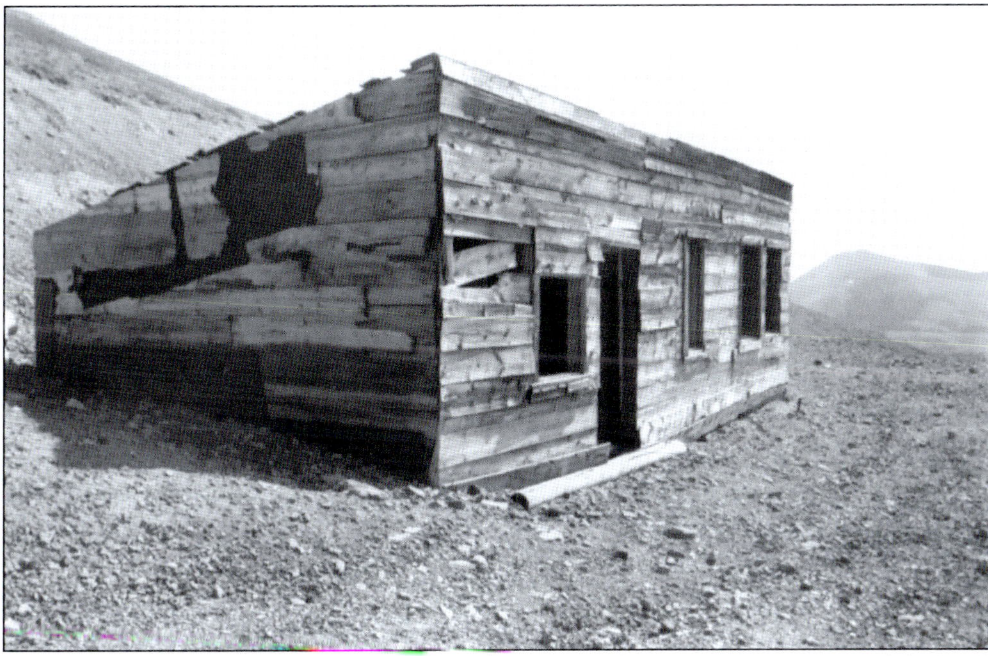

The boardinghouse at the Dolly Varden mine, located on Mount Bross, has withstood the harsh elements at over 12,000 feet. Discovered in 1873 by Assyria Hall and George W. Brunk, the mine produced approximately $3 million in silver before reducing operations in 1884. At one point, a tram and mill contributed to the large mining operation.

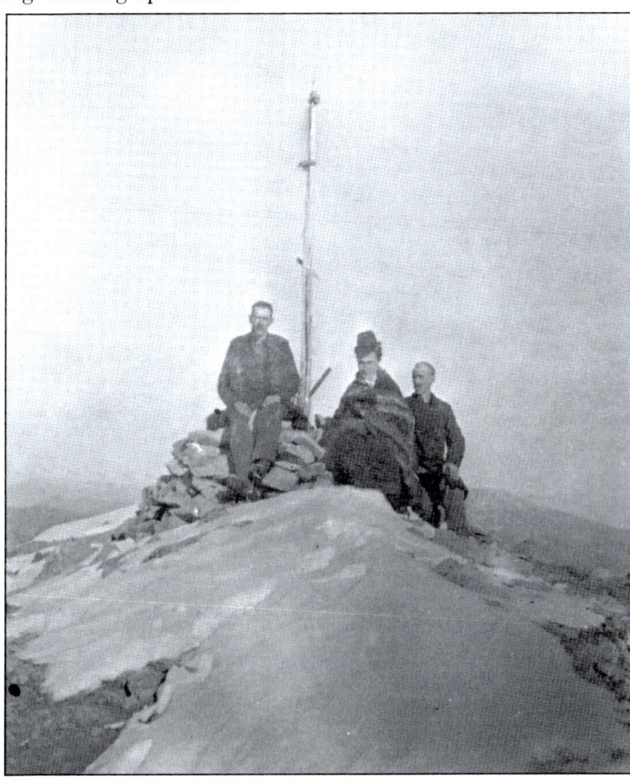

Seen here in the 1880s, three unidentified mountain climbers sit atop Mount Lincoln. Even in the summer, climbing a "fourteener" can be chilly, with sudden rain or snowstorms. Mount Lincoln was named in 1861 in honor of President Lincoln by local miner Wilbur F. Stone, who later became a Colorado Supreme Court justice.

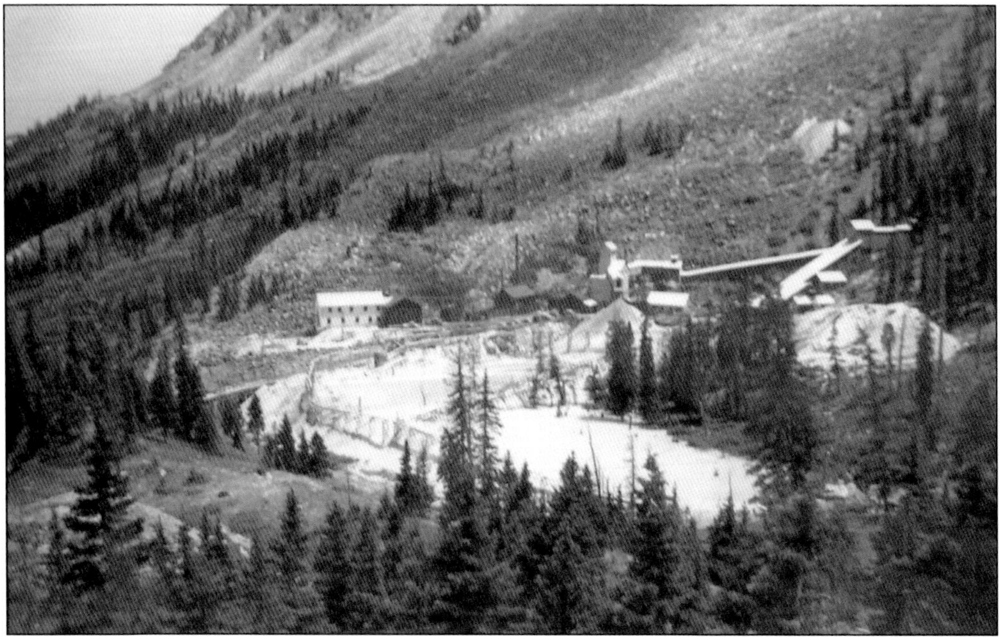

The enormous London Mine Group, consisting of three mines—the North and South London and the London Butte—was discovered in 1874. From 1895 to 1931, total output was a whopping $8 million in both gold and silver, according to a 1941 US Geological Survey report by Quentin D. Singewald and Bert S. Butler.

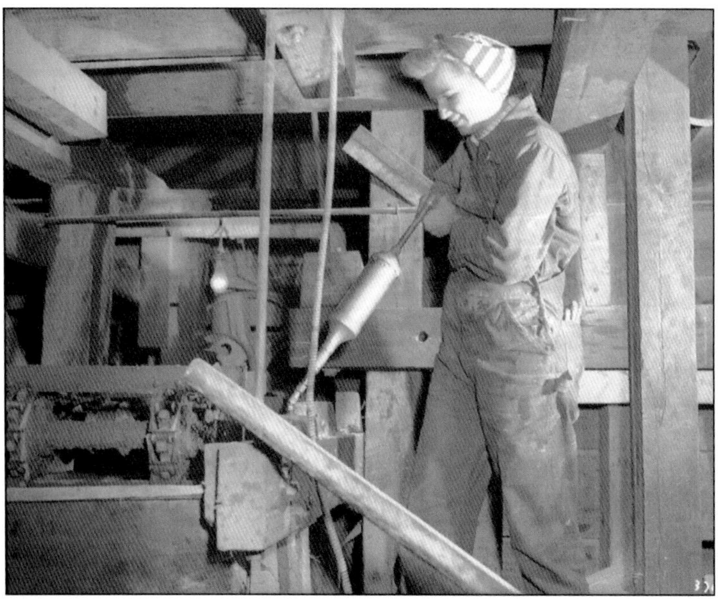

Women were frequently employed at the London Mine. Here, a woman works on a piece of machinery inside the mill building. Note the flag-motif scarf in her hair. This photograph was taken in 1941, during World War II. Other women worked at the mine in a variety of capacities, including sorting ore on a conveyer belt. (Courtesy Bob Zellers Collection, Ph.00493, scan no. 20005751, History Colorado, Denver.)

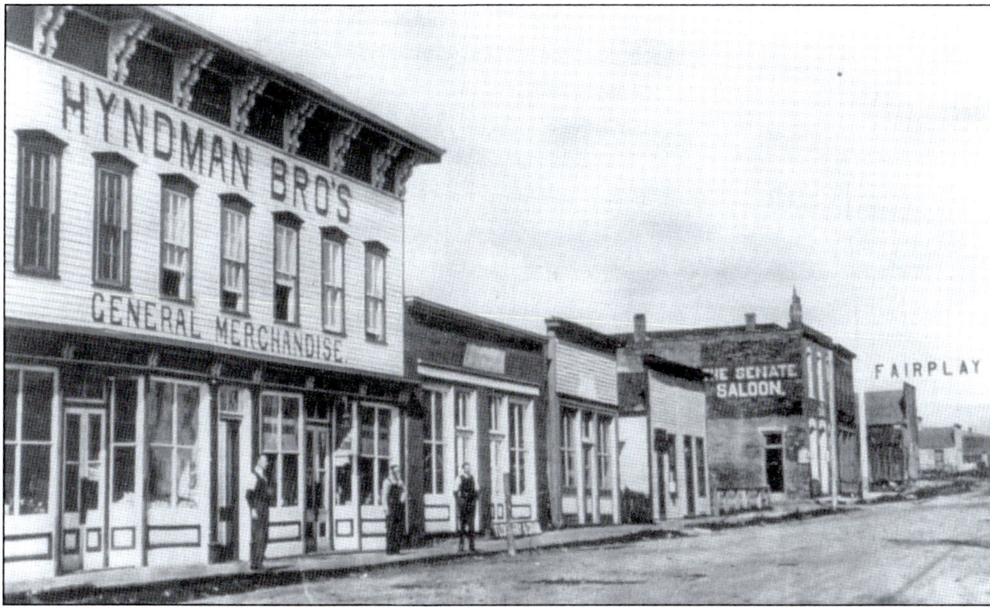

The town of Fairplay was established in the early 1860s as a mining and supply center for the "Fairplay Diggings," as the early mining operations were called. General merchandise stores, such as the one at left, carried many necessities. Brothers Archie and William Hyndman bought this establishment in 1911. The ever-present saloon, at right, was another staple on the mining frontier.

A large Chinese population lived in the Fairplay area and worked the placers at the riverbeds of the South Platte River. Large iron nozzles, or "giants," were used to wash down the soil to extract the gold, a form of placer mining. Placering left permanent scars in the creek beds that are still visible today.

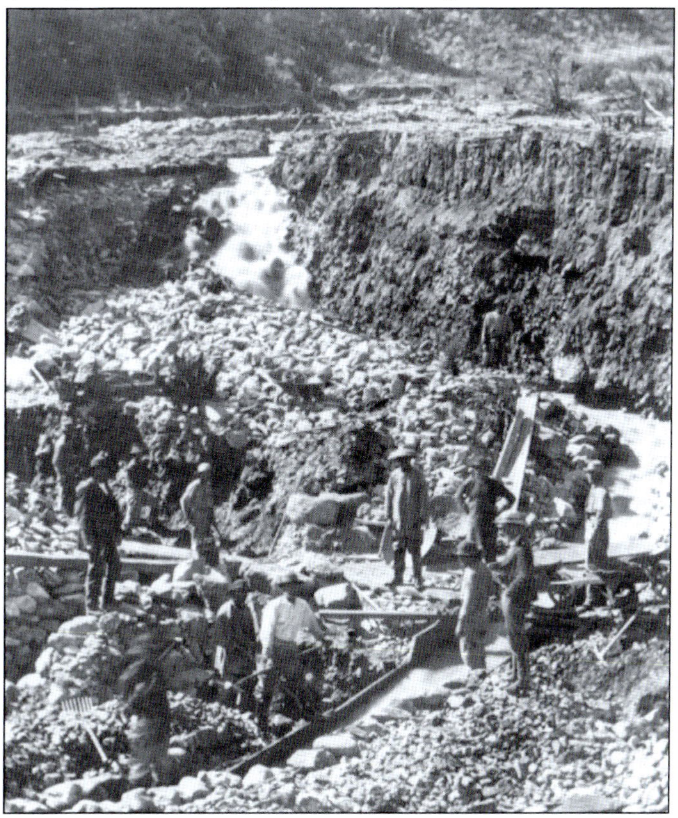

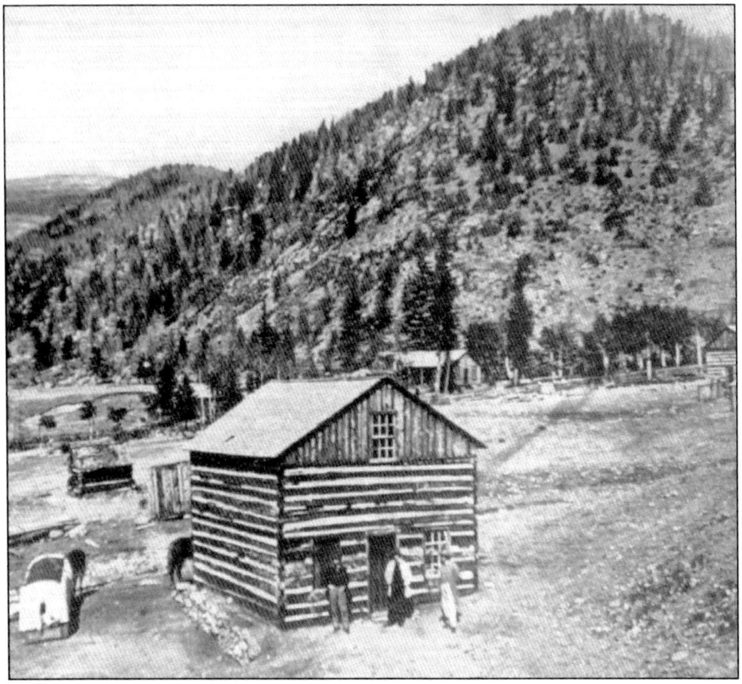

Hamilton was another early mining camp, named after Earl Hamilton. Located northwest of present-day Como, its rival sister town of Tarryall was within shouting distance on the other side of Tarryall Creek. The area yielded $2 million in gold between 1859 and 1872, but water shortages affected the ability to placer mine, and the miners moved on.

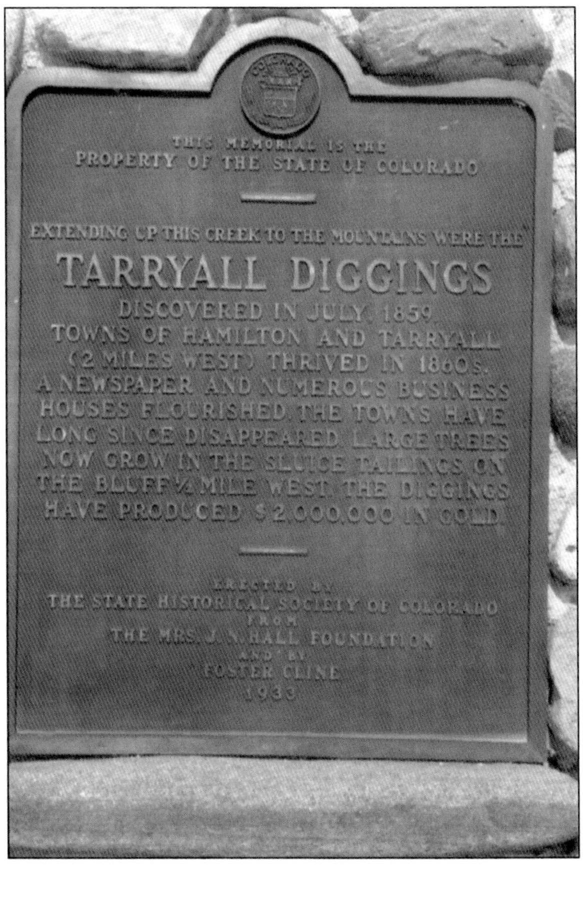

A state waymark sign was installed by the Colorado Historical Society and two private parties in 1933 to commemorate the importance of the "Tarryall Diggings." The monument sits approximately two miles east of the original Tarryall townsite at the entrance to the Cline Ranch State Wildlife Area on US Highway 285.

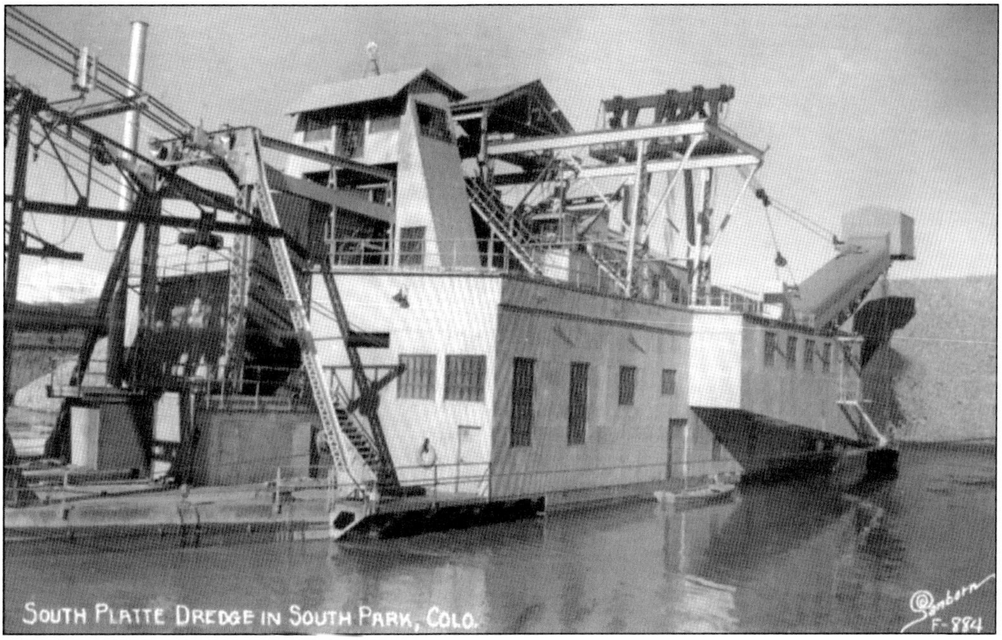

The South Park Dredging Company owned this enormous "gold boat," a floating dredge operation installed in the 1940s near US Highway 285 and Colorado State Highway 9. The behemoth weighed 2,400 tons and mined up to 15,000 cubic yards of gravel per day with 103 buckets. It was removed from the area in the 1980s.

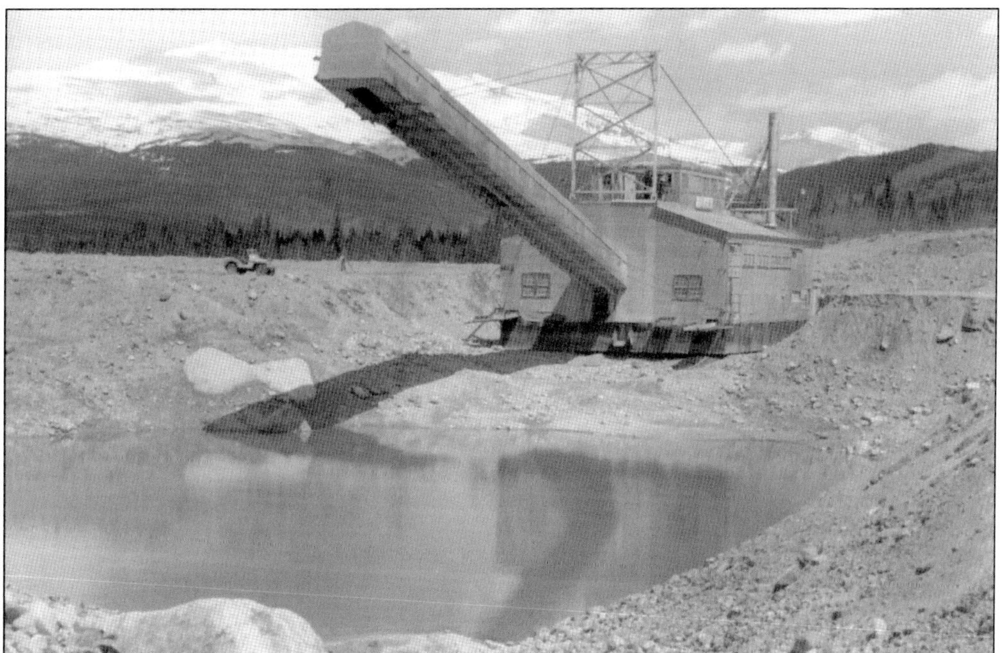

The Snowstorm Dredge, a floating gold-washing machine, sits in its original location between Fairplay and Alma. Constructed in 1941 for the Timberline Dredging Company, it is the largest and most recent dredge of its kind in the United States. The dredge last operated in 1976 and was listed as one of the top Endangered Places by Colorado Preservation Inc. in 2001.

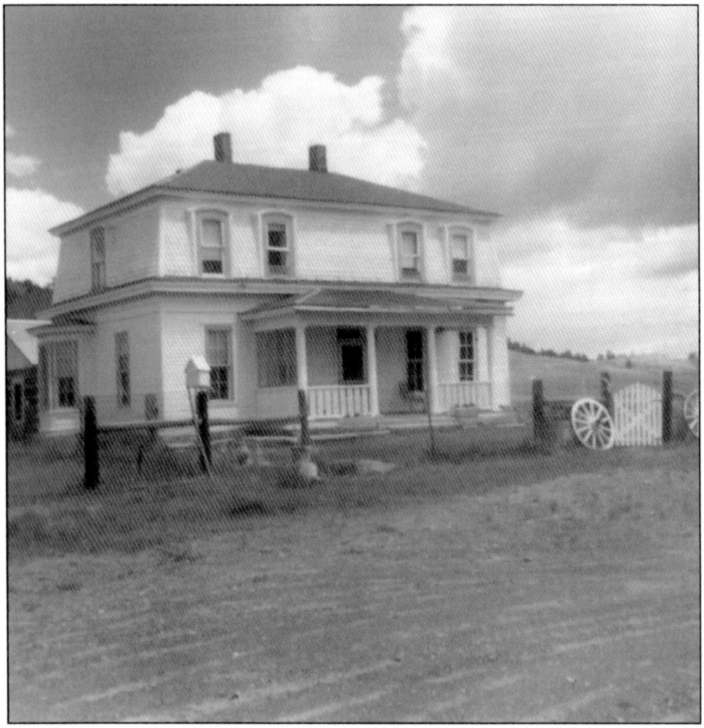

The Salt Works ranch house is an early 1860s home built by Charles L. Hall and his wife. They operated a commercial salt business. The natural salt marshes found on the property were dubbed "Bayou Salade" by the early French traders; Native Americans took advantage of the mineral as well. The ranch has remained in the same family for generations.

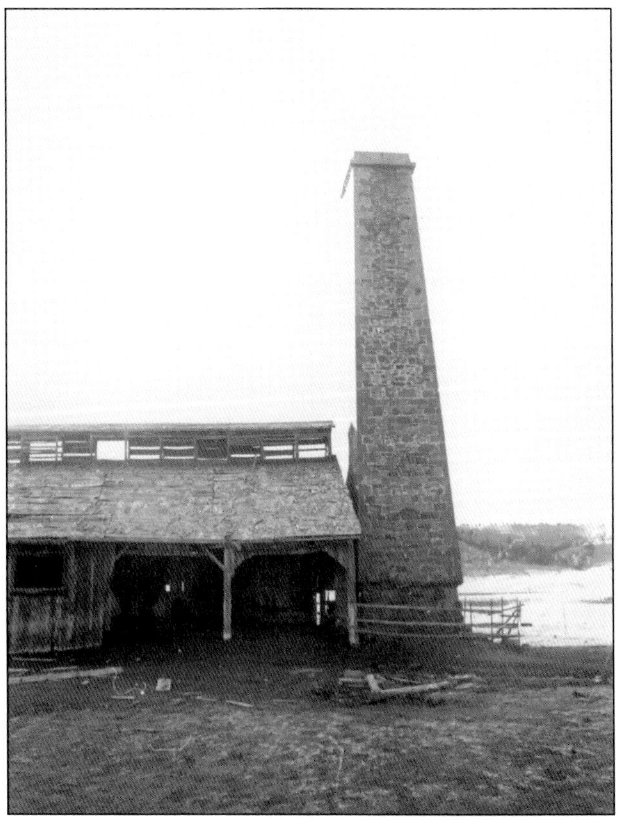

A 50-foot chimney is seen in this 1870s–1880s photograph of the Kettle House at the Salt Works ranch. The ranch is the only remaining structure of an 1860s kettle-and-pan salt facility in the United States. Brine water was boiled in the kettles to capture the white mineral, which was then dried, bagged, and sold.

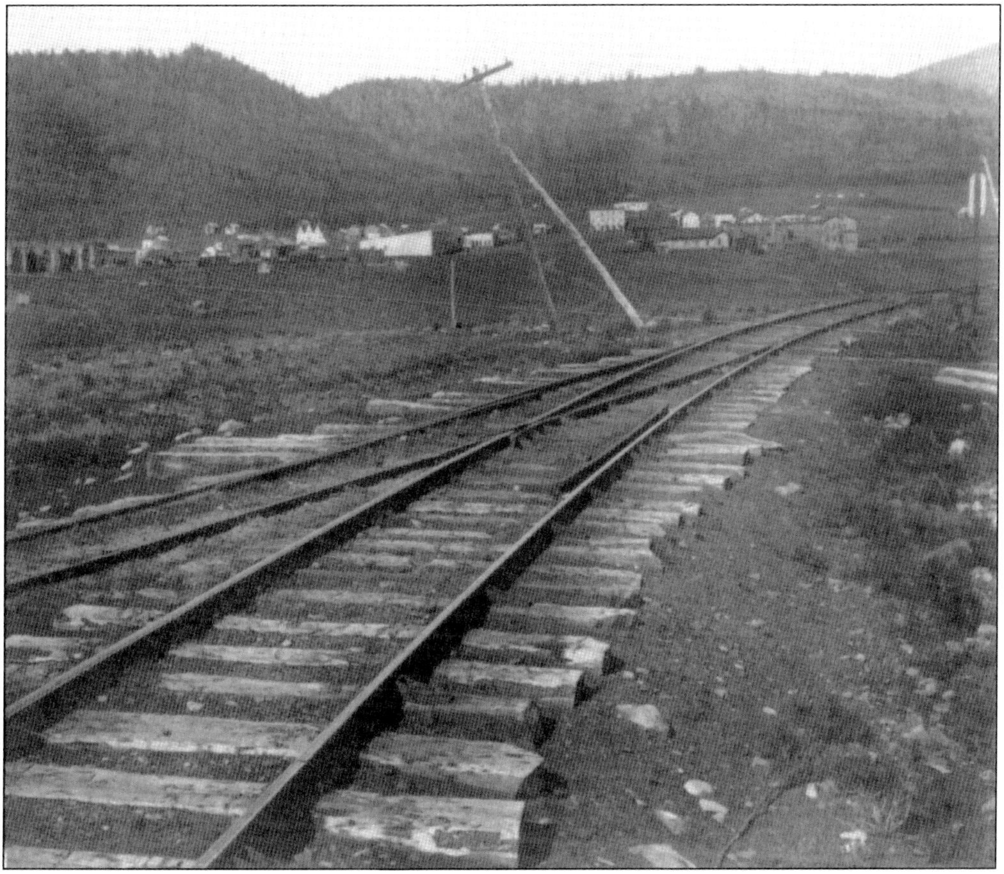

Como sprang up in 1879 as a railroad hub and supply center for the Denver, South Park & Pacific narrow-gauge railroad. County pioneer George Lechner previously owned the property and discovered rich coal deposits in the area. Several historic buildings are being renovated in a sign of the town's enduring significance.

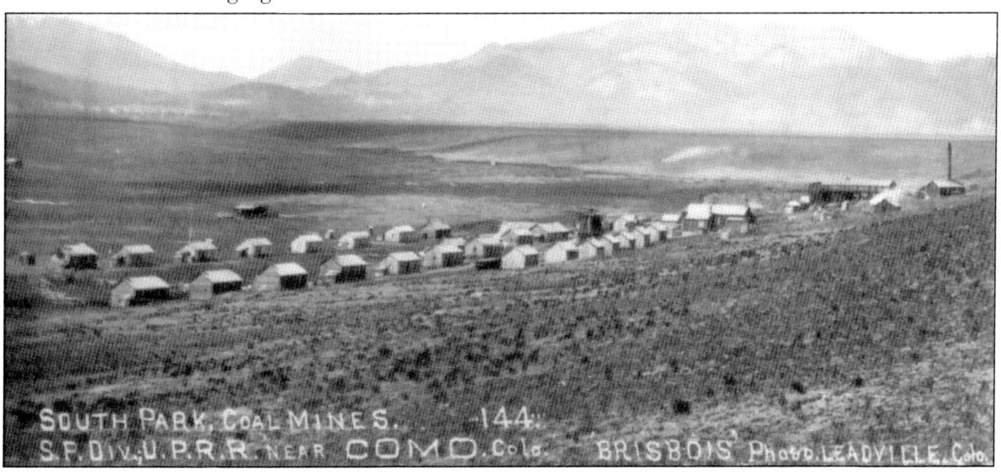

The town of King was named for Park County's clerk, A.J. King, who ran the general store and post office. Originally the coal-mining camp for George Lechner's South Park Coal Company, it was later owned and mined by the Union Pacific Coal Company.

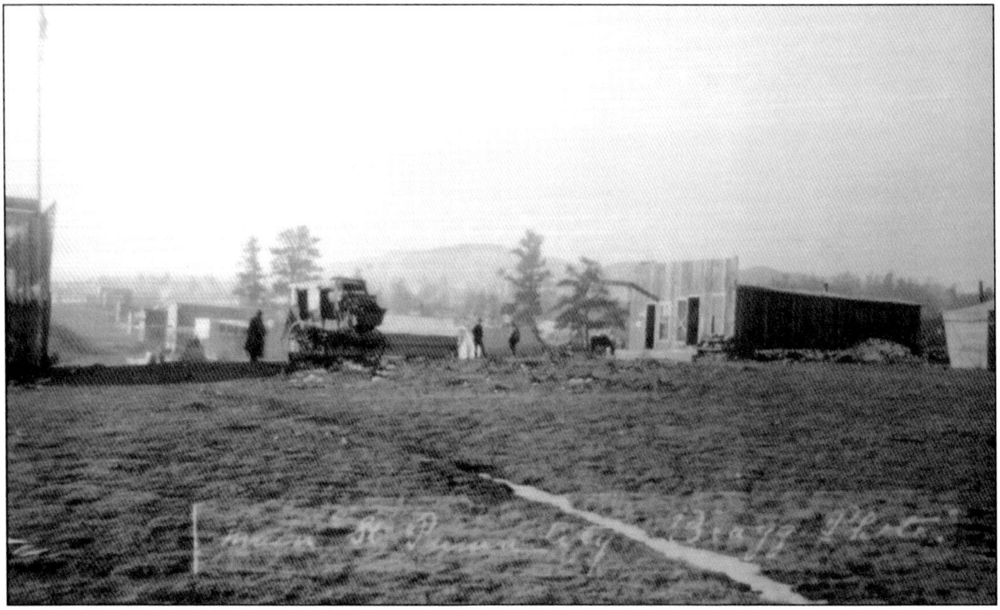

Puma City was developed in 1896 by Cripple Creek prospectors looking for new gold fields. It was located between the town of Jefferson and Lake George. The Pemberton & Moore stage line ran a route from Lake George to Puma City. It took three hours to travel the 10 miles.

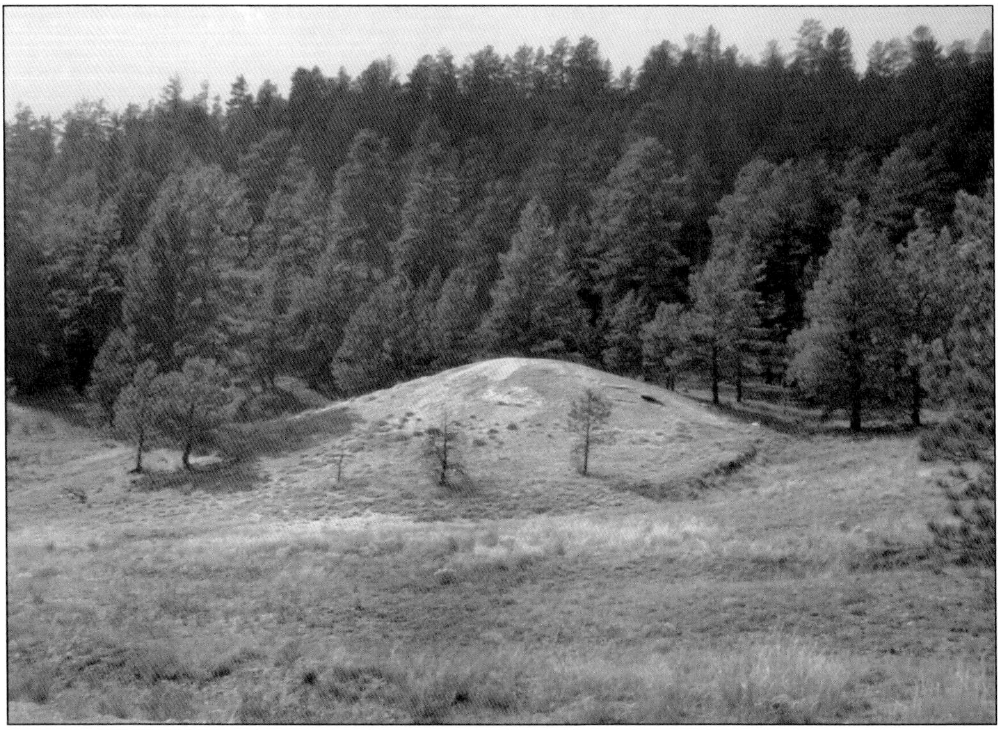

Originally called Mound Spring, this soda spring, located a mile south of Guffey, was initially used to water livestock. Settled in the 1890s by Cripple Creek miners, Guffey was initially called Freshwater and included a mining district; other nearby districts were Fourmile, Alhambra, and Red Ruth. (Courtesy of Christie Wright.)

Two

RANCHING

After the 1859 gold rush subsided, those who had come to the Rocky Mountains either left for other locations or settled down to occupations that supported the population. Samuel Hartsel was one of the early pioneers who started a cattle ranch after gold fever left him less than rich. He bought oxen cheaply; the animals had become emaciated as they brought covered wagons across the plains, then were fattened up to sell to hungry miners.

Ranchers discovered that diverting water from the river into irrigation ditches allowed them to produce four or five cuttings of hay each season. Growing hay to feed the cattle was not only a profitable venture, but South Park hay became a lucrative commodity of its own.

Homesteaders attempted to grow vegetables, but they found that the short growing season was suitable for only certain crops. Potatoes were grown for commercial use; gardens with cold-weather plants such as lettuce, radishes, and parsnips flourished, as they produced crops for home use and local markets. Grains like oats, barley, and rye were grown.

In the 1920s, ranchers began to replace cattle with sheep. They sheared sheep for the wool and sold the animals for meat. Many ranchers hired experienced Mexican sheepherders. Wars between cattle ranchers and sheep ranchers did not occur in the area, because most of the same ranchers had raised both and learned which pastures worked for which livestock. Erecting and maintaining fences was a way of life, in order to keep livestock either in or out. The fence law dating back to the 1870s is still a part of Colorado law.

During the 1930s and later, ranchers began to sell off their water rights to cities such as Denver, Colorado Springs, and Westminster. Ranchers found it much easier to accept the generous payments for their land and the accompanying water rights than to continue with the backbreaking work of running a ranch.

Although buffalo freely roamed the plains in the early days, they were killed almost to extinction. In this way, the Indians who depended upon them for their existence were forced to move to designated reservations. Raising buffalo for commercial use is a recent phenomenon, as markets have developed a taste for the delicacy.

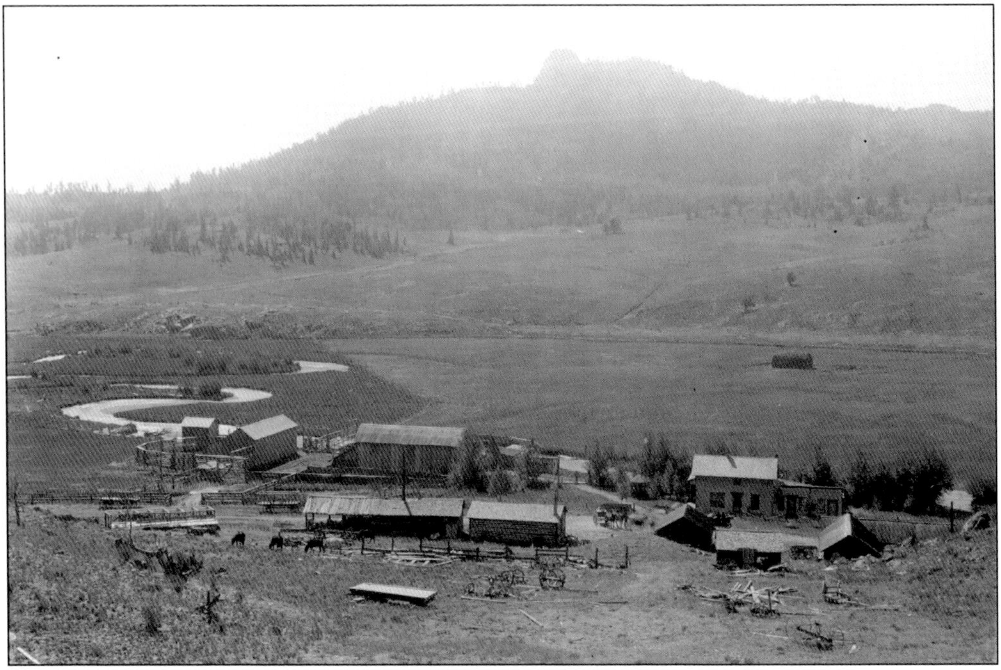

Cattle are shown in the corral at the Tim Borden ranch in the early 1900s. The Borden ranch, located east of the town of Jefferson, was situated along the Tarryall River. Tim and his brother Olney were early Park County settlers, moving to the Tarryall area in 1865. Tim Borden's homestead, 20 years later, encompassed over 1,300 acres.

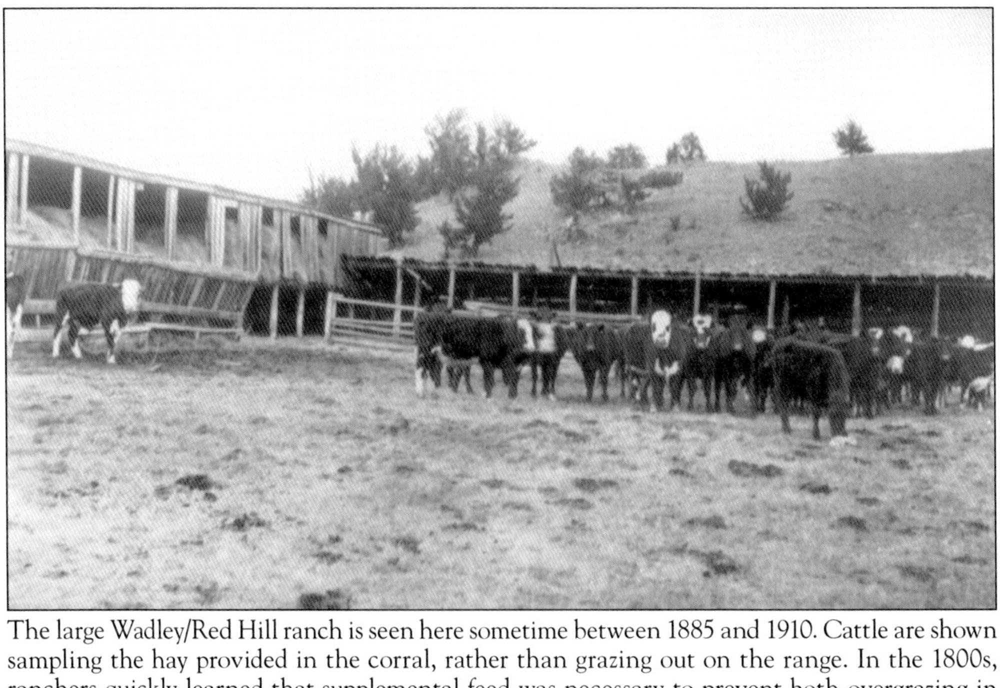

The large Wadley/Red Hill ranch is seen here sometime between 1885 and 1910. Cattle are shown sampling the hay provided in the corral, rather than grazing out on the range. In the 1800s, ranchers quickly learned that supplemental feed was necessary to prevent both overgrazing in the summer and herd loss in the winter. From 1885 to 1887, summer droughts plus snowy winters resulted in huge cattle losses for the county's ranchers.

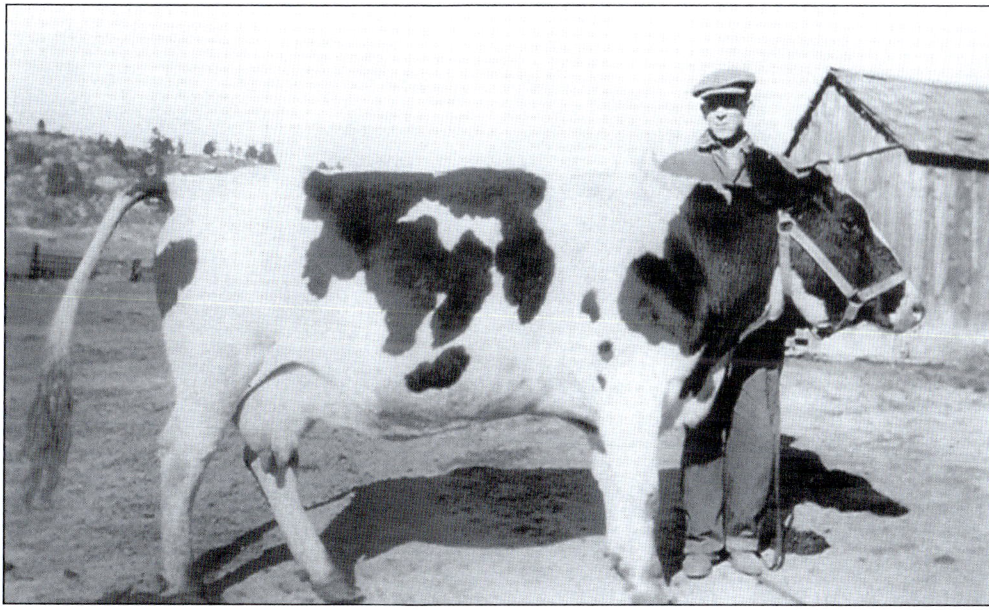

Local cattleman Pearl Oakley poses with his prize Holstein cow in the 1930s. Dairy farming was an important component of South Park's ranching industry, especially after the arrival of the Denver, South Park & Pacific Railroad and the Midland Railroad. Workers for the railroads and at the mining camps were local customers for dairy products.

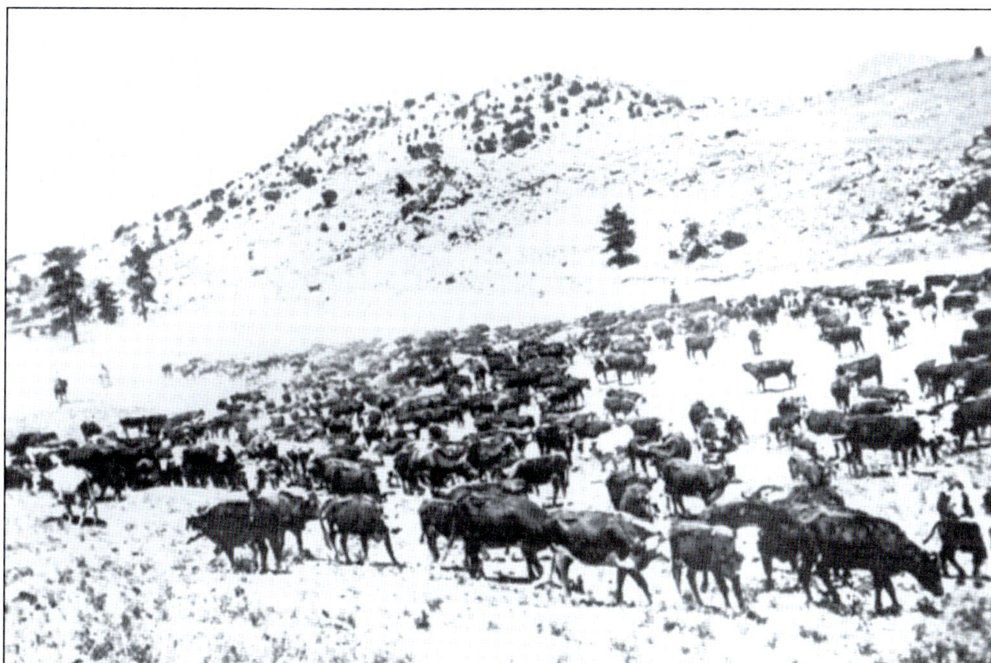

Roundups were held annually to gather the cattle that had strayed from their home ranges. They were then separated by brand and returned to their owners. This roundup occurred near Guffey in the southeast section of the county. By the late 1870s, there were approximately 150 ranches in Park County whose primary business was either raising cattle or growing hay.

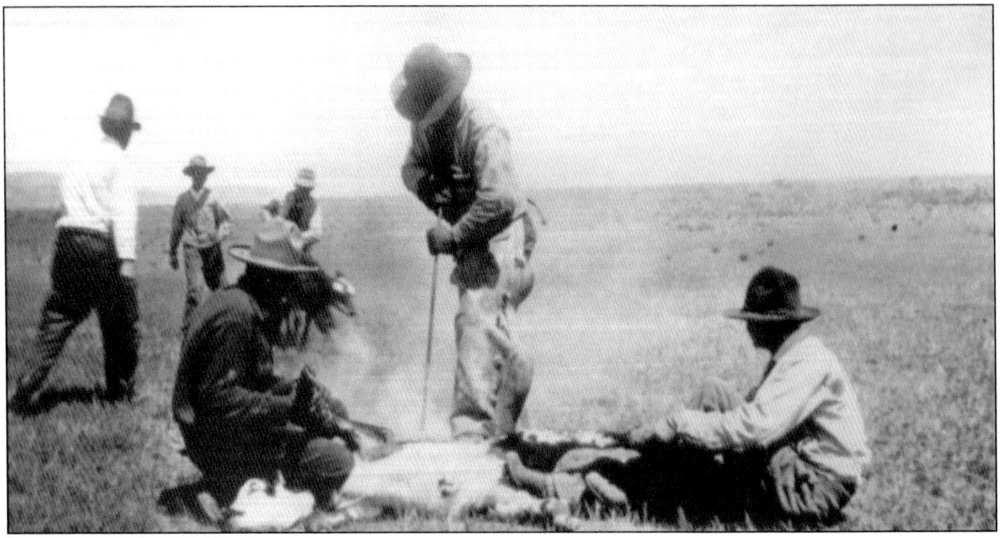

Cattle ranching was a major business in the county beginning in the early 1860s, serving to supplement protein to the mining camps. In order to tell one rancher's cattle from another's, each rancher used his own brand, which had to be approved by the Colorado Stockgrower's Association. The branding iron was heated to the point of leaving a permanent mark on the hide. These cowboys are branding in 1922.

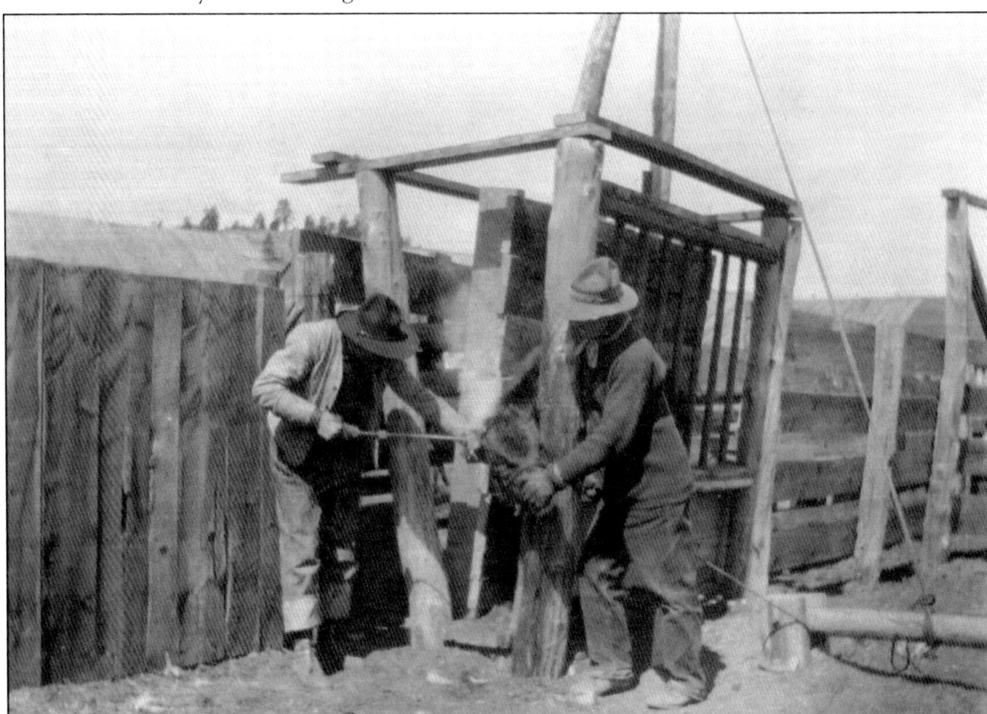

Albert Lafferty (left) and William Norton work to dehorn cattle on their Park County ranch around 1916. Longhorn cattle could sometimes injure themselves and one another, so in addition to branding them, the rancher sawed off the horns. Some cattle were born without horns, called polled cattle. A shorthorn breed of cattle was developed in the United States in the 1870s.

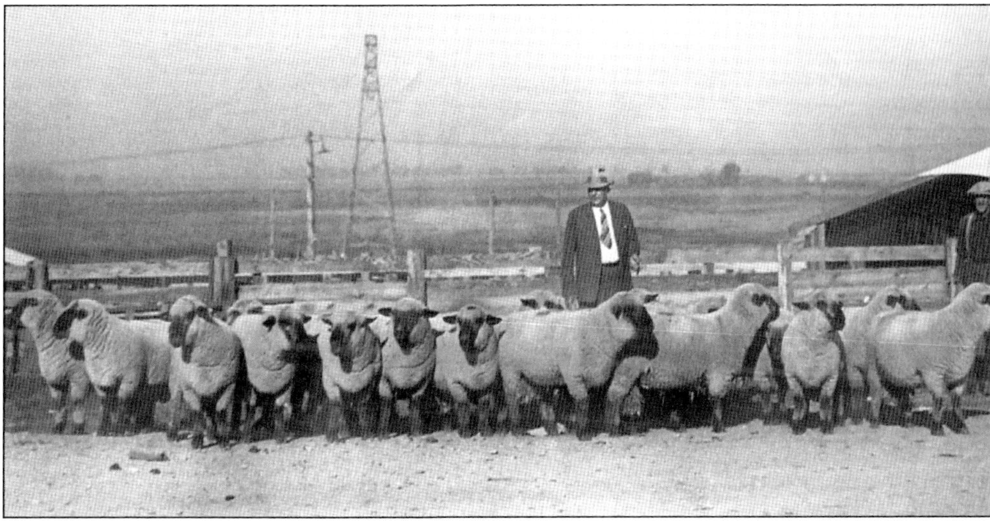

Hollis Mills, one of the county's main sheep men in the 1920s, stands amid his sheep at the Hartsel ranch. As the cattle industry waned, ranchers began raising sheep instead. Many of the ranchers installed extensive fencing to keep cattle and sheep herds separate. The Park County Woolgrowers was active during this time in promoting its stock.

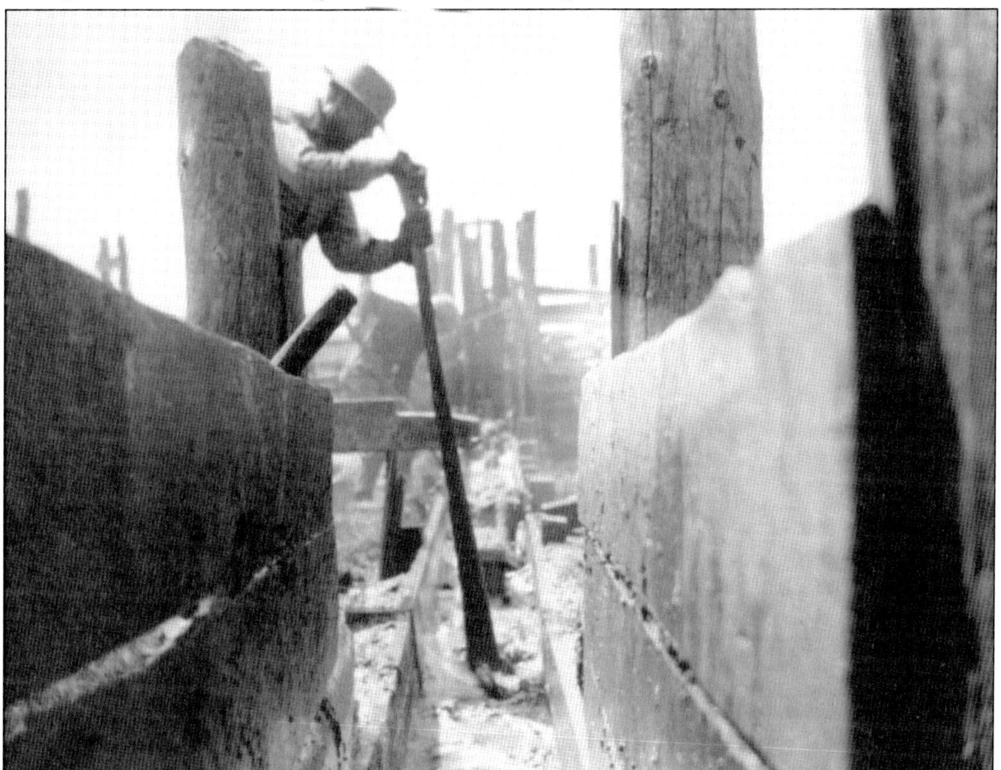

The dip works at the Hartsel ranch is seen here in the 1920s. After the shearing operation, the sheep were run through a trough of heated water. The water contained disinfectant, which helped to heal any cuts that occurred during the shearing. The ranch comprised a total of 9,000 acres of patented ranchland, with plenty of room to raise both sheep and cattle.

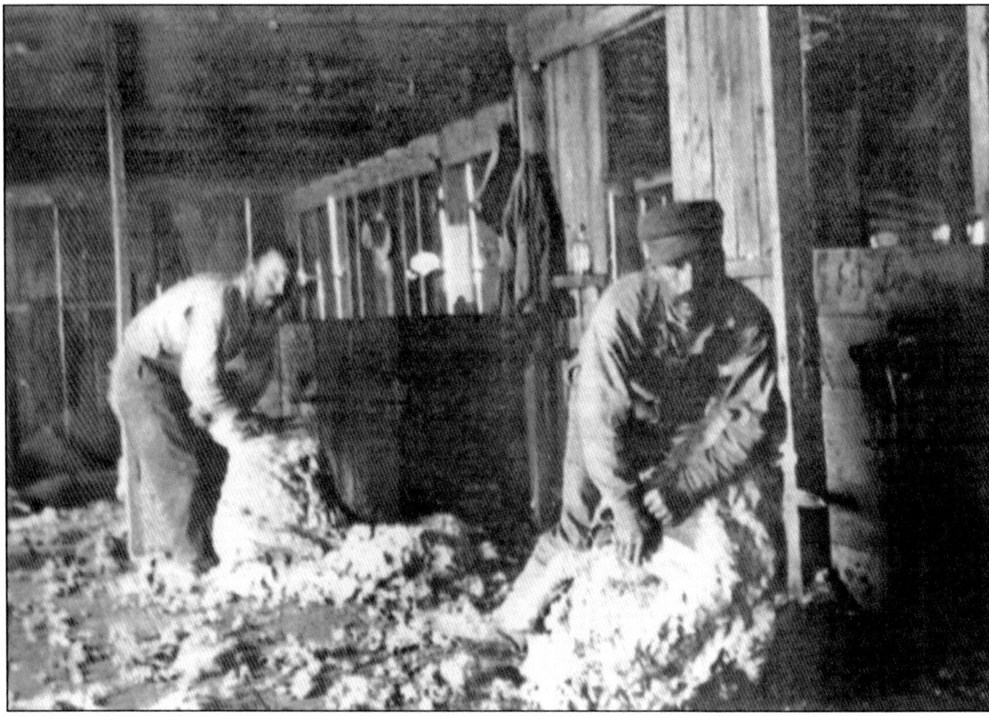

Sheepherders from New Mexico were frequently hired to take care of the herds and perform the shearing. These unidentified men shear sheep at the Wadley/Red Hill ranch sometime between 1885 and 1910. The ranch was located on the east side of present-day Red Hill Pass on US Highway 285.

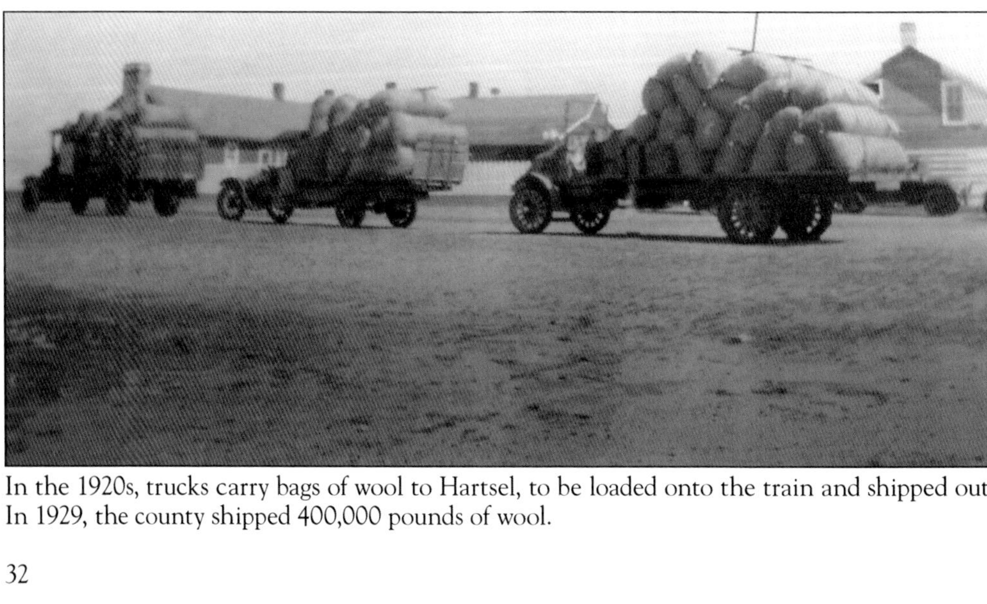

In the 1920s, trucks carry bags of wool to Hartsel, to be loaded onto the train and shipped out. In 1929, the county shipped 400,000 pounds of wool.

Rams were kept for breeding at the Wadley/Red Hill ranch, located at the east base of Red Hill Pass on US Highway 285. In 1929, 40,000 lambs were shipped. At that time, Park County was recognized as one of the leading wool and mutton growers in the West.

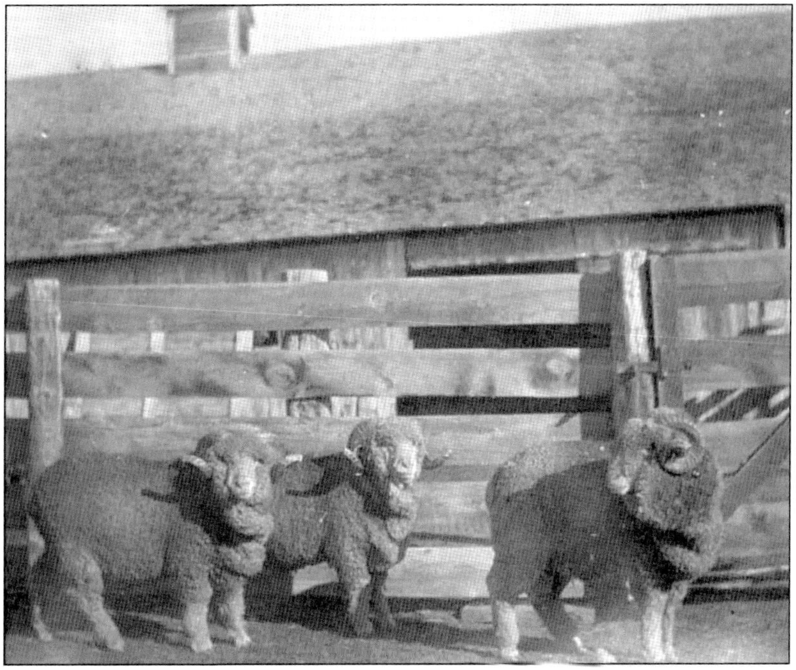

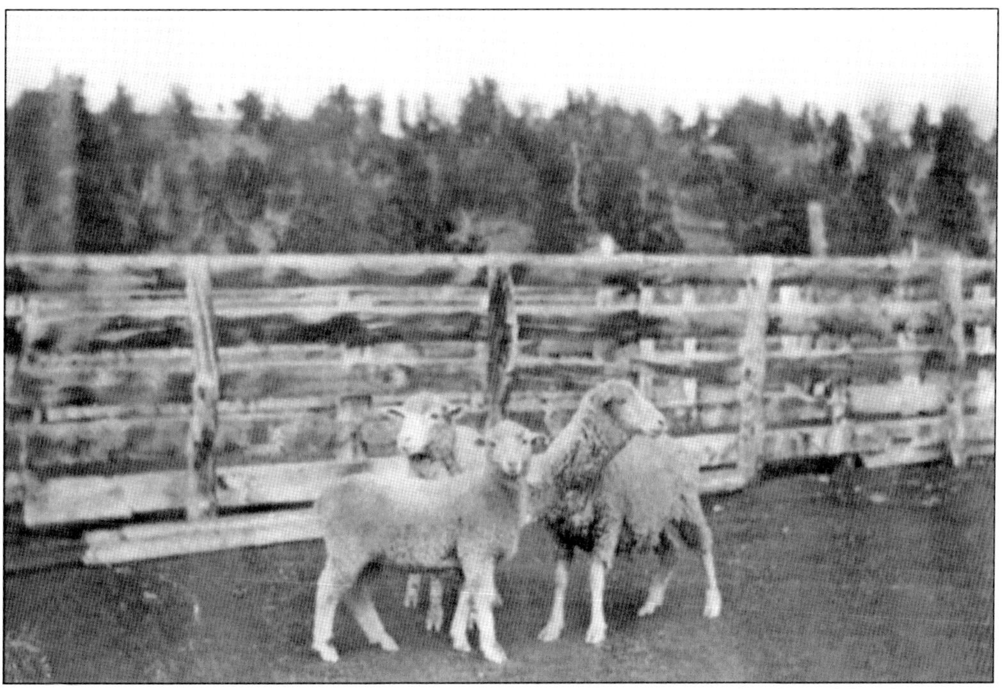

Although young lambs look like pets, they also went to market to be butchered for their meat, which was a delicacy. Sheep ranching has declined in the county, according to 2012 US Department of Agriculture statistics. The county now has only 11 sheep or goat farms.

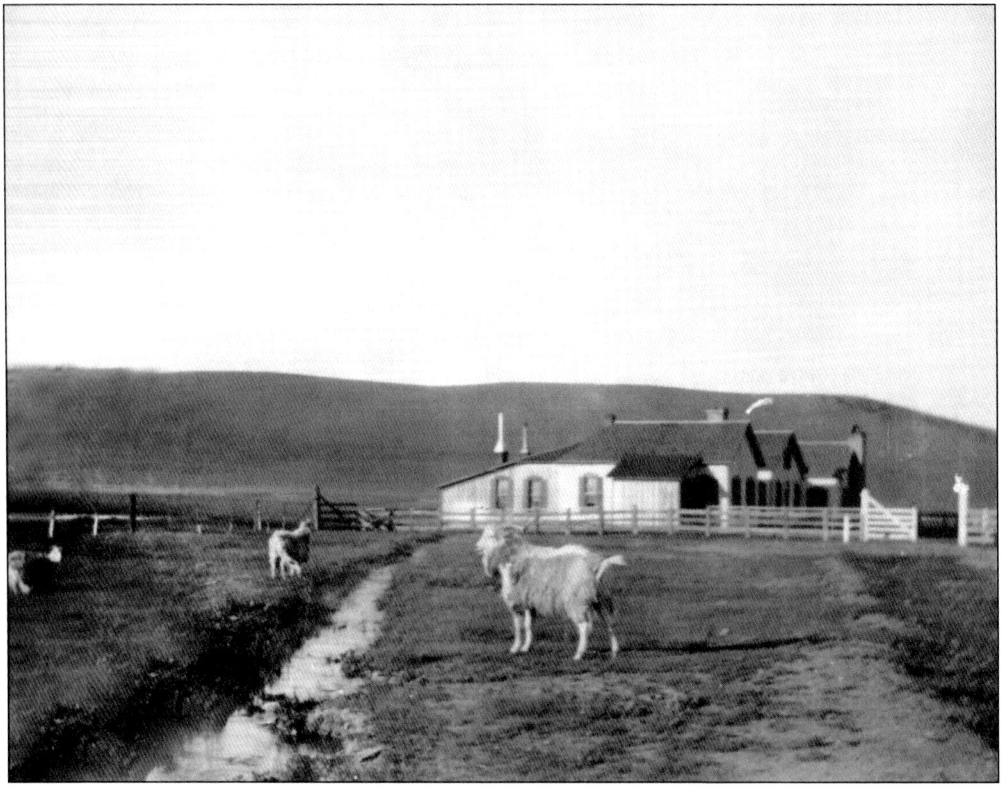

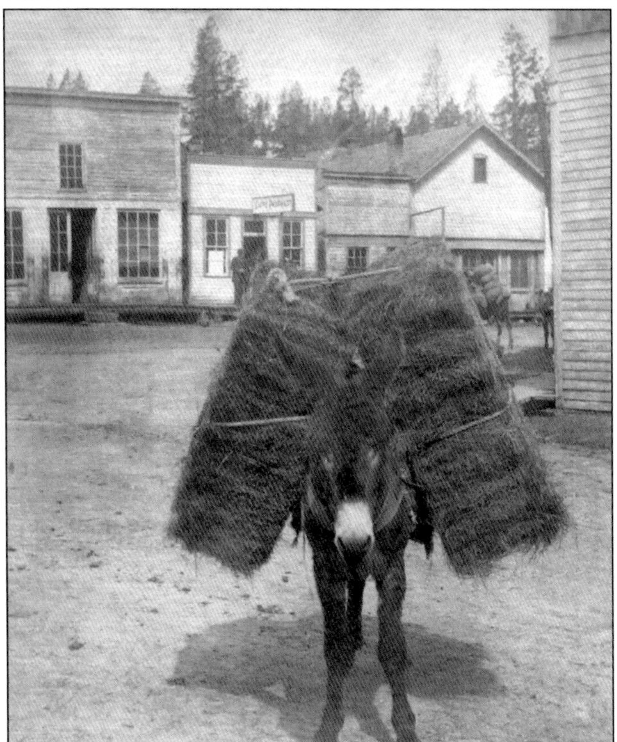

Goats were kept on some farms for milk as well as meat. Young kids' meat was highly prized. According to the US Department of Agriculture, over 37,000 goats were being raised in Colorado by 1900, compared to a quarter of a million in the state of New Mexico.

This 1880s photograph shows how burros were used to freight hay to places only their sure footing could navigate. Hay was vital in the mining camps to feed livestock that the miners relied on, such as horses and mules. Any extra hay was often used to fill makeshift mattresses.

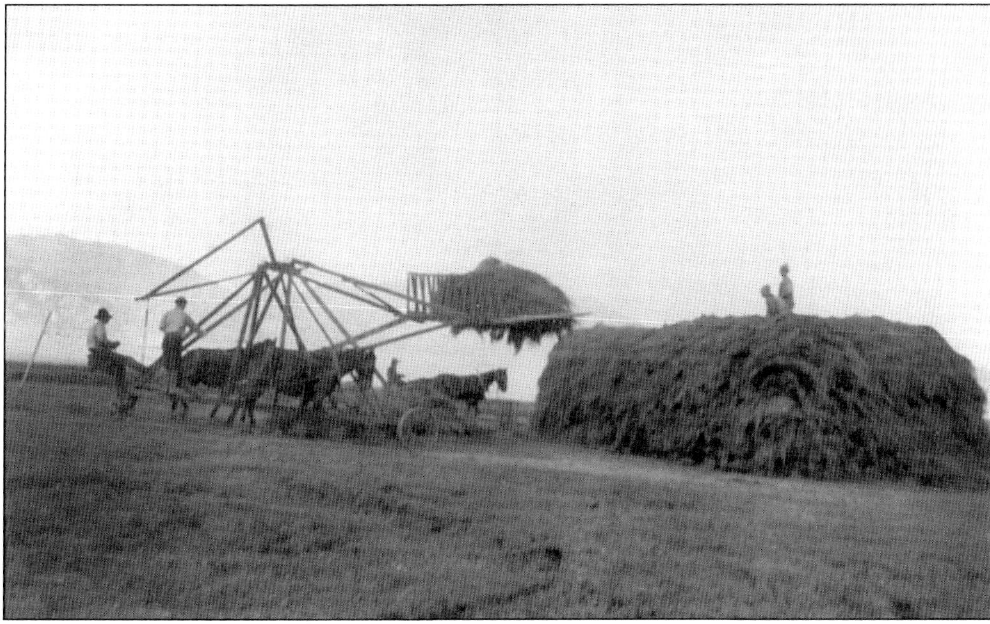

Machinery was necessary to harvest and stack, as well as cut, hay. South Park's very lucrative hay crops were prized for their high quality. The January 1, 1884, issue of the *Rocky Mountain News* asserted, in regards to the region's hay, that, "the quality . . . is unsurpassed by any known, if indeed, it is not superior to any other."

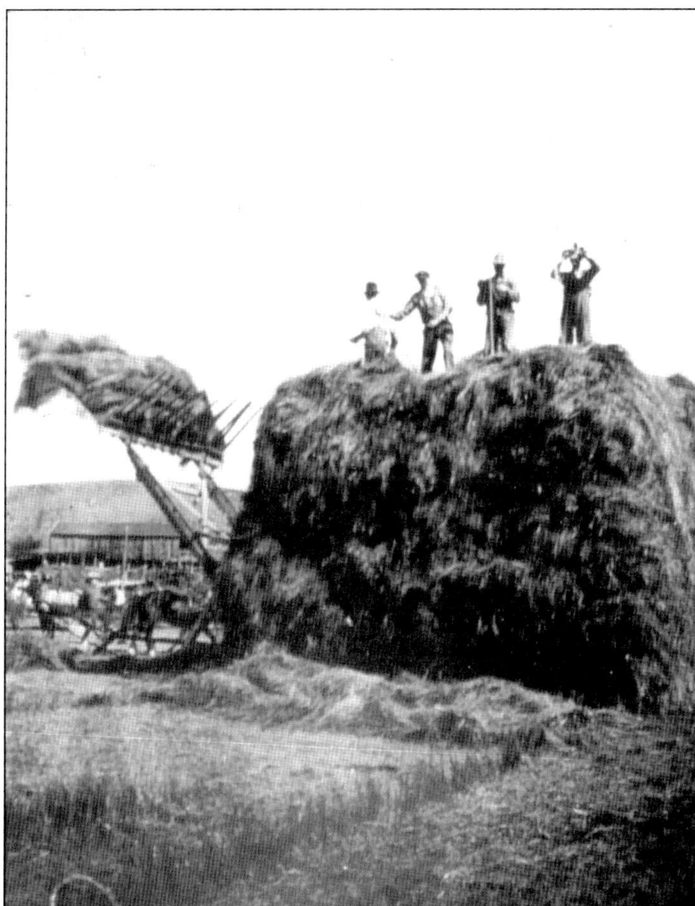

This stacker could bring hay up from either side without the wind affecting it, reaching up to 20 feet. Basic homemade stackers could be built by the ranchers themselves, although they were not as effective. The cost of a manufactured stacker around 1920 was approximately $75. These men stand poised to receive the incoming hay.

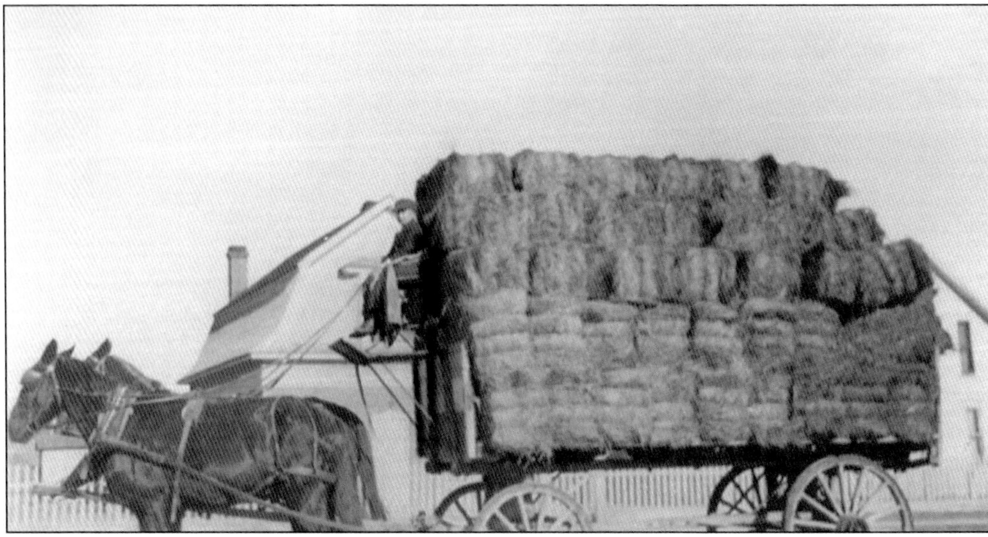

Bill Lewis rides atop Wilbur Lewis's hay wagon in 1921. Bales of hay were delivered to a location on Front Street in Fairplay, the main thoroughfare in town.

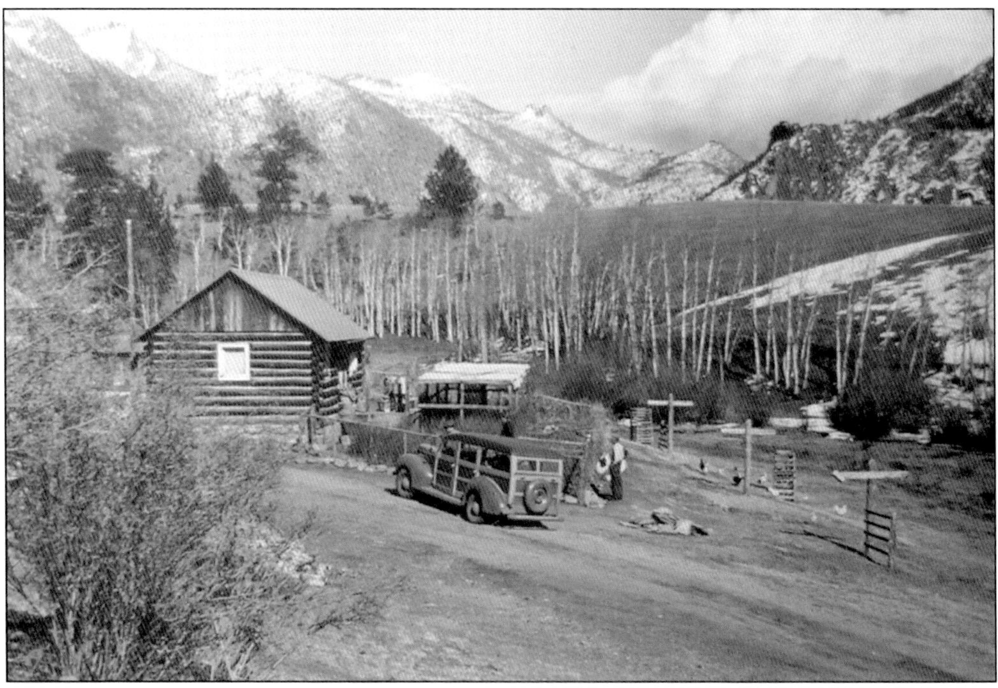

This picturesque cattle ranch, located along the Tarryall Road, was owned by the John E. Williams family. An early Park County pioneer, Williams first worked as a miner and freighter before purchasing the ranch in the 1880s. After Williams's death in 1887, one of his sons married a nearby homesteader, Edith Gold, and the ranch became known as the Williams/Gold ranch. It remains in the Gold family today.

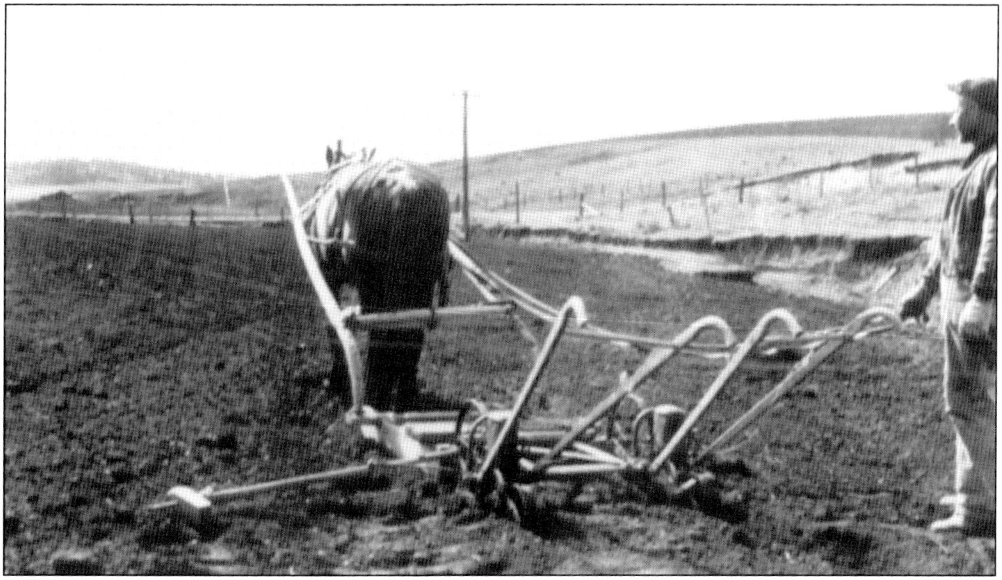

One of the earliest settlers on West Four Mile Creek, located northeast of Guffey, was the Tremayne family. Horses were frequently used to pull plows to till the soil. There were approximately 150 ranches in Park County in the late 1870s.

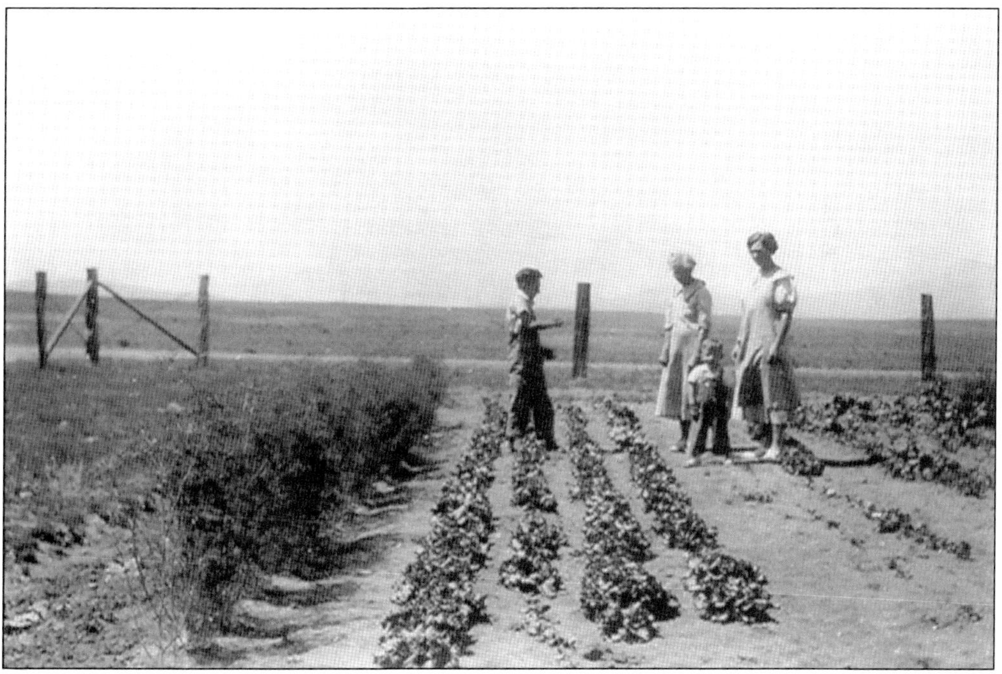

The Oakley family is shown in 1934 in the garden at their homestead. Farmers grew truck gardens for their own use, and the leftovers were sold in the local market. Lettuce, potatoes, and other root vegetables were favored, because they could survive the high altitude and early frosts.

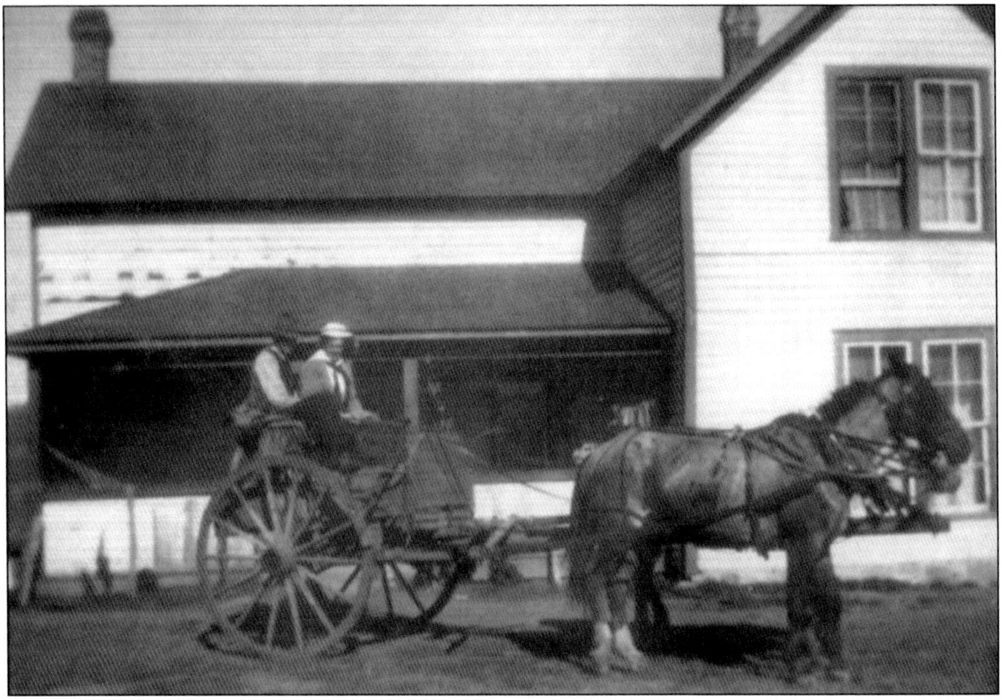

This horse pulls an unusual-looking carriage for members of the Epperson family. Horseback, buggies, and wagons were the primary modes of travel in the West before the advent of the automobile. The Eppersons owned considerable acreage in central South Park and were a well-known ranching family.

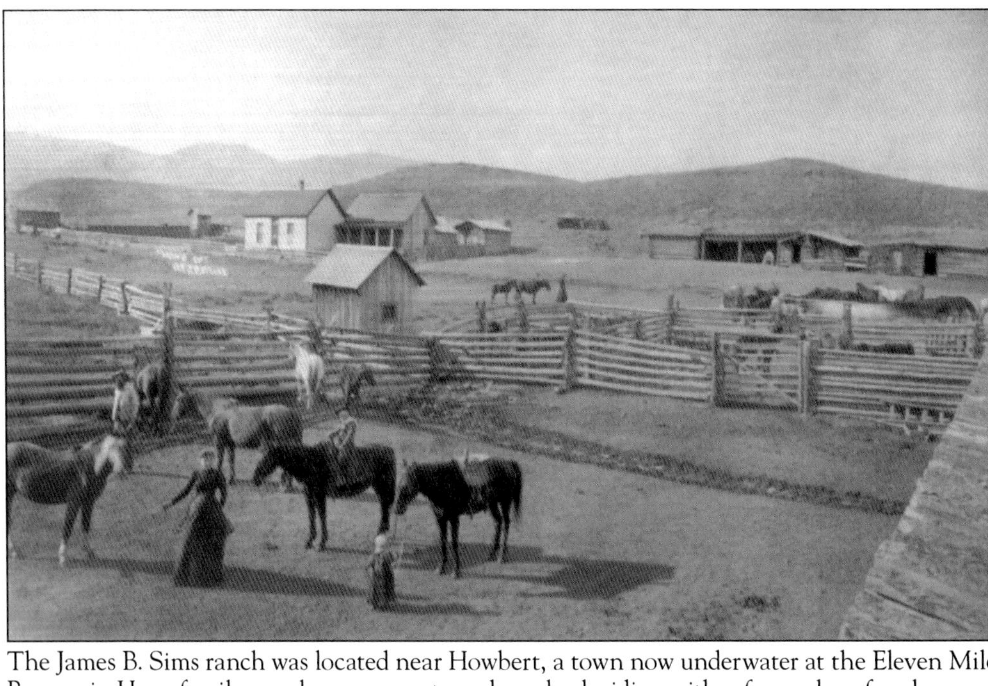

The James B. Sims ranch was located near Howbert, a town now underwater at the Eleven Mile Reservoir. Here, family members prepare to go horseback riding, either for work or for pleasure.

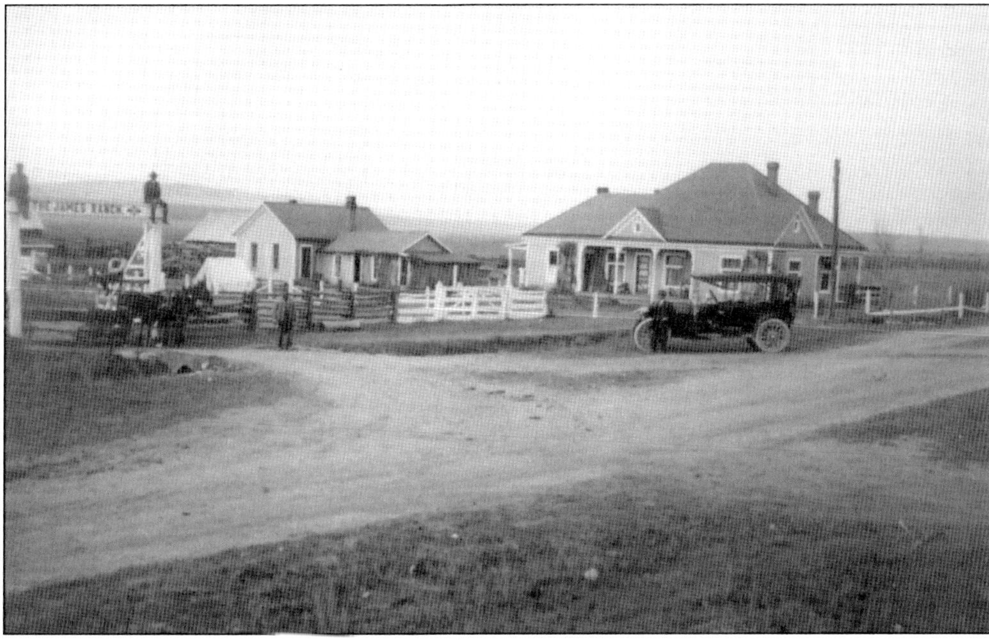

The 640-acre James ranch was located on Colorado State Highway 9, between Hartsel and Fairplay. It was purchased by Dr. William C. James and Dr. A.C. Donovan in 1883 for $13,000 from Hardy Epperson, a well-known Park County rancher.

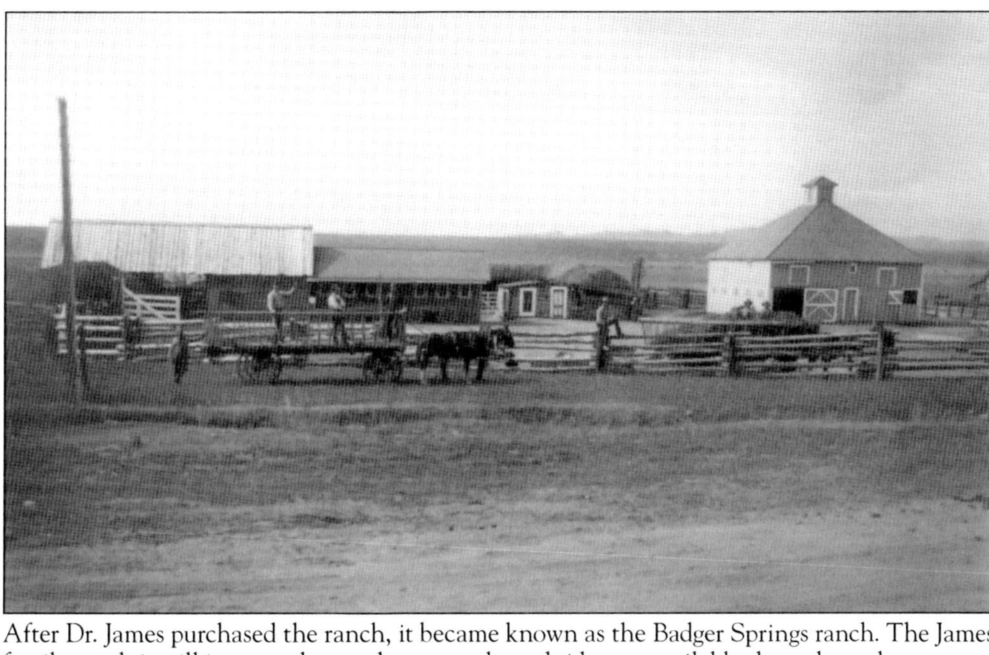

After Dr. James purchased the ranch, it became known as the Badger Springs ranch. The James family ranch is still in use today as a horse ranch, and rides are available throughout the summer. Both photographs on this page were taken around 1912. Shown here are the outbuildings, a barn, and corral.

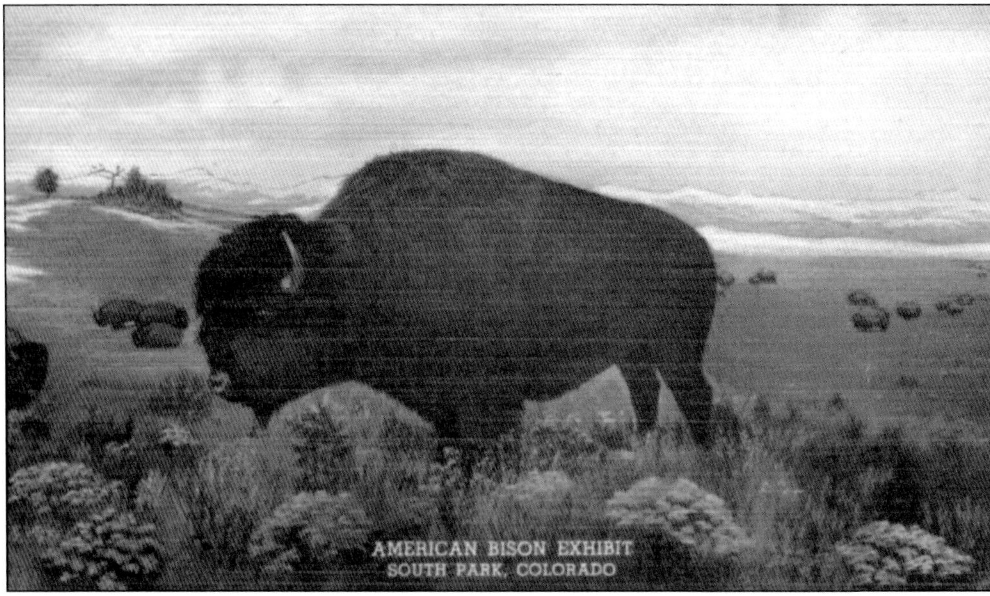

This vintage postcard replicates the American Bison exhibit that was at the Denver Museum of Natural History, the Chars. Boettcher Colorado Hall, in the 20th century. Bison were plentiful in South Park in the 1800s, until the remaining four were killed in the Lost Park area in 1897.

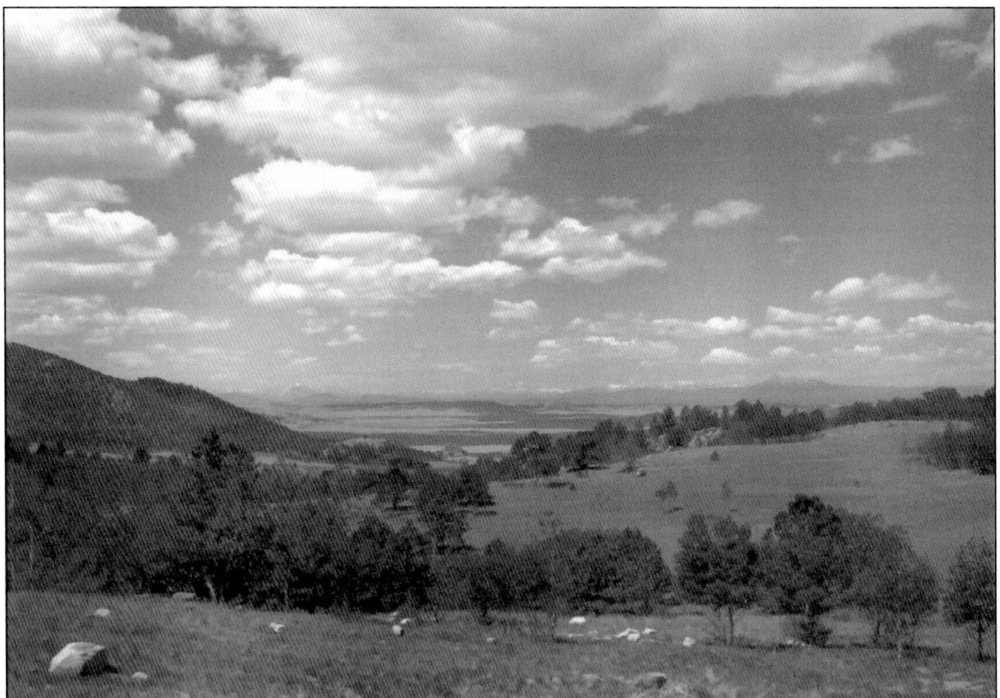

The South Park Basin, located in the center of Park County, has long been the subject of glowing pastoral accounts. Many writers have expounded on its unique geography. Samuel Bowles wrote during his 1868 Colorado expedition: "This [the South Park] is the more beautiful of the parks. . . . It offers a remarkable combination of the beauties of the Plains and those of the Mountains." (Courtesy of Christie Wright.)

Three

Transportation

Transportation within Park County has run the gamut, from the Ute Indians and French fur trappers traveling on foot, to modern times and the automobile. In between came pack mules, horses, freight wagons, stagecoaches, railroads, and an occasional airplane. South Park (originally spelled "Parc"), along with Middle and North Parks, was named by French fur trappers.

The need for more efficient travel kicked into high gear when the Colorado gold rush began in 1859. People needed to move, and supplies needed to be delivered. Stagecoaches brought the people to Park County, and freight wagons brought the supplies to sustain them. The horse-drawn conveyances provided the fastest means of transportation for nearly 20 years, until the arrival of the railroads. Locomotives pulling the coaches over the iron rails upped the ante on speed and efficiency, and the stages and freighters continued to operate, but altered their routes to coordinate with the railroad's advance. In 1878, the Denver, South Park & Pacific Railroad was the first to enter Park County on its way to the Gunnison Valley. It was built as a narrow-gauge railroad. This gauge (36 inches between the rails versus 56.5 inches for standard gauge) was widely utilized in Colorado in the early years, as the equipment was smaller and cheaper to build and operate, and thus more conducive to mountain operations. In 1887, the Colorado Midland, built to standard gauge, also crossed Park County on its way to Salt Lake City. Both railroads had their eye on points beyond South Park, but were quick to take advantage of local demand along the way. By 1938, the last of the railroad tracks in Park County were removed.

As the 20th century progressed, automobiles and the roads they utilized steadily improved. This, combined with a sharp decline in mining activity, rendered all prior forms of transportation in Park County obsolete. Today, the county has over 3,300 miles of public roadways, which it maintains.

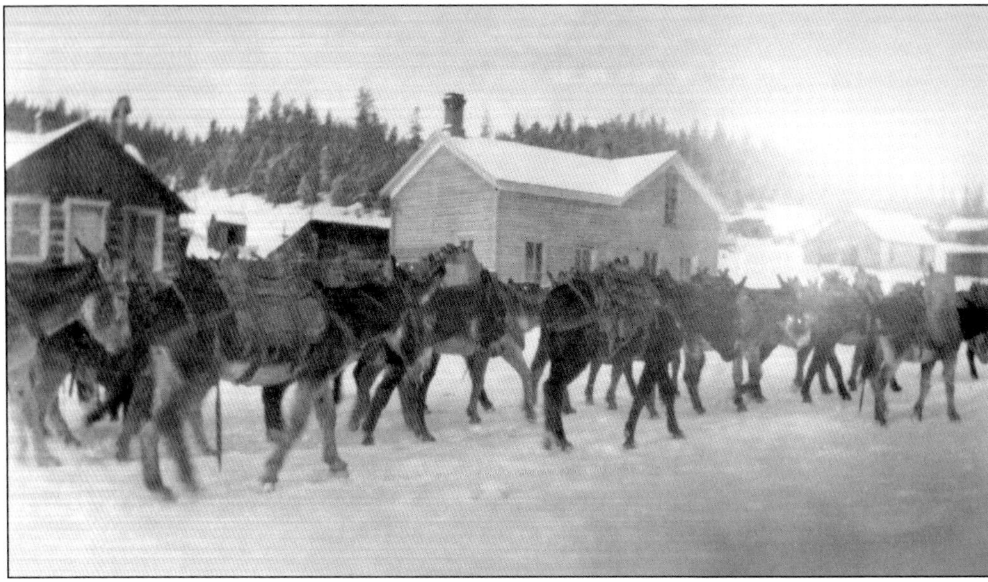

Burros and mules were the all-terrain vehicles of their time. They hauled anything, anywhere. They were the primary means of moving supplies and ore to and from the mines, as evidenced here by a "jack train" ready to head out from Alma.

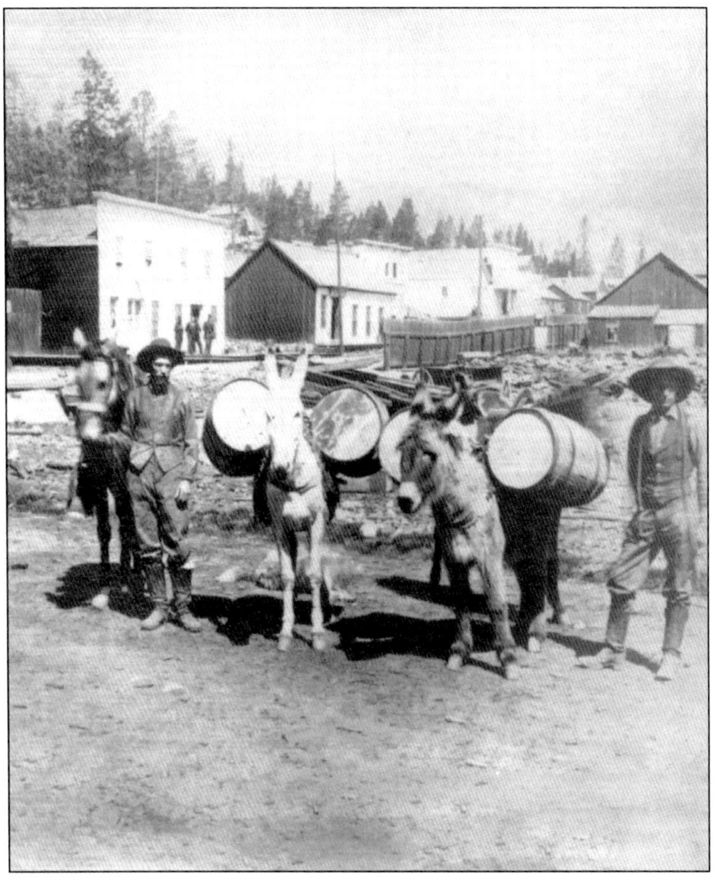

Burros, sometimes referred to as "jacks," carry large barrels in this early photograph of Alma. Founded in 1872, the town was a major supply center for the Mosquito Range mines, including the large and profitable Dolly Varden, Moose, and Russia Mines located on Mounts Bross and Lincoln.

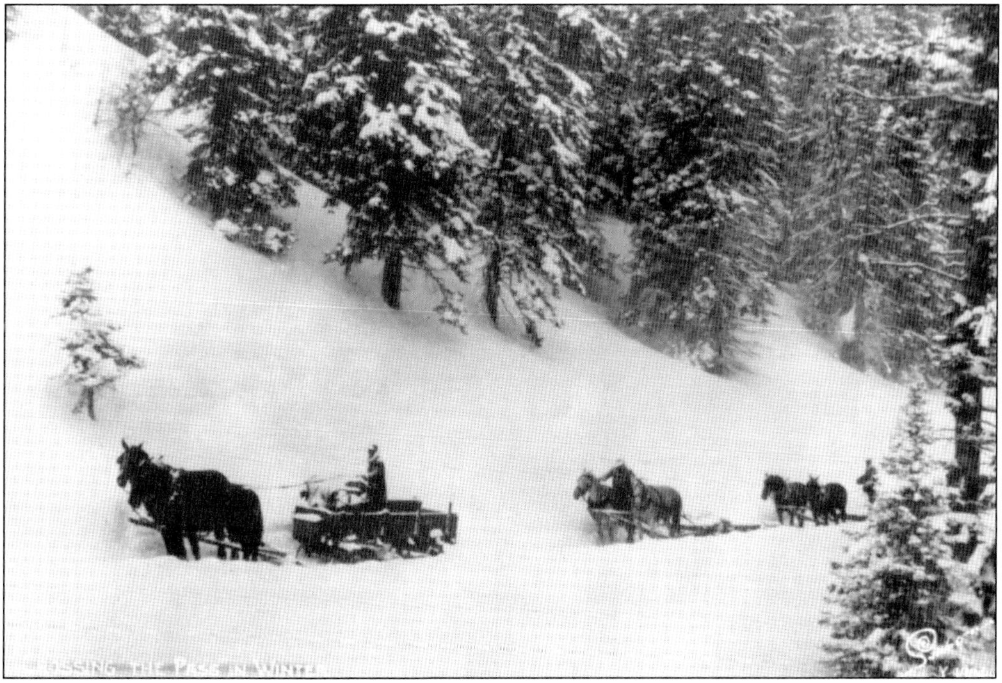

Hoosier Pass could be crossed in the wintertime via horse teams outfitted with sleds. Today, the pass is paved. Colorado State Highway 9 connects Park and Summit Counties along the Continental Divide and is a popular scenic roadway. At over 11,500 feet, it can still be a difficult crossing in the wintertime.

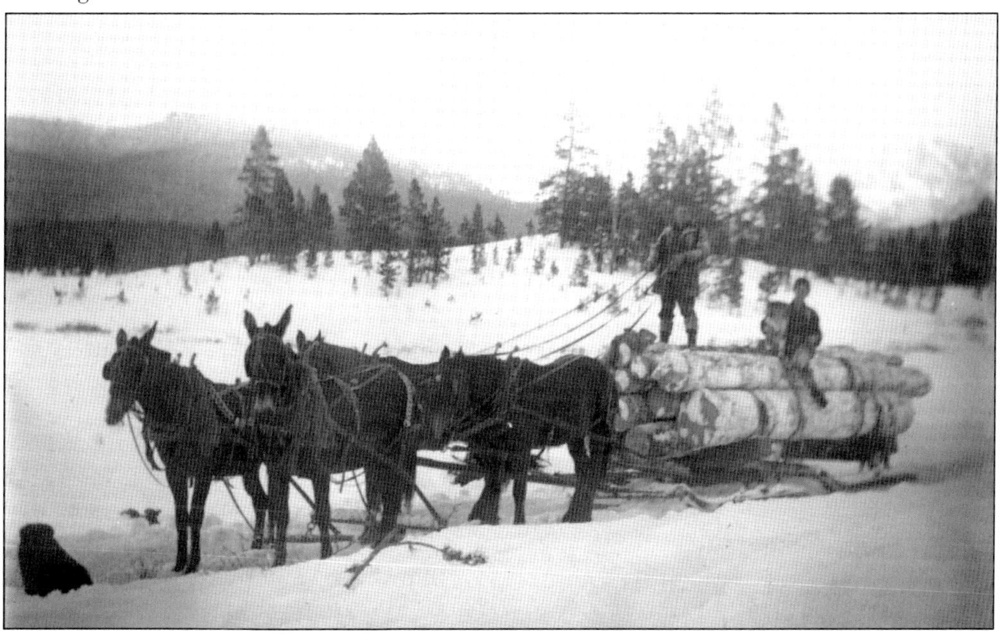

A freight wagon on skis proved that winter weather did not stop these freighters engaged in winter timber operations in Park County. Utilizing wheels in the summer and skis in the winter, the freight wagons moved the heavier, bulkier items between towns and the railroads. (Courtesy of AADSP&PHS.)

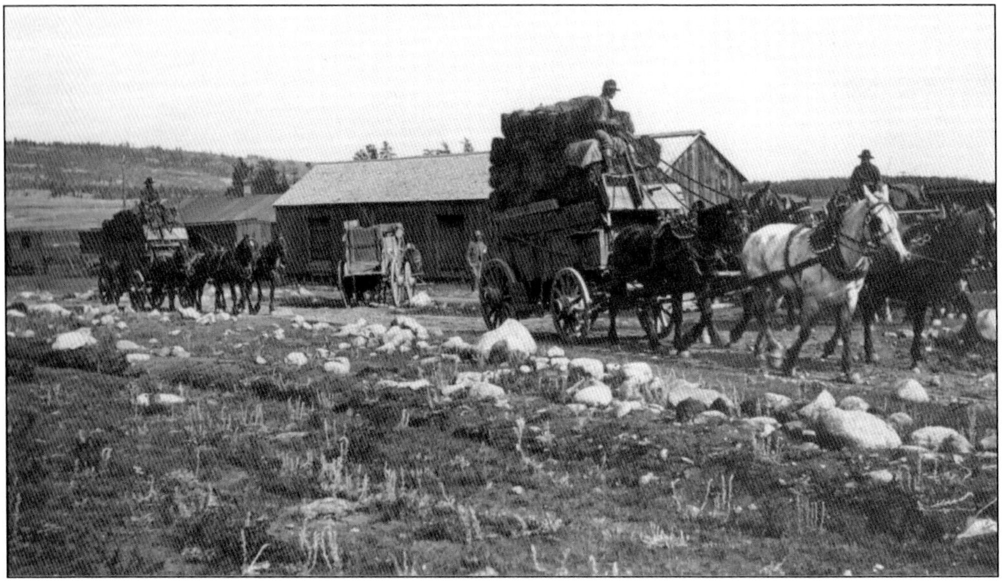

Teamsters and their freight wagons haul supplies from the Colorado & Southern train at London Junction (later Alma). After the demise of the London, South Park & Leadville Railroad (later the South Park & Leadville Short Line), freight wagons also hauled ore from the London Mine to the smelter at the Colorado & Southern railhead at London Junction/Alma. (Courtesy of AADSP&PHS.)

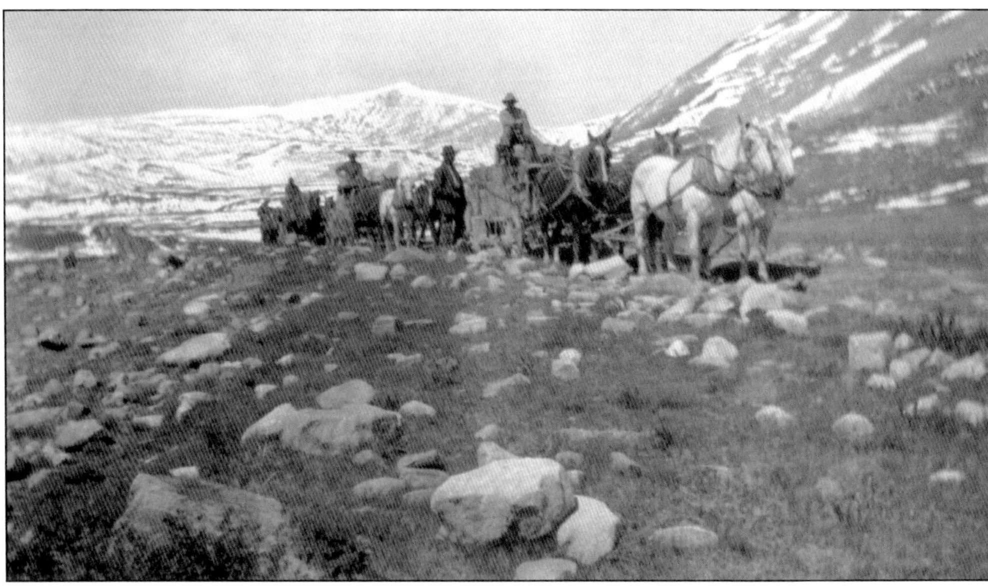

Ore wagons were used to haul precious gold and silver from the hard-rock mines high in the Mosquito Range down to the towns, where several mills and smelters were located. The ore was then processed for sale. This horse team is descending from the American Flats area, located just southwest of London Mountain.

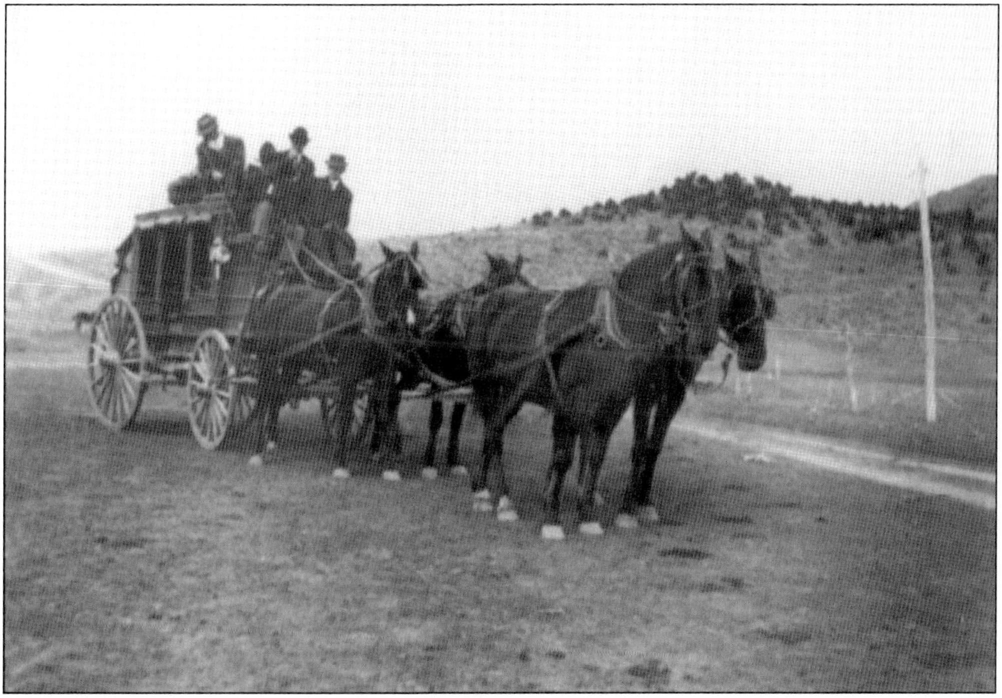

Stagecoaches moved people to all points not directly served by the railroads, until the advent of the automobile. The stage lines serving Park County included companies such as the Pioneer Stage Company, Denver & South Park Stage Company owned by Spotswood and McClellan, Wall & Witter, McLaughlin, and Quiggle Stage Line.

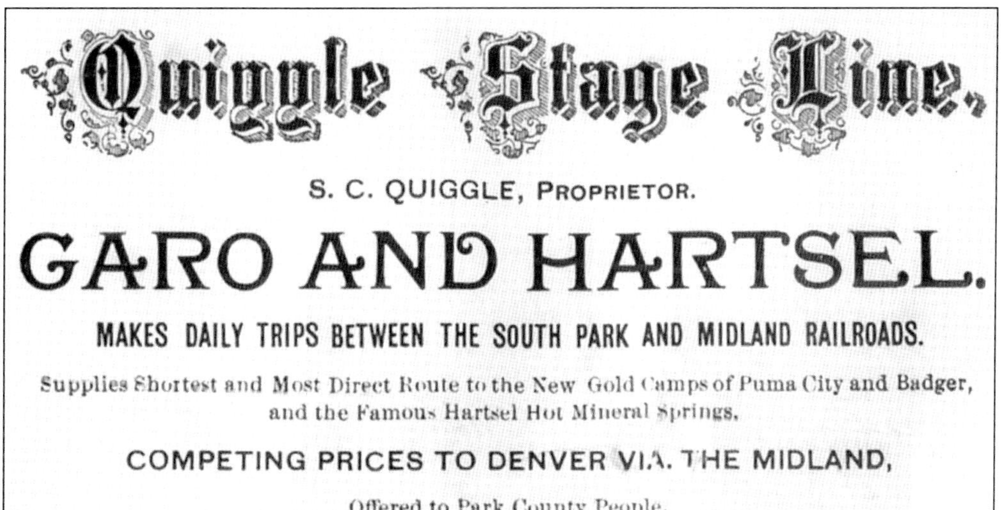

Shown here is a business card for the Quiggle Stage Line, around 1890. This line provided a stagecoach connection between the depots of Park County's two railroads, and served other locations in the area, such as Hartsel. One eastbound stage left for Denver and Colorado Springs at 3:20 a.m., according to an 1897 notice in the local newspaper. (Courtesy of AADSP&PHS.)

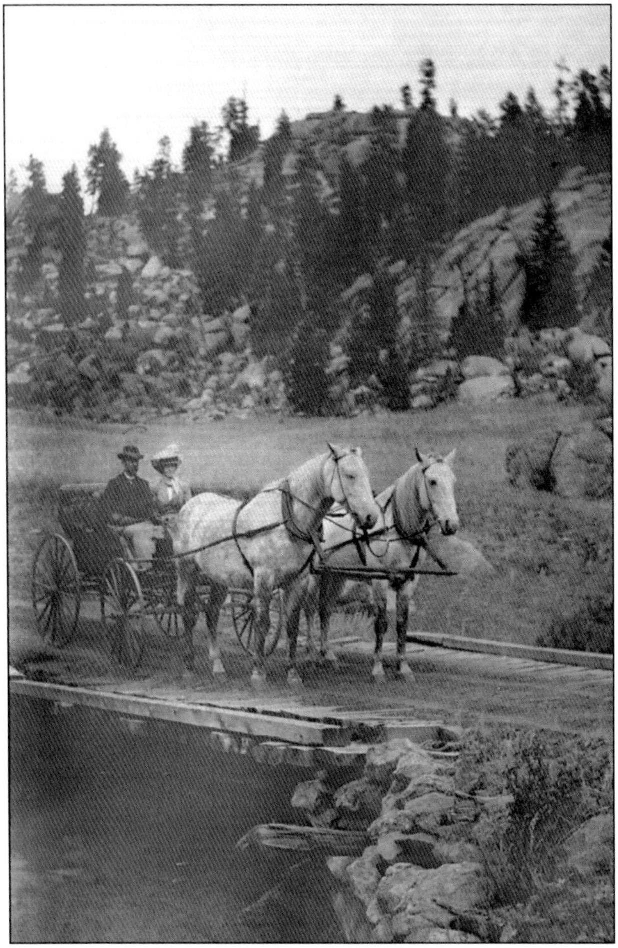

A more genteel mode of transportation was a buggy pulled by a span of horses. This couple, dressed in their Sunday best, might have been out for an afternoon outing along the Tarryall Road that connects the towns of Jefferson and Lake George, 42 miles in length.

Deep Park County snows required keeping up with snow removal to keep the roadways passable. Here, a buggy is fitted with a plow underneath to clear away a recent snowfall in the 1930s in the town of Guffey. Guffey homesteader Amos Hardy stands on the rear of the wagon as a four-horse team pulls the plow along.

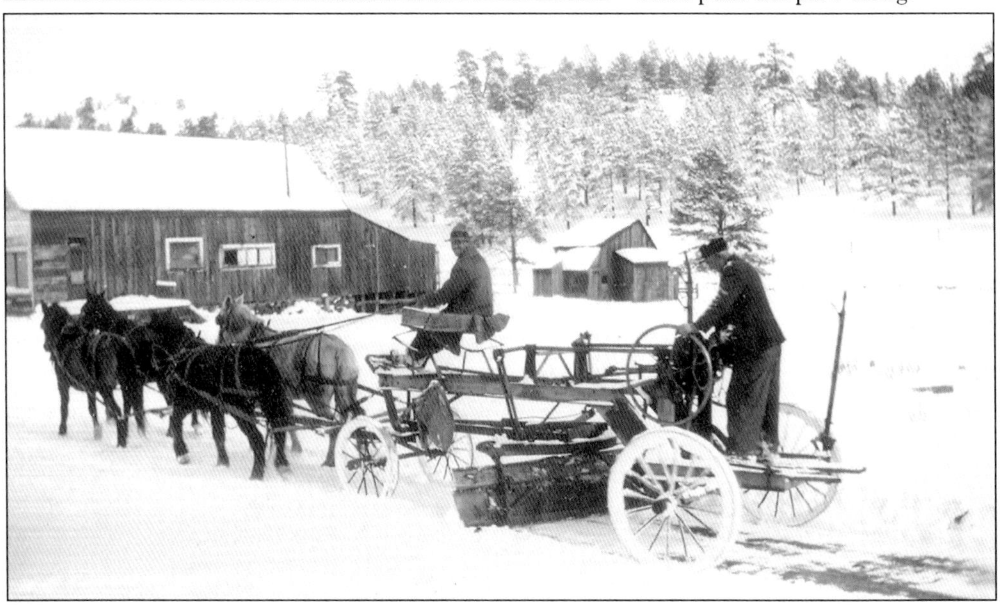

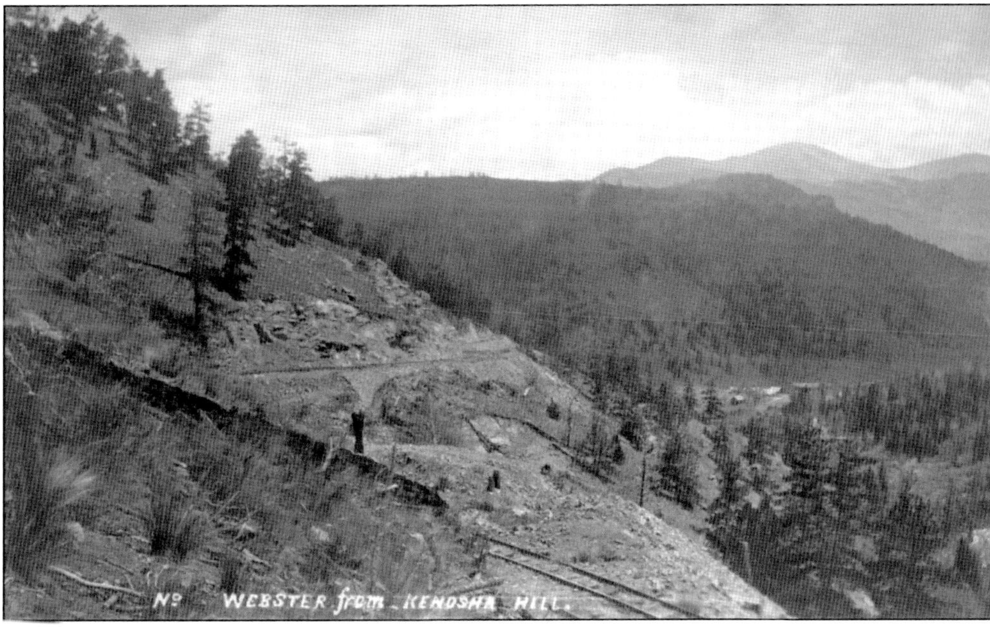

The town of Webster, located several miles west of Grant, is shown when it was the end of the track in 1878–1879. Webster was extremely busy during this period, as people and supplies were transferred from the train to stagecoaches and freight wagons to continue to all points west. (Courtesy of DSP&PHS.)

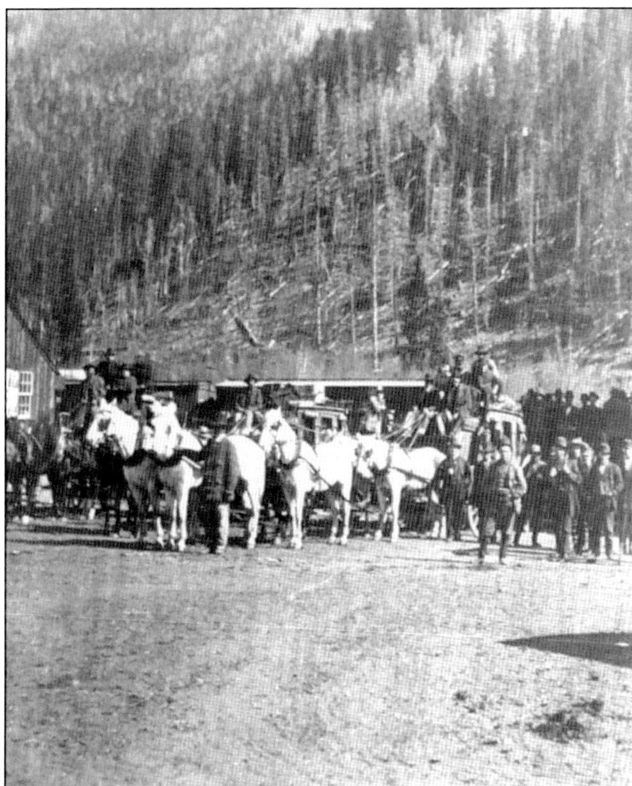

The Webster area was named after an early Colorado legislator, William W. Webster, a "fifty-niner," who was a Constitutional Convention delegate in 1876 when Colorado achieved statehood. To the west of the town is Webster Pass, coincidentally named after two other men, William and Emerson Webster, who built a road over the Continental Divide connecting Summit and Park Counties in 1878 to more easily ship mining freight.

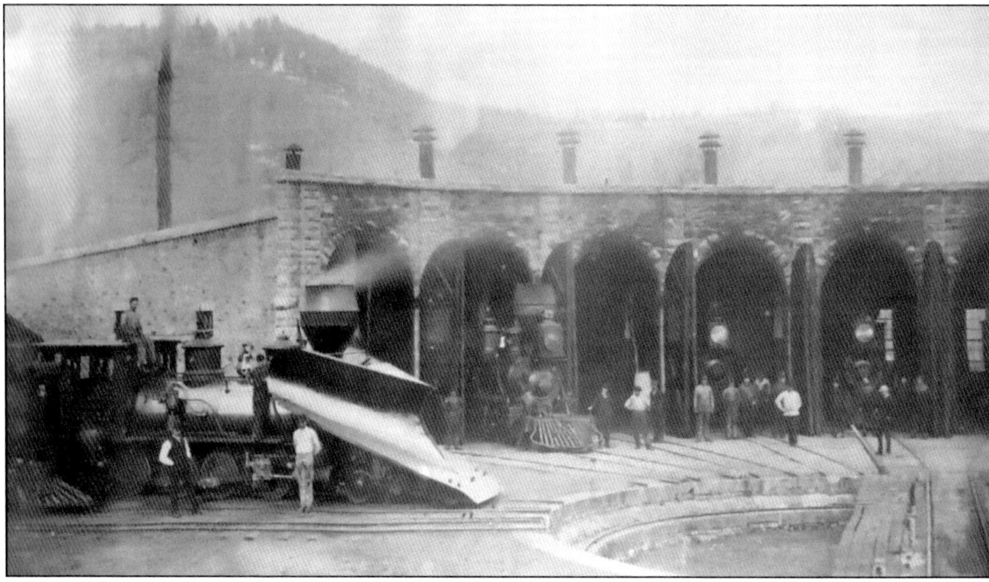

The Como roundhouse is a beehive of activity in this c. 1885 photograph. The turntable was manually pushed by hand. With all of the roundhouse doors open, many locomotives and employees pose for the camera. Built in 1881, this cut-stone roundhouse still stands today. (Courtesy of DSP&PHS.)

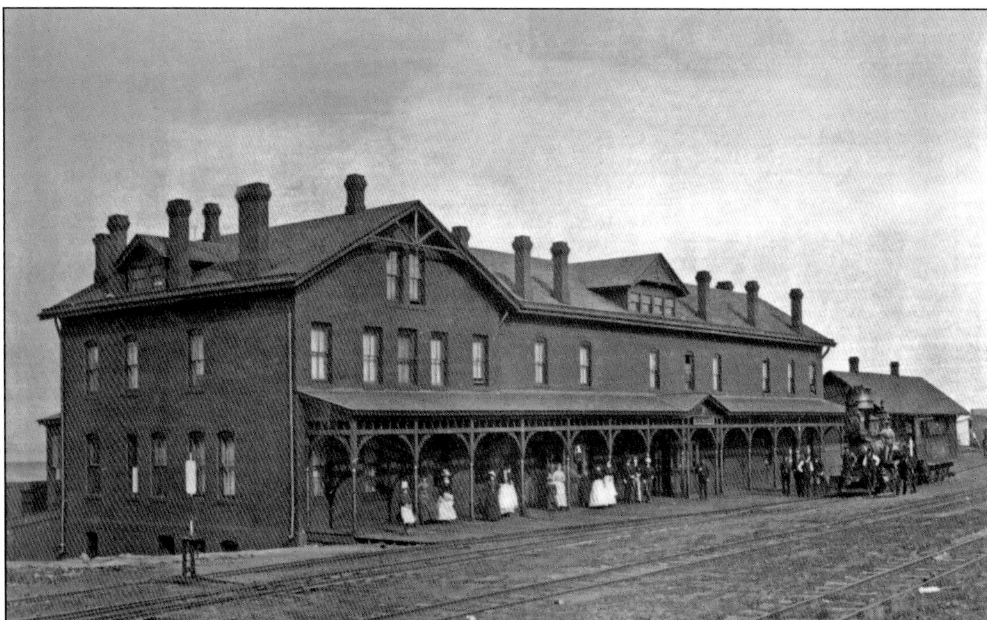

The Pacific Hotel accommodated Park County travelers and was Como's premiere hotel from 1885 to November 1896, when it burned down. Much like the Harvey Houses along the Santa Fe Railroad, the Pacific Hotel company managed the eating houses along the Union Pacific Railroad. This photograph was taken on July 18, 1886, by George Mellen.

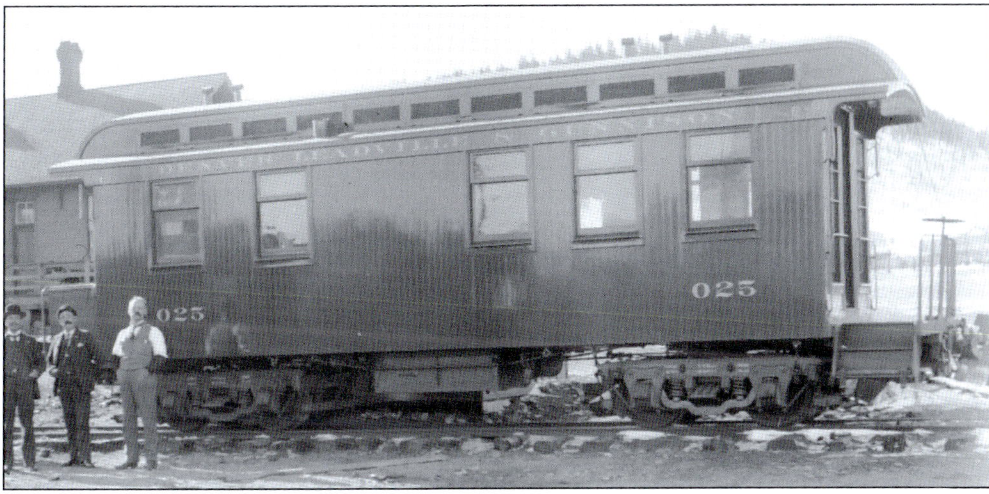

Railroad management, also known as the "Brass Hats," of the Denver, Leadville & Gunnison Railroad liked to travel in style. Here, they visit Como around 1898. The car's staff pose in front of the car, whose sides are so shiny, the men's reflections can be seen. This narrow-gauge railroad was known as the Denver, South Park & Pacific from 1872 to 1889, when it reorganized into the Denver, Leadville & Gunnison. (Courtesy of DSP&PHS.)

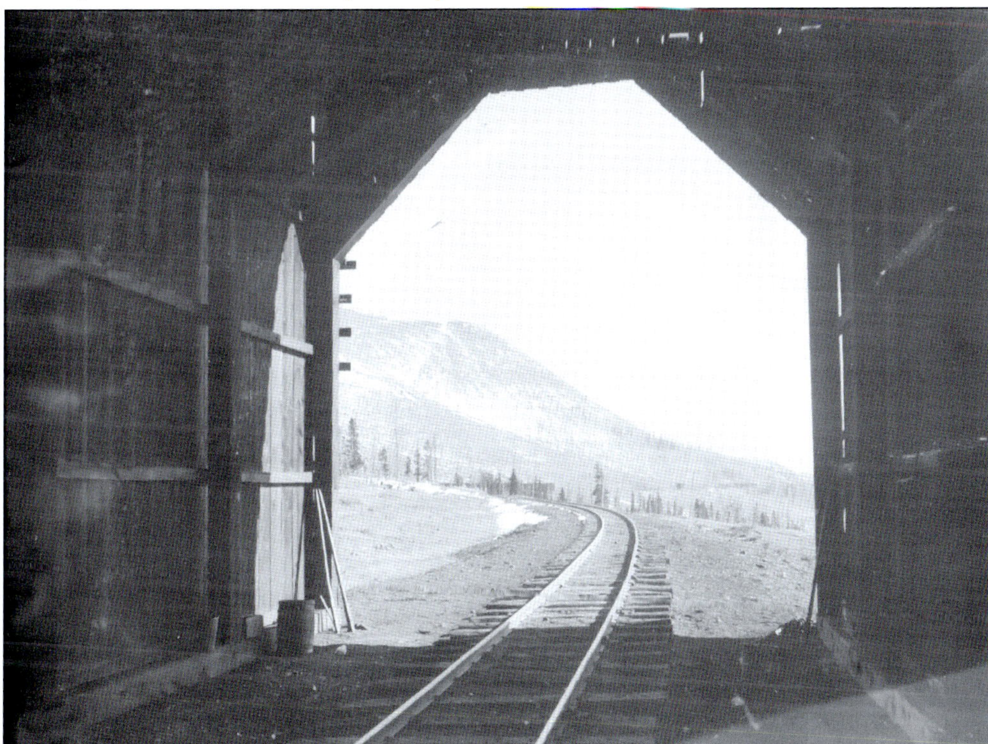

Taken from the top of Boreas Pass, at the county line between Park & Summit Counties, this photograph looks south into Park County from inside the summit snow shed. From here, the track goes down into South Park and Como. Boreas Pass was named for the Greek god of the north wind, and the railroad employees who lived there at 11,493 feet knew it was well named. (Courtesy of DSP&PHS.)

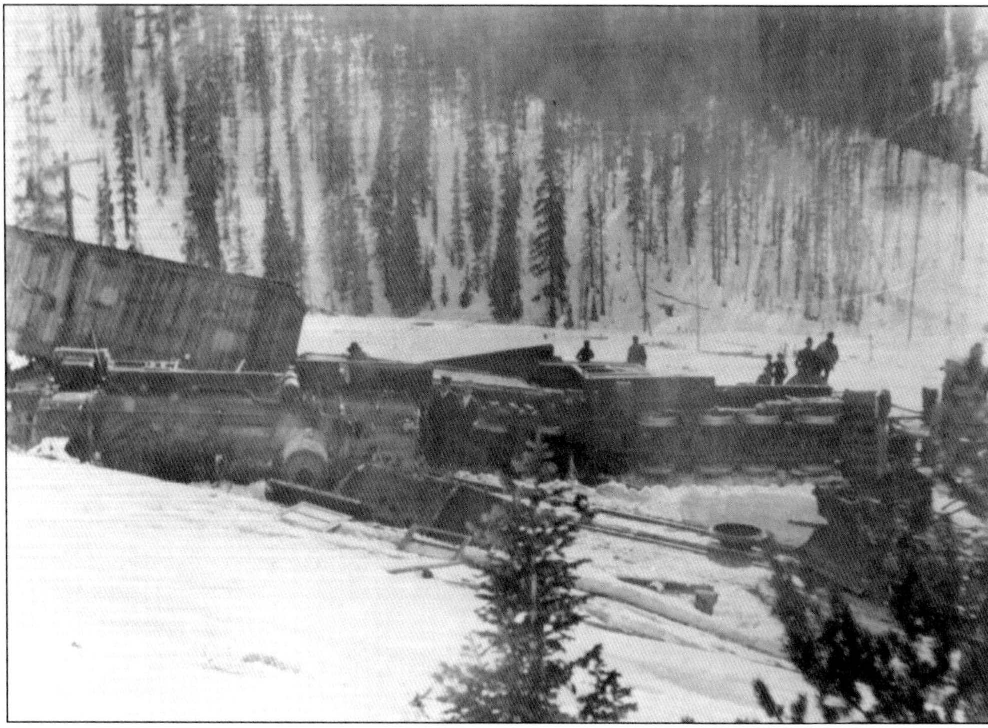

Mountain railroading, especially in winter, could be very unforgiving. Runaway trains usually resulted in a wreck, such as this one on Boreas Pass. Even limiting downgrade speeds to eight miles per hour did not guarantee that a train would not get away from the crew. Before air-brake systems were implemented, the crew would jump from car to car to tighten the brake wheels. (Courtesy of AADSP&PHS.)

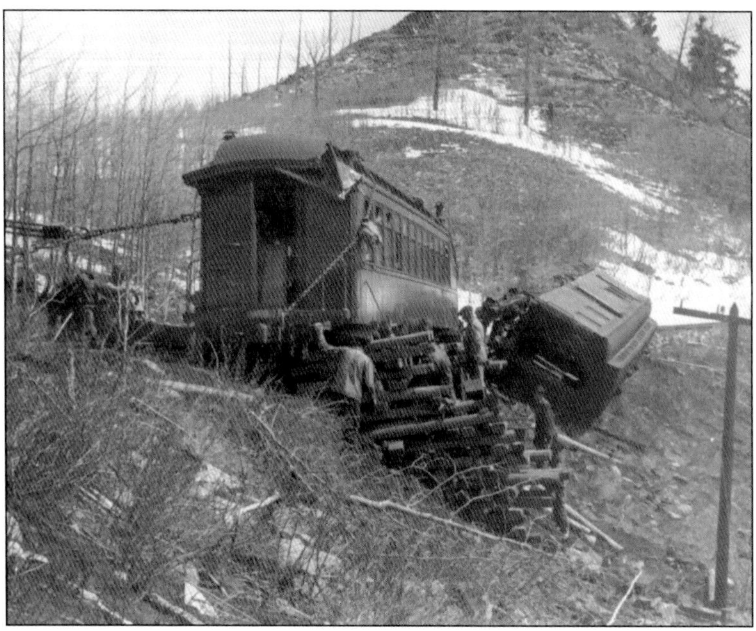

Cleaning up wrecks took a lot of men, muscle, rope, chain, timbers, block and tackle, time, and a bit of luck. Unfortunately, such events were not at all rare, resulting in the wreck crew becoming quite proficient at their job. This accident occurred on the Park County side of Boreas Pass. (Courtesy of DSP&PHS.)

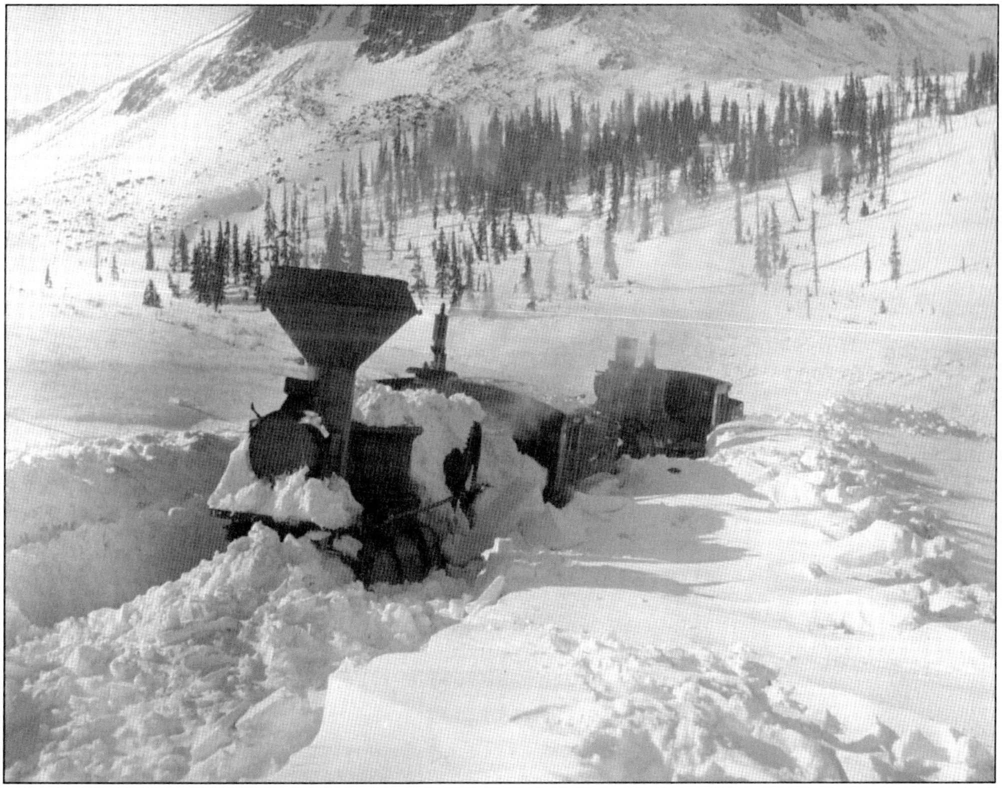

Snow proved to be a formidable impediment to conducting railroad operations, as these snowbound locomotives indicate. The worst winter was that of 1898–1899, when the line over Boreas Pass was closed for three months. (Courtesy of AADSP&PHS.)

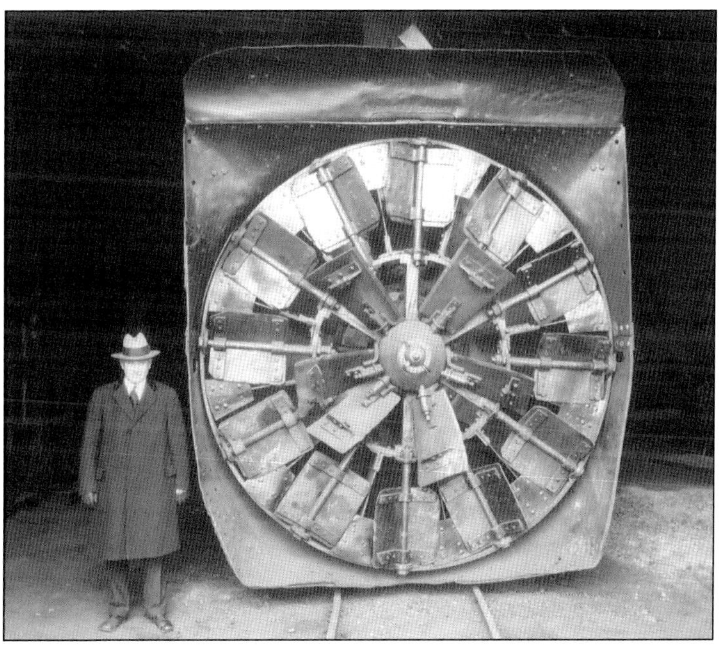

When the Leslie brothers patented the rotary snowplow, it rapidly became the railroad's most successful snow-fighting tool. These machines were powered by a steam boiler that drove a great steel wheel. The machines could throw the snow a considerable distance, doing the work of hundreds of men. This photograph shows the fearsome face—and great size—of the rotary in the Como roundhouse. (Courtesy of DSP&P.)

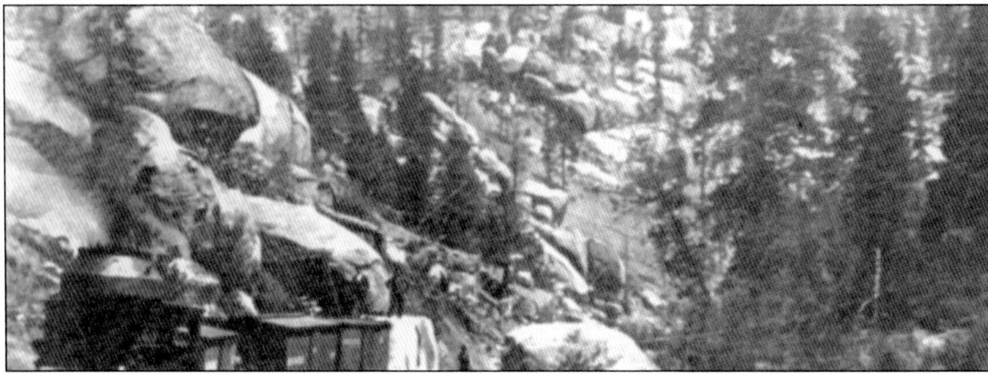

The Denver, South Park & Pacific train chugs its way through the winding Platte Canyon, which follows the north fork of the South Platte River. The train made numerous stops along the way for ranchers to load boxcars with vegetables, dairy products, and other commercial items.

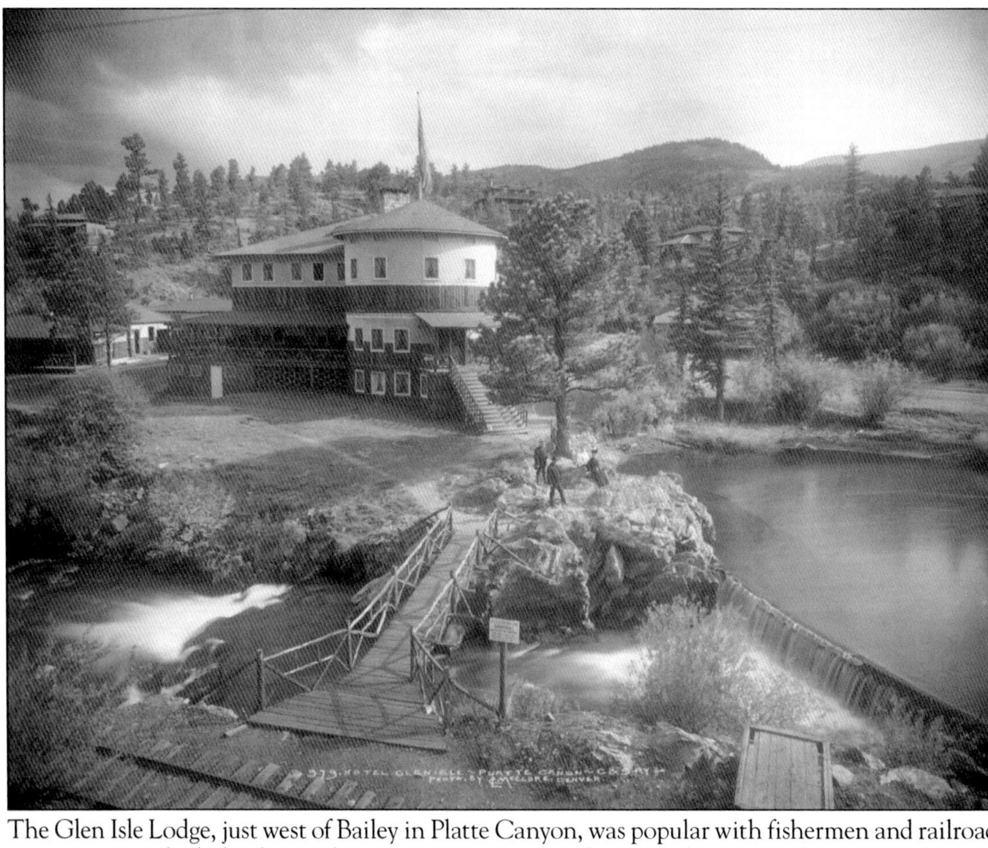

The Glen Isle Lodge, just west of Bailey in Platte Canyon, was popular with fishermen and railroad excursionists. The lodge featured its own open-air railroad stop. Today, US Highway 285 is located on the old railroad right-of-way (foreground). (Courtesy of DSP&P.)

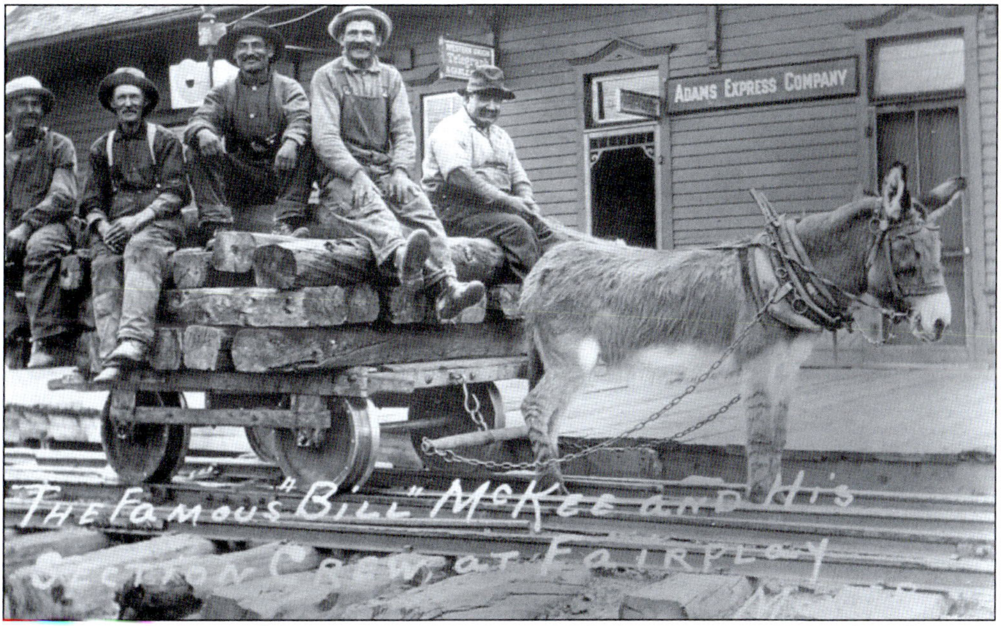

The arrival of railroads did not necessarily mean that the burros were out of a job. Bill McKee (far right), section foreman between Garo and London Junction/Alma for many years, prepares to leave the Fairplay depot with new rail, ties, and crew in 1910. The faithful burro Vanderbuilt is ready to pull the "train" out of the station. This depot burned down on August 12, 1912.

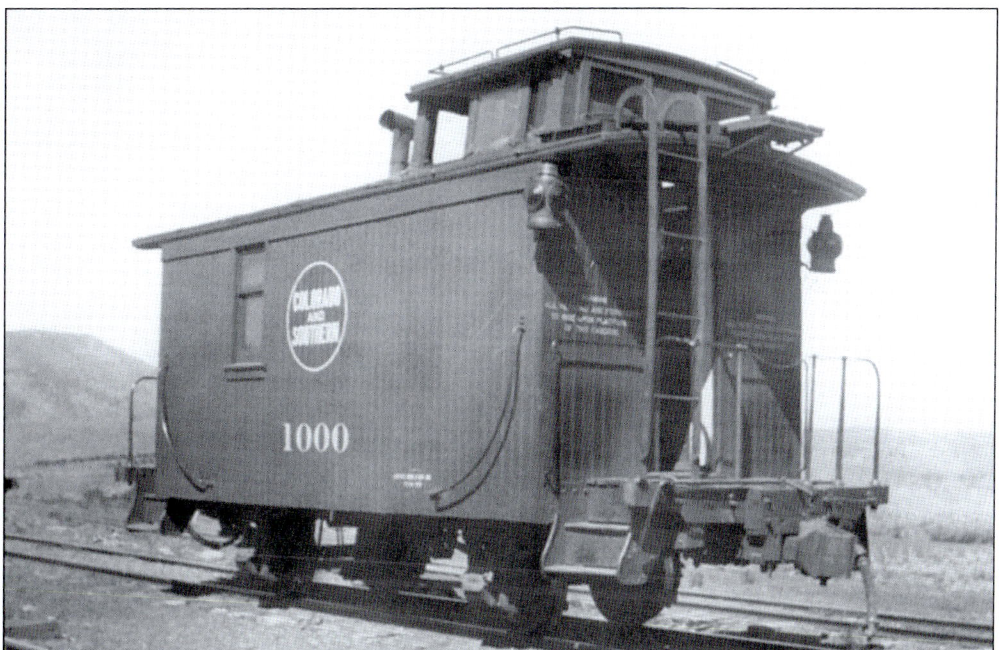

The caboose was the railroader's home away from home. The Colorado & Southern caboose No. 1000 is shown at the north end of the Como yard on the line to Breckenridge and Leadville. The conductor and rear brakeman would ride in this car and inspect the train while it was in motion. (Courtesy of DSP&P.)

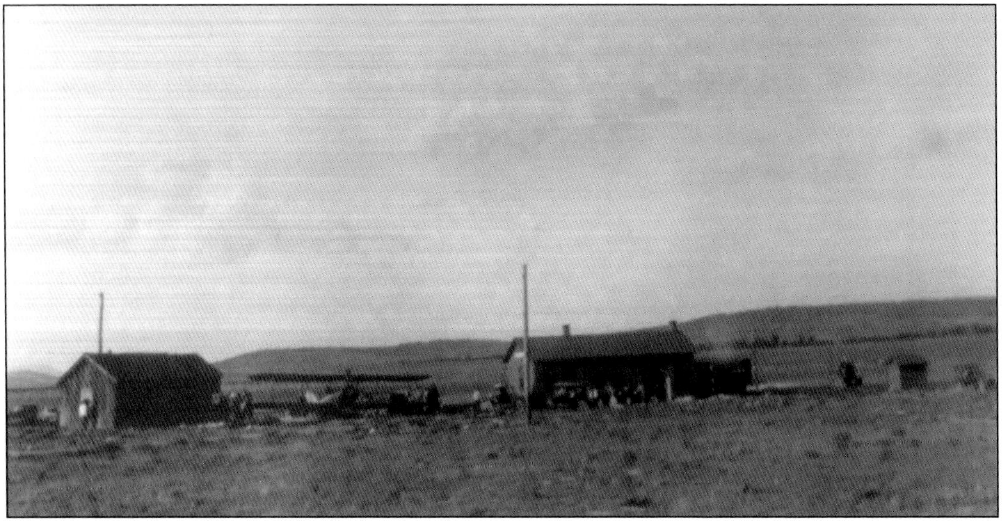

A biplane has landed by the Fairplay railroad depot in the 1920s. Several people arrived to witness this unusual event. Park County never had a formal airport, but several informal airports have served the needs of aviators over the years. (Courtesy of DSP&P.)

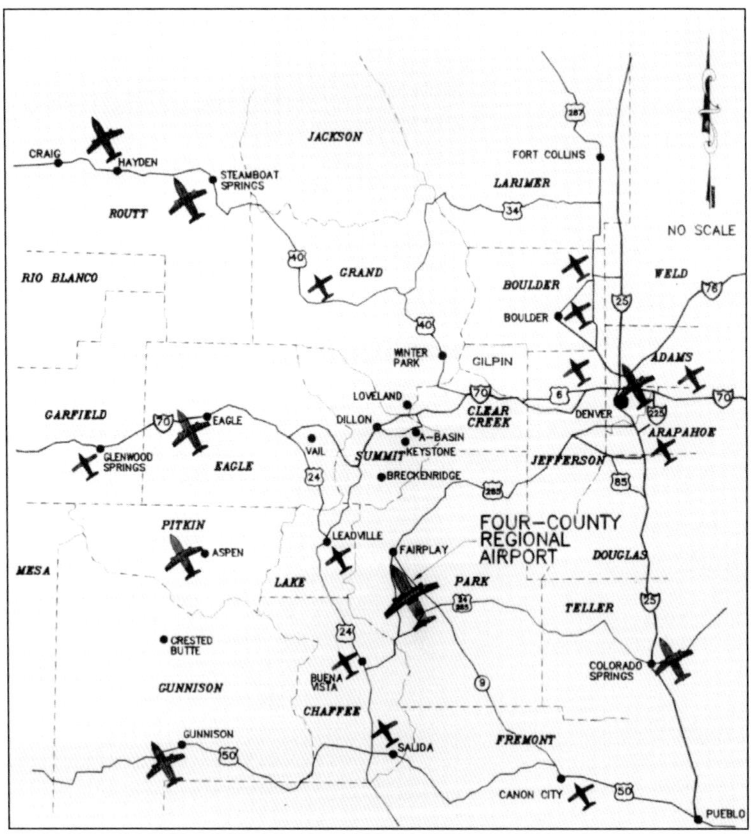

An airport was planned in South Park in 1995 to serve a four-county area. Called the Central Colorado Regional Airport, it was voted down by residents concerned about noise, traffic pollution, and the impact the 1,400-acre facility would have regionally. The issue was revived 10 years later, but the airport again was not approved.

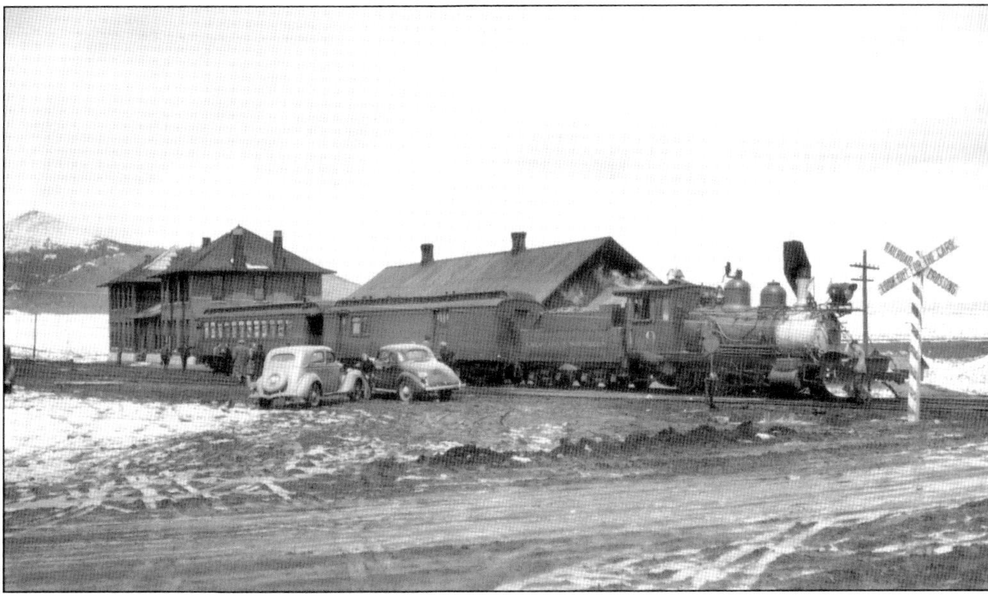

This photograph was taken on April 10, 1937, an important and sad day in Como. The very last passenger train from Leadville to Denver prepares to depart. This ended an era of passenger trains in Park County that spanned 58 years. Due to declining business, the Colorado & Southern Railroad tried to abandon service for many years. (Courtesy of DSP&P.)

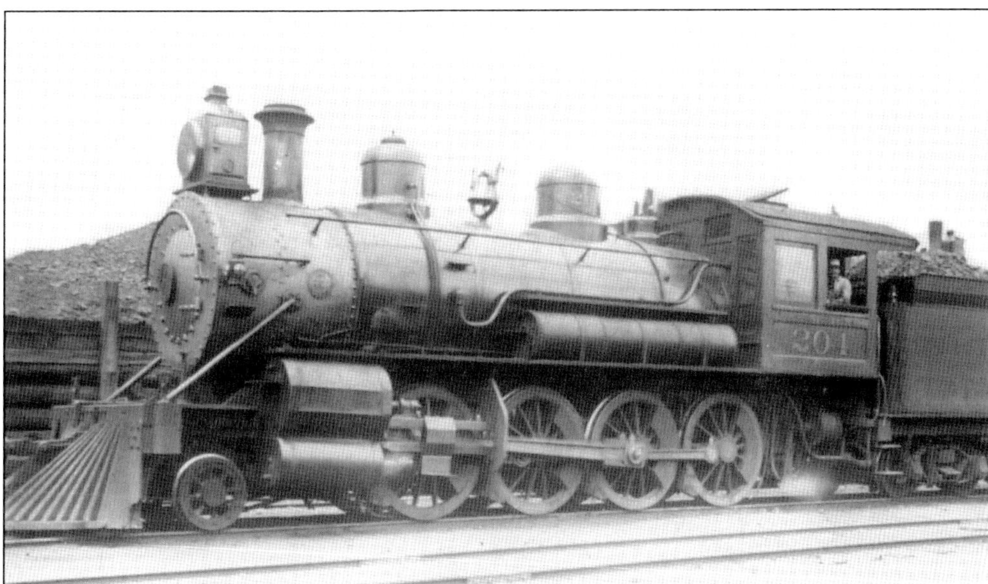

Colorado Midland engine No. 204 was built in 1901 by Baldwin Locomotive Works in Philadelphia as a compound engine. This design used the steam twice, in high- and low-pressure cylinders. While more efficient, the design proved problematic, and the model was rebuilt to a traditional single-cylinder design. The standard-gauge Colorado Midland had five of this class of locomotive; they were the second most powerful engines on the line. (Courtesy of DSP&P.)

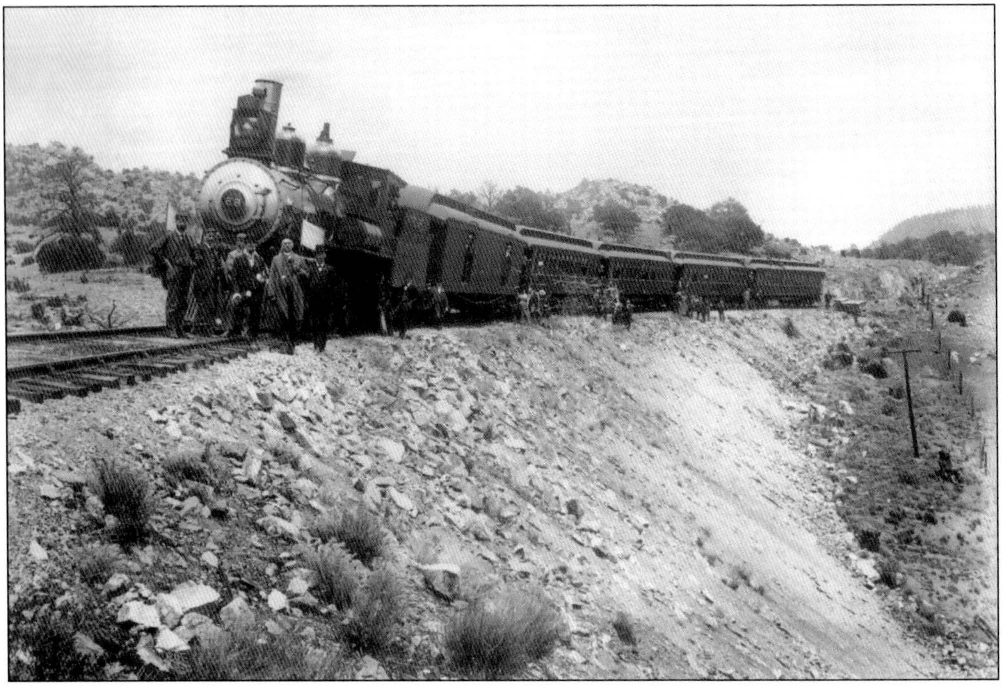

A westbound Colorado Midland passenger train pauses near the summit of Trout Creek Pass for a photograph. Trout Creek Pass marked the boundary between Park and Chaffee Counties. Here, the Colorado Midland crossed over the South Park Line. Engine No. 28 was a 4-6-0 passenger locomotive built in Schenectady, New York, in 1888. (Courtesy of DSP&P.)

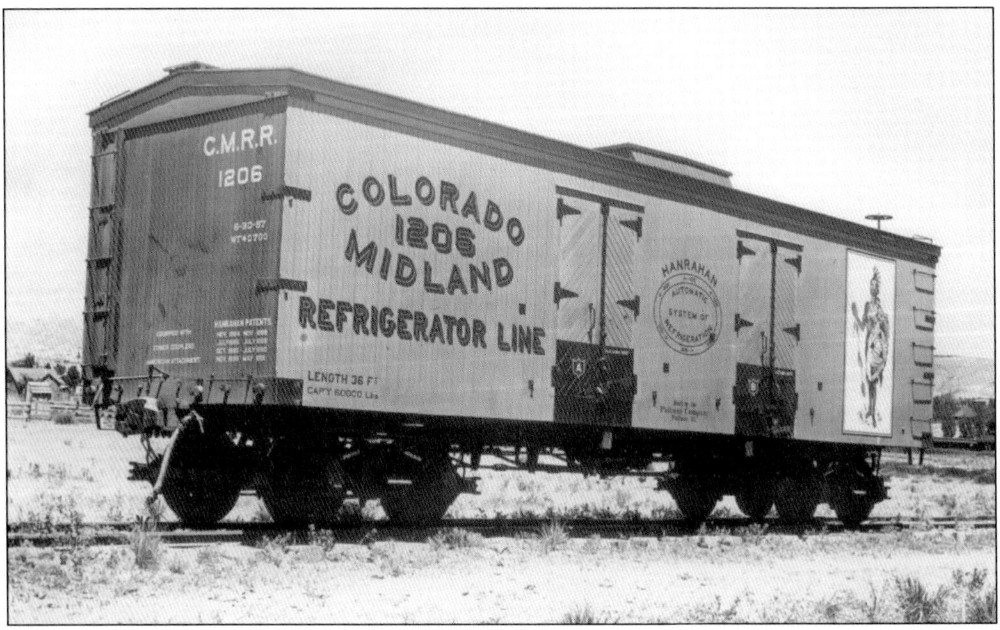

The Colorado Midland delivered perishables in refrigerated cars like this new Hanrahan refrigerator car. These cars, also known as "reefers," had thick insulated walls with ice bunkers inside to keep the contents cold in any weather. As indicated on the side, this car was built by the Pullman Company in Illinois. (Courtesy of DSP&P.)

The Colorado Midland "brass hats" traveled in luxury, as evidenced by this Pullman business car, developed by George Pullman for more comfortable train travel. The rear end of such cars usually featured a lounge area with large windows to view the passing countryside and an end platform for even better views. (Courtesy of DSP&P.)

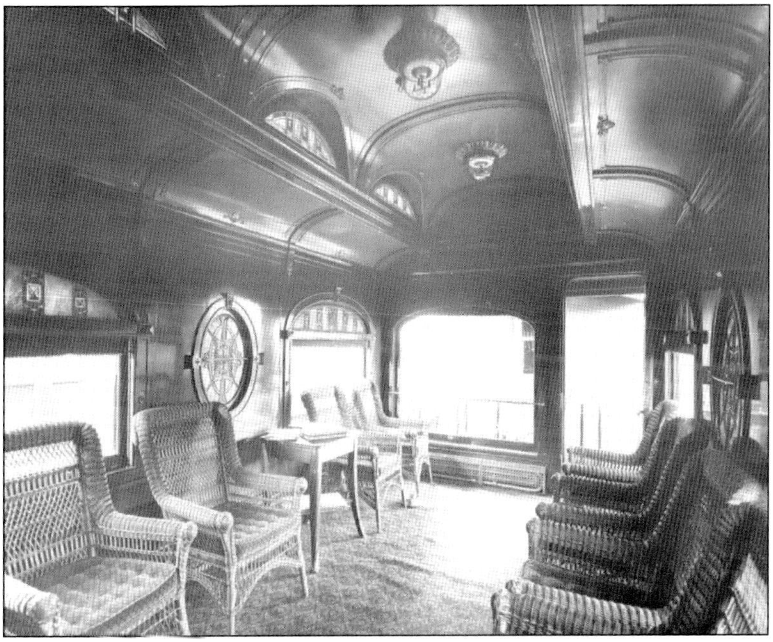

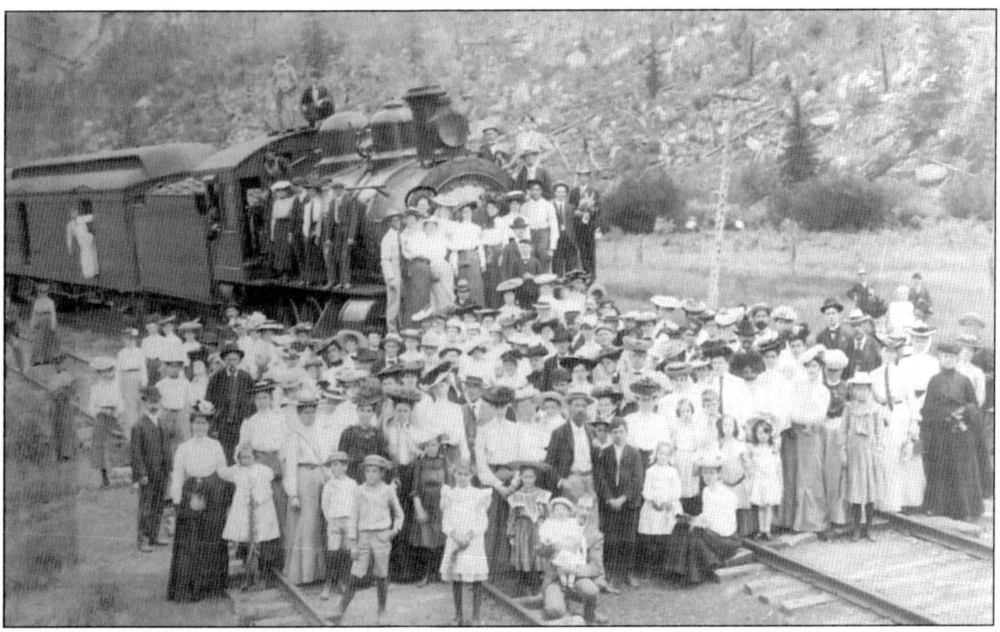

A significant part of the Colorado Midland's summer business was the wildflower excursions. Long trains of picnickers would spend a Sunday afternoon gathering flowers and enjoying the pleasant mountain scenery. This excursion took place in July 1903. According to one of the railroad's advertisements, the cost was only $1. (Courtesy of DSP&P.)

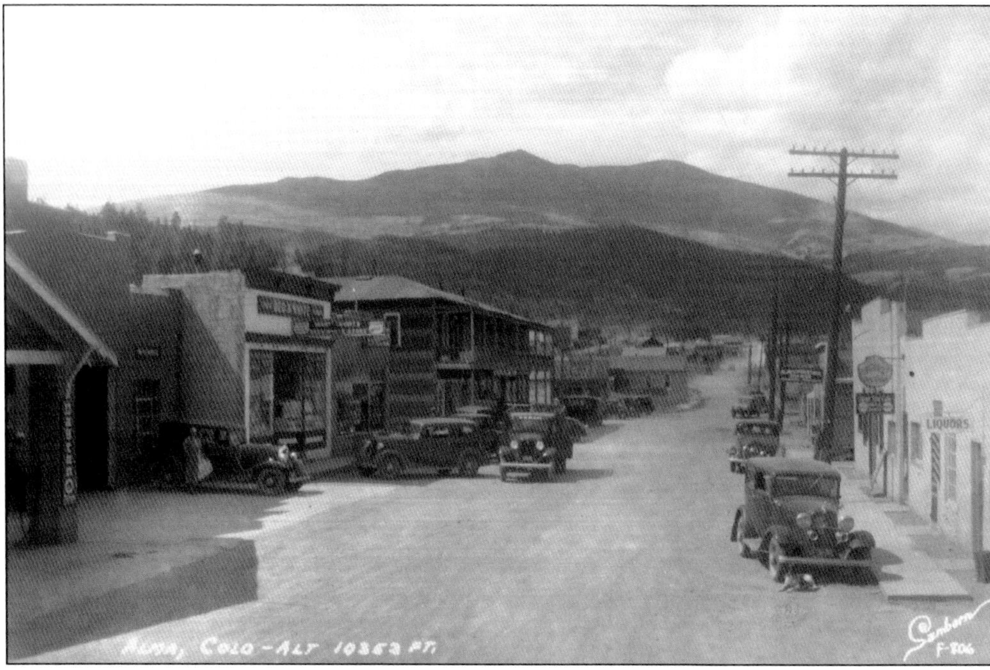

The advent of the automobile in mountain towns greatly enhanced residents' ability to travel quickly to outlying areas and to Denver and beyond. The county comprised over 2,200 square miles. A trip from Bailey to Guffey meant a drive of over 85 miles. Here, early automobiles line the streets of Alma in the 1920s.

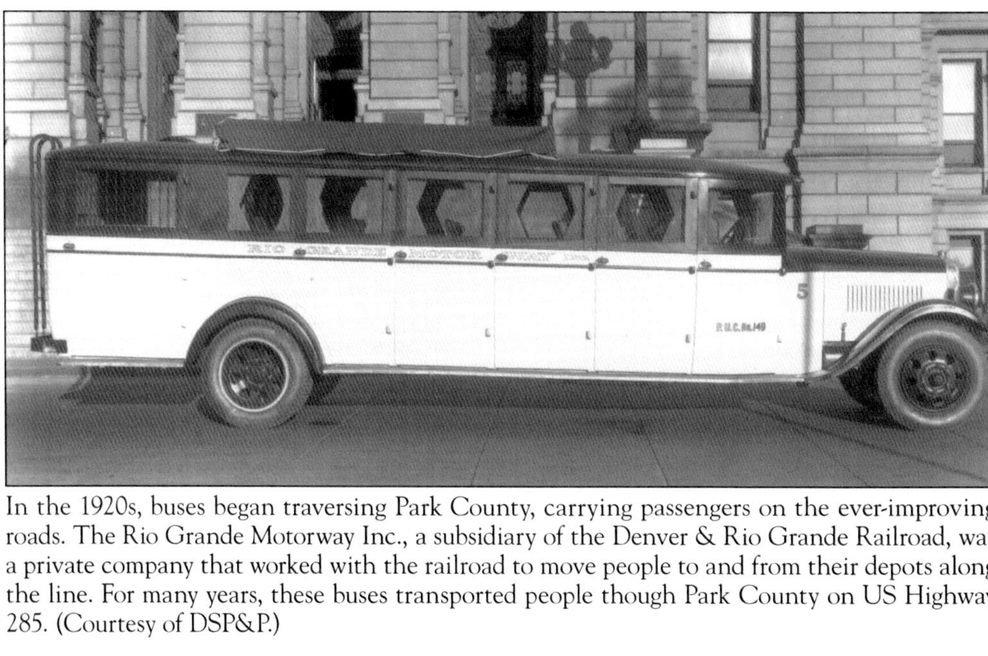

In the 1920s, buses began traversing Park County, carrying passengers on the ever-improving roads. The Rio Grande Motorway Inc., a subsidiary of the Denver & Rio Grande Railroad, was a private company that worked with the railroad to move people to and from their depots along the line. For many years, these buses transported people though Park County on US Highway 285. (Courtesy of DSP&P.)

Four

Timbering

Timber is a great natural resource in Park County, which is home to at least nine varieties of conifers and three kinds of deciduous trees. This resource has produced fuel, structures, fencing, mine timbers, railroad ties, food, furniture, flagpoles, paper, excelsior, and a scientific record, and has served as an artists' medium as well as a feast for sightseers, painters, and photographers, and even an occasional hanging tree. Park County's Native Americans used timber largely as a basic, subsistence product. Fuel for warmth and cooking, poles from aptly named lodge pole pines, edible pine nuts, pitch to seal woven vessels, and tree bark for medicine and/or food were common uses for timber resources.

After Euro-American settlement, timber use—and sometimes abuse—became much more intensive. Forest products eventually assumed an important role in Park County's economy. The coming of rail transportation greatly increased commercial cutting. Logging's power sources evolved, from water, steam, and animals to internal combustion.

Early logging was often a somewhat lawless enterprise. Many operators exploited public lands at will, or made very liberal use of the homestead laws to carry on with little interference. But the railroads also brought passengers who became offended by such sights as denuded hillsides stripped by the charcoalers. The 1880s gave rise to Colorado's early "tree huggers;" public pressure contributed to the establishment of the federal Forest Reserves and eventual regulation of public-land logging by both federal and state agencies.

Logging for lumber has now greatly receded in Park County. However, wood heat still serves many homes and even commercial buildings. The ancient, weatherworn bristlecone and limber pines, some 1,000–2,500 years old, have become quite a source of pride.

From early times to today, many a view would be blank or sorely lacking if timber and its products were removed. It is hoped that the photographs in this chapter will serve to validate the significance of the trees and their bounty that residents all too often take for granted. From basic survival to feeding the soul, timber has played a vital role in human progress. This chapter is a reminder of that role in the history of Park County.

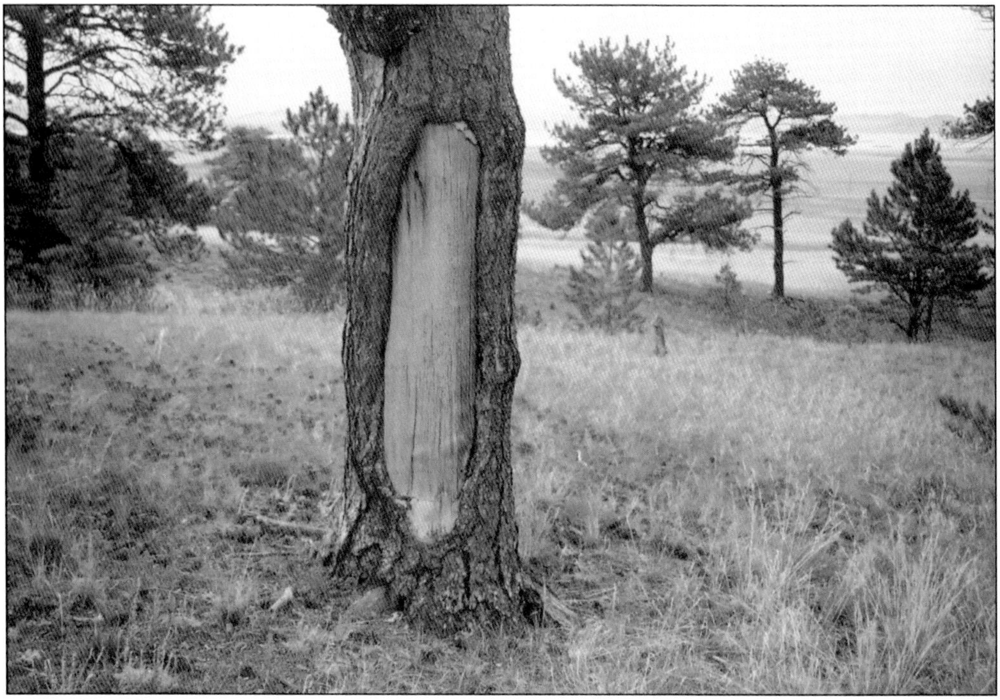

Scarred ponderosa pines, such as this survivor south of Fairplay, are often called "medicine trees." The scars were made by Native Americans in the early to mid-19th century. The inner bark was reportedly used for food, medicine, and sweetener. Literal tree huggers who embrace large ponderosas will often notice a sweetish, vanilla-like odor, suggesting that there might indeed be something tasty under that outer bark. (Courtesy of Jerry Davis.)

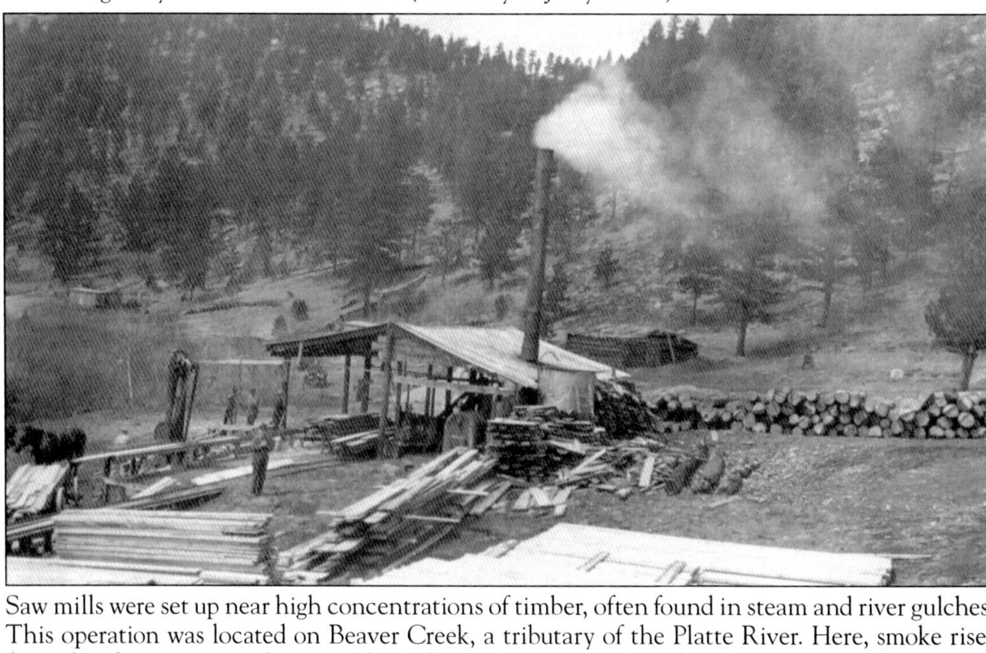

Saw mills were set up near high concentrations of timber, often found in steam and river gulches. This operation was located on Beaver Creek, a tributary of the Platte River. Here, smoke rises from the chimney as workers run the mill machinery. Large stacks of wood can be seen in the foreground and behind the main building.

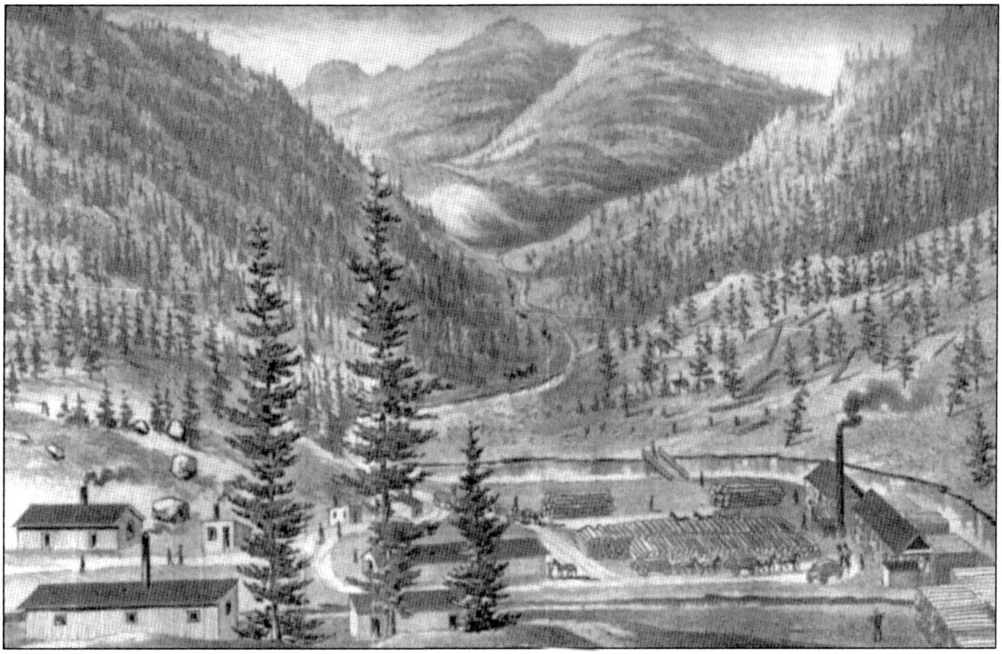

This c. 1888 drawing depicts the Laws Sawmill on the Platte River, downstream from what is now Lake George. This was a more orderly, organized site than most short-term sawmills of the day. Few, if any, of the residents currently living near the site are aware that it ever existed.

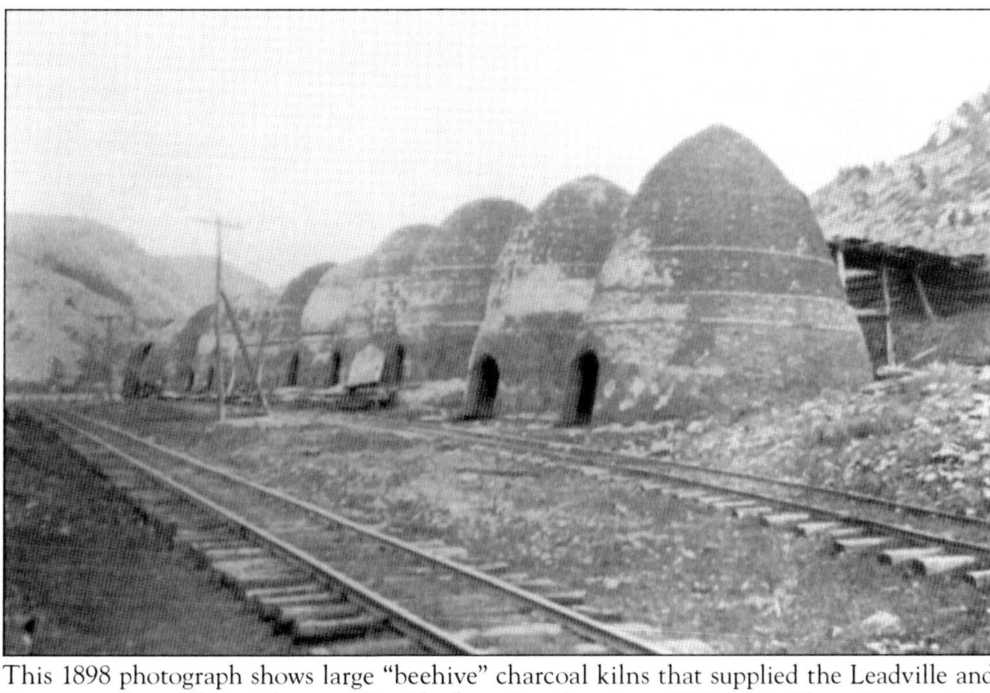

This 1898 photograph shows large "beehive" charcoal kilns that supplied the Leadville and Denver smelters. These kilns stand beside the railroad tracks at Webster in Platte Canyon. The charcoalers often slashed off every burnable stick of wood over large expanses of land. Much of their extreme clear-cutting was visible to railroad passengers, and such sights may have played a part in forest conservation efforts.

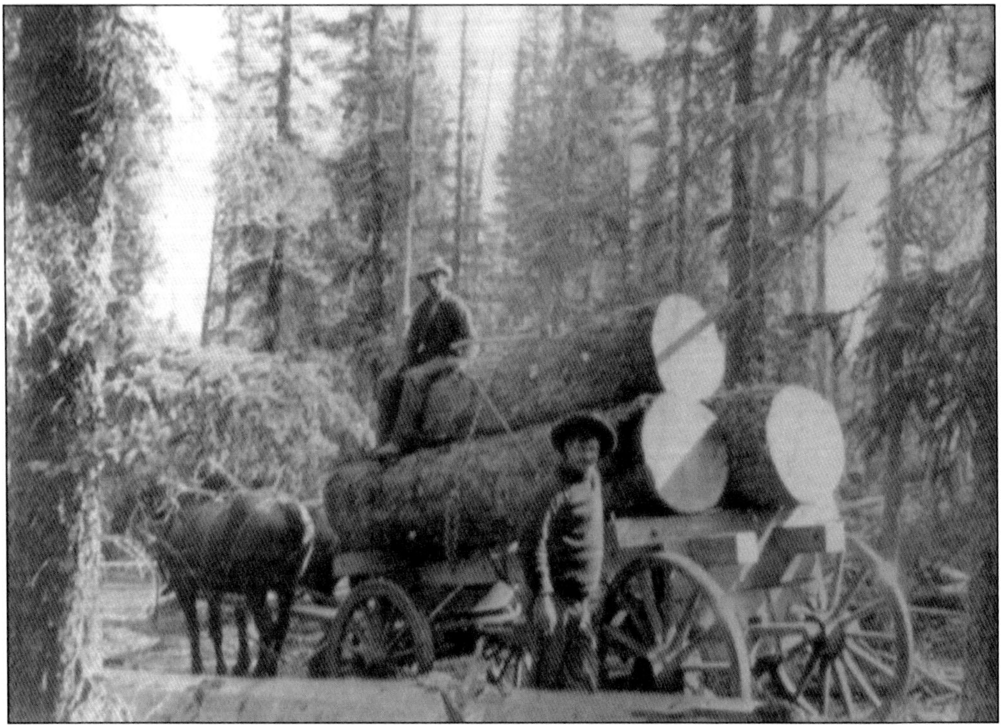

Unusually large spruce logs are headed for the sawmill in North Lost Creek in 1898. Manpower and horsepower got the job done in the days before chainsaws provided cargo for snorting diesel loaders and trucks. This operation was an illegal trespass on Forest Reserve (later National Forest) lands. Probably unknown to these loggers, photographer J.G. Jack was working under contract with the Interior Department.

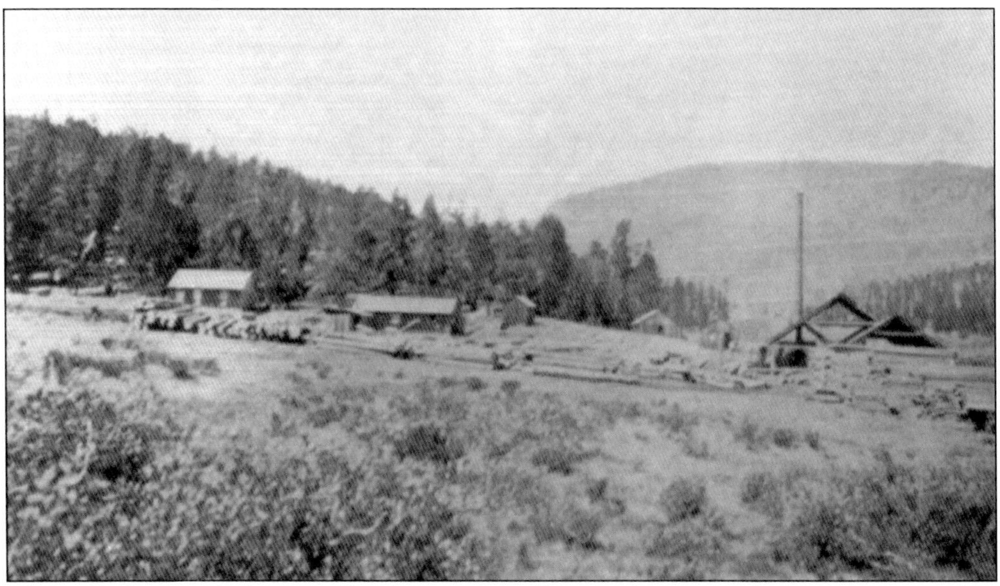

This 1898 photograph shows an illegal steam sawmill in North Lost Creek. It was not unusual for such logging/sawmill operations to simply carry out their activities on the public domain until they moved on or were caught. This mill was shut down by General Land Office authorities.

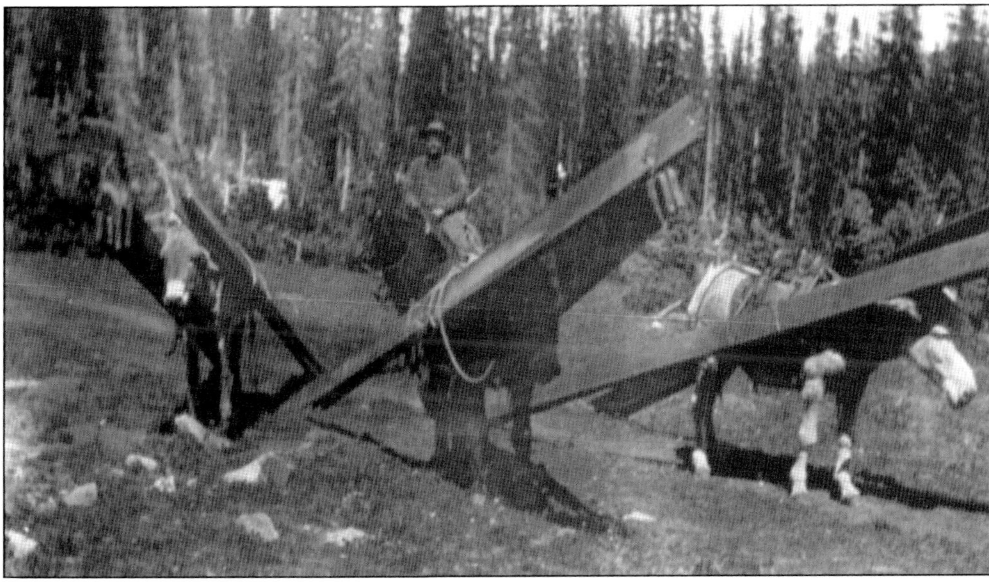

Sometimes, loggers needed to get a load of very long lumber to places beyond the reach of wagons. The amazing burro was up to the task. The presence of old mine buildings clinging to a mountainside high above timberline raise the question of how that lumber was transported. This early 1900s photograph, possibly taken near Jefferson Creek, shows how it got up there.

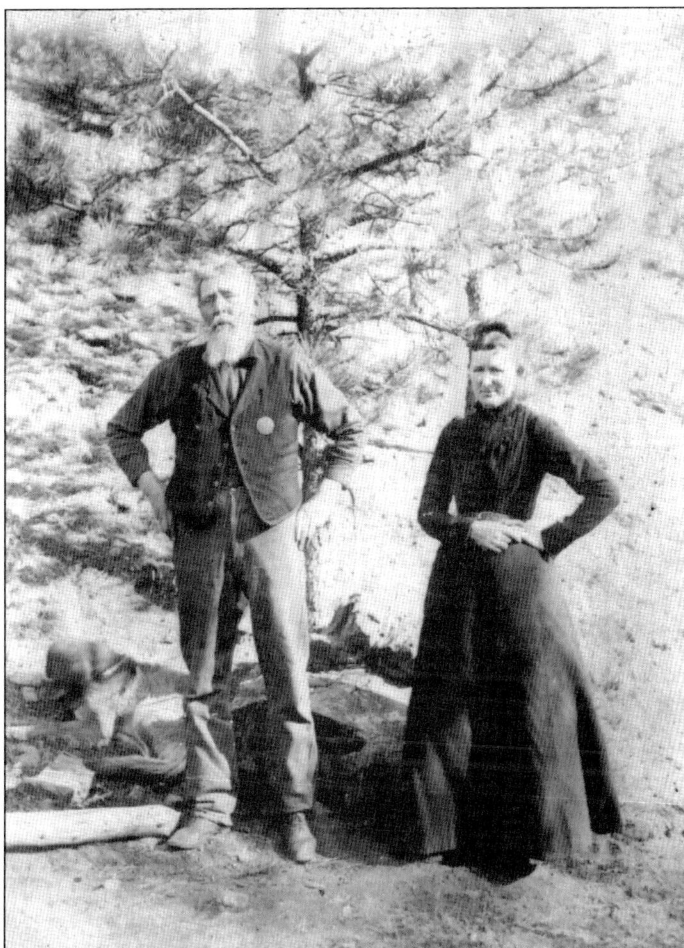

William Watts Hooper and his wife pose for a photograph around 1900. Hooper was in the logging business around Bailey for some years before working for the Interior Department's General Land Office; note his badge. He transferred to the US Forest Service after timber piracy finally faded from the public lands in favor of forest conservation.

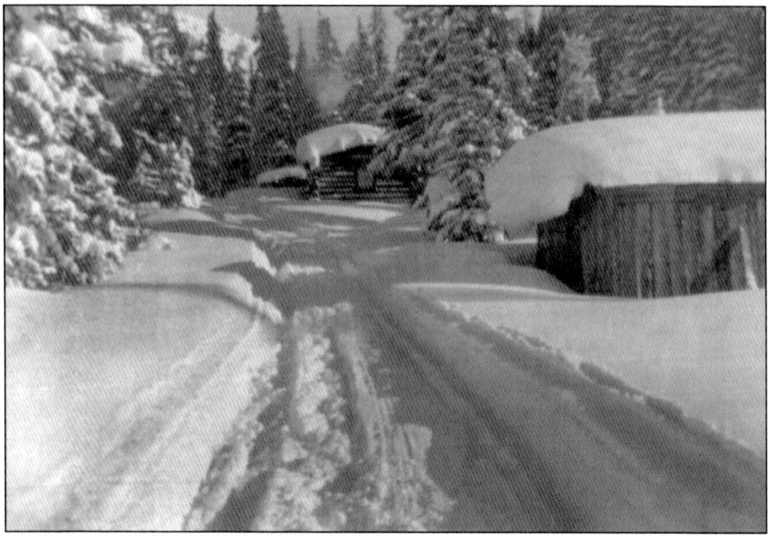

Some very hardy loggers just kept at it, snow or shine. Busy sleds made the tracks in this early 1900s photograph of a logging camp near Mount Silverheels, north of Fairplay.

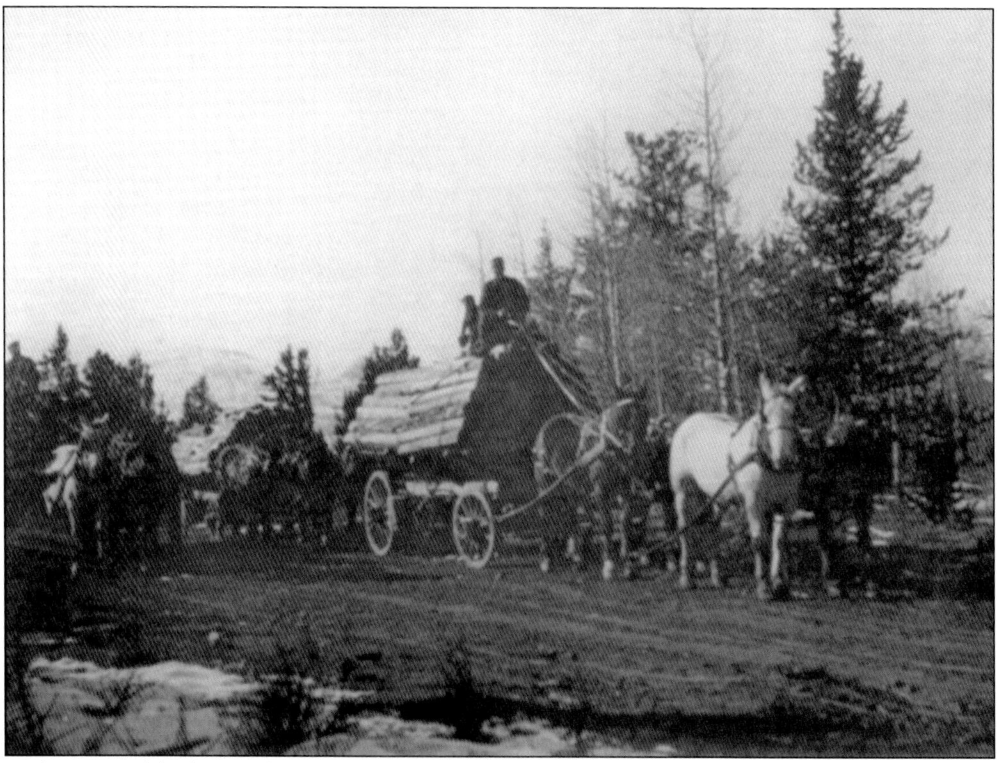

Today, it would take 100 horsepower to handle this 4-horsepower load of railroad ties. Decades after sawmills were established, the hand-hewn ties turned out by the tie hack or tie chopper were still competitive, since these artists with axes were sending a finished product directly from stump to market. This photograph was taken near the Almgren brothers' 1920s logging camp on Jefferson Creek.

In the early 1920s, Earl Almgren (left) and J.R. Tooher pose with the tools of their trade in Jefferson Creek. The two-man crosscut saw at left was often called a "misery whip." Bending over to make countless horizontal stump cuts with one of those was not for the weak of back or arm. Stoop labor was defined!

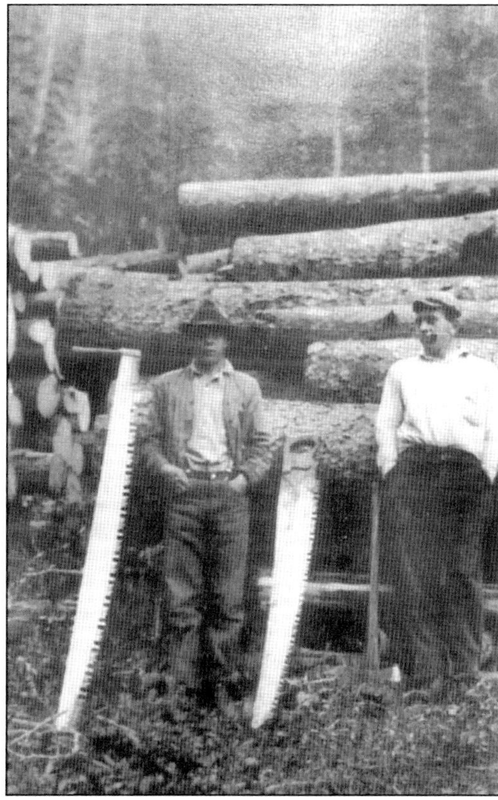

Roy Davenport stands with his log-hauling team near Chase in Platte Canyon around 1920. The rather complex harness required no small degree of knowledge. And plenty of "horse sense" was then needed to coax the steeds from point A to point B. These folks were every bit the equal of the very best of today's commercial truckers.

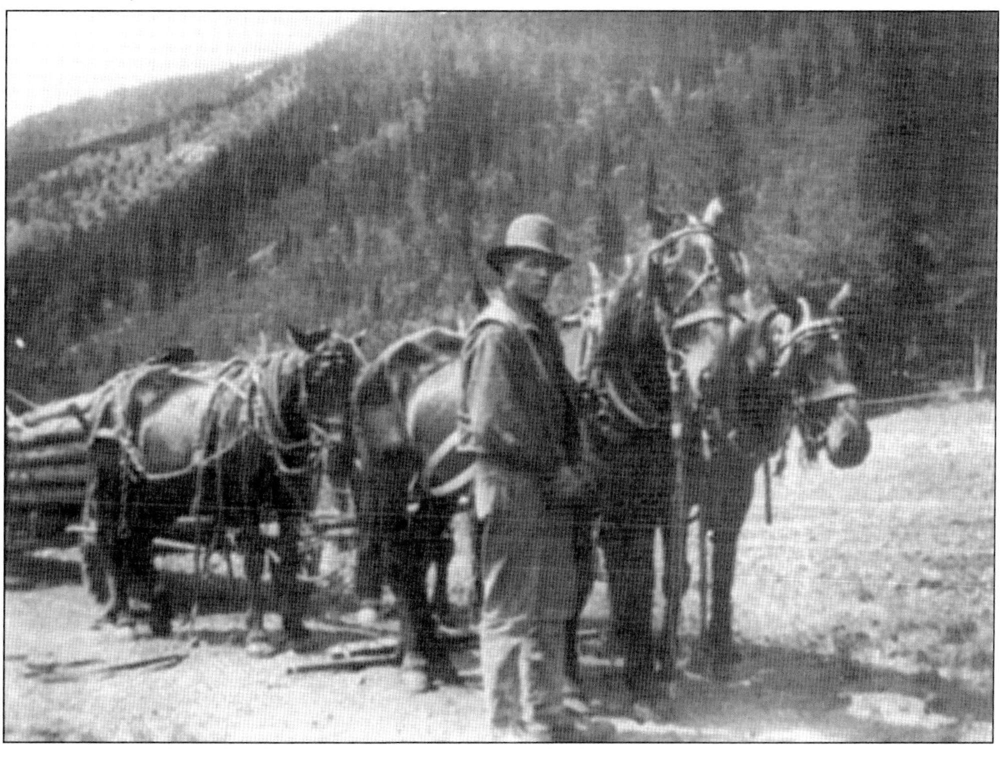

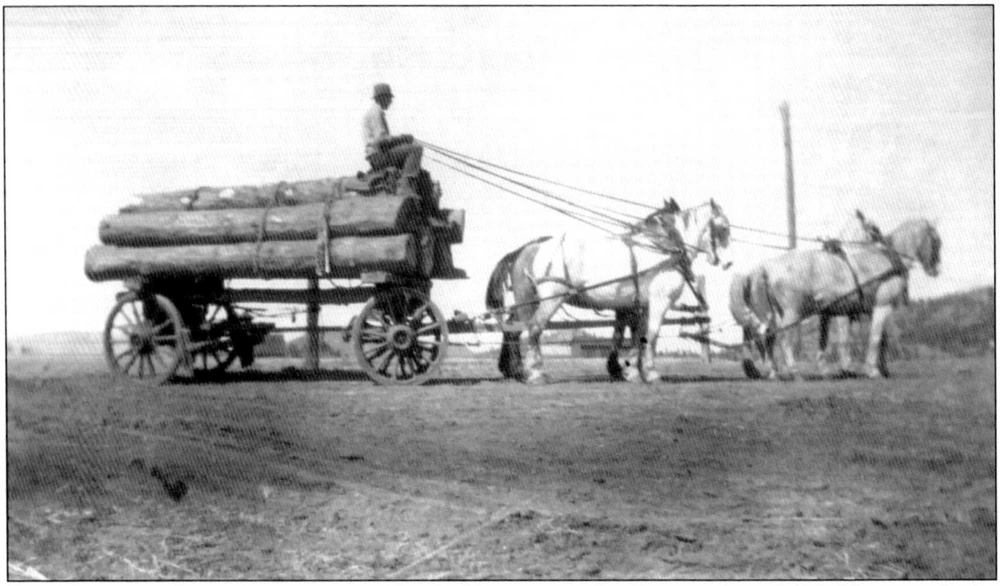

Frank Norton rides with a substantial load of logs near Lake George about 1918. The term "rides like a lumber wagon" is amply illustrated. His jacket no doubt provided scant relief on a conveyance with no spring seat or spring suspension.

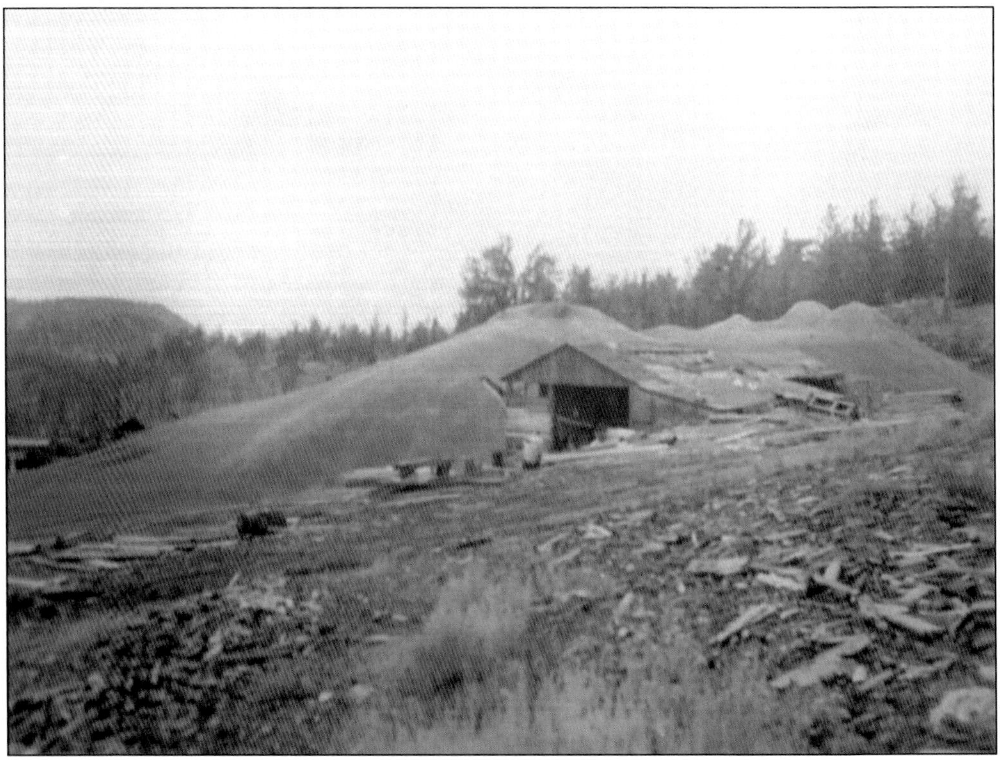

This 1941 photograph shows the remains of the Achord Sawmill in Packer Gulch not long after the operation moved west to nearby Turner Gulch. It operated here for 10 years and even had an occasional on-site school because of its remoteness. Having caught fire several times, the sawdust pile was the bane of Smokey Bear's existence before heavy equipment finally mixed it with dirt.

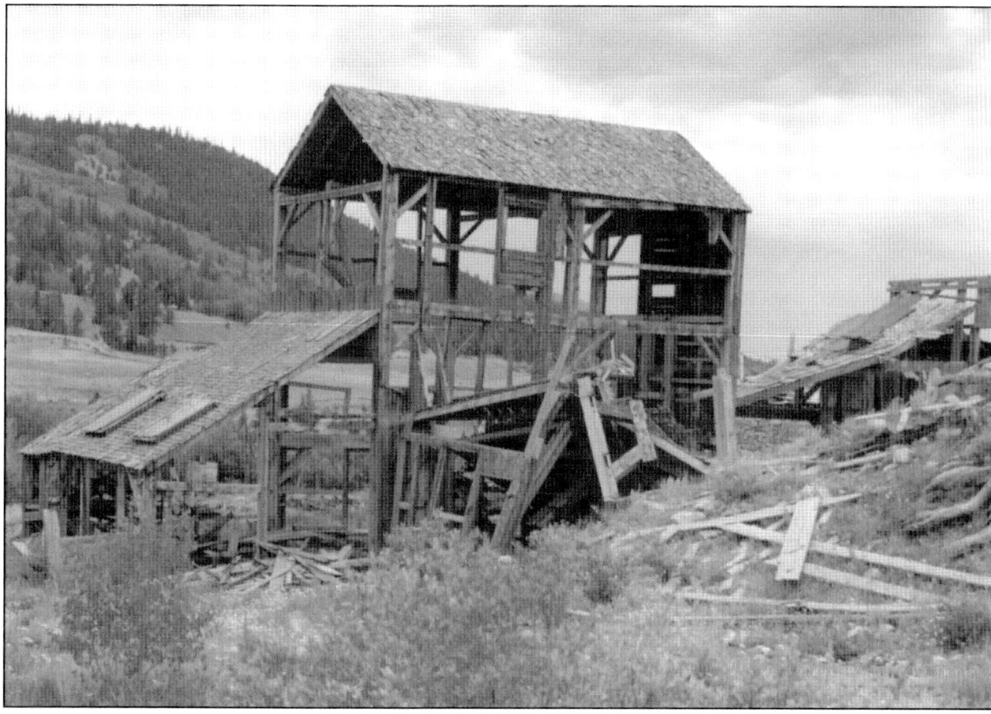

Shorn of its protective siding, this timber skeleton from the smelter complex at Dudley, located near the base of Mount Bross, awaits its demise in the 1940s. Scores of large structures in early Park County featured timber framing, another testament to what was, and is, arguably the most cost-effective, versatile material on earth.

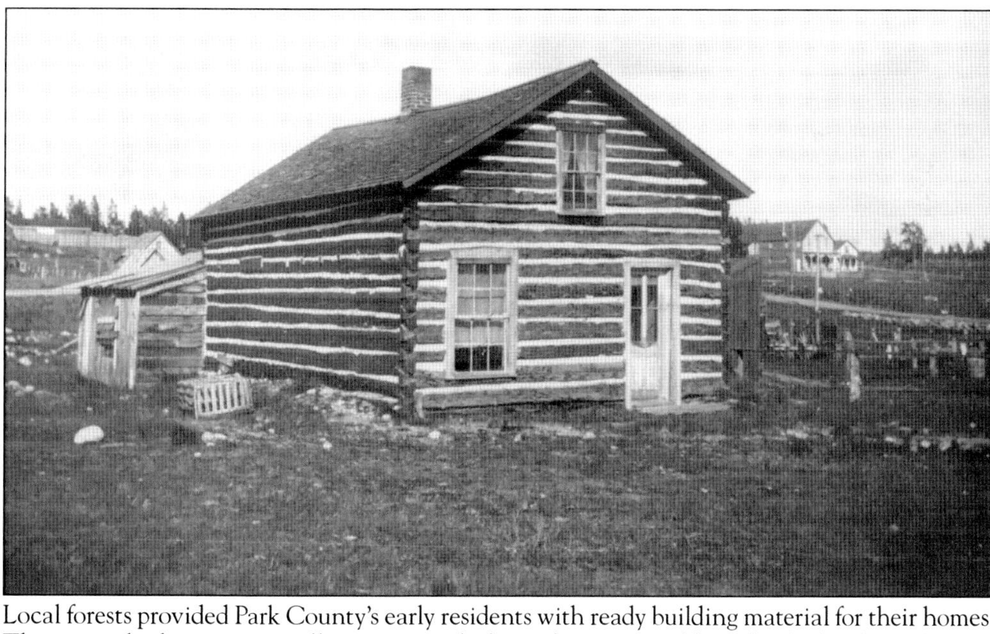

Local forests provided Park County's early residents with ready building material for their homes. The rustic abodes were typically constructed of round, untrimmed logs chinked with mud, while more refined residences like this cabin in Fairplay featured hand-hewn square logs connected by complex dovetail joints.

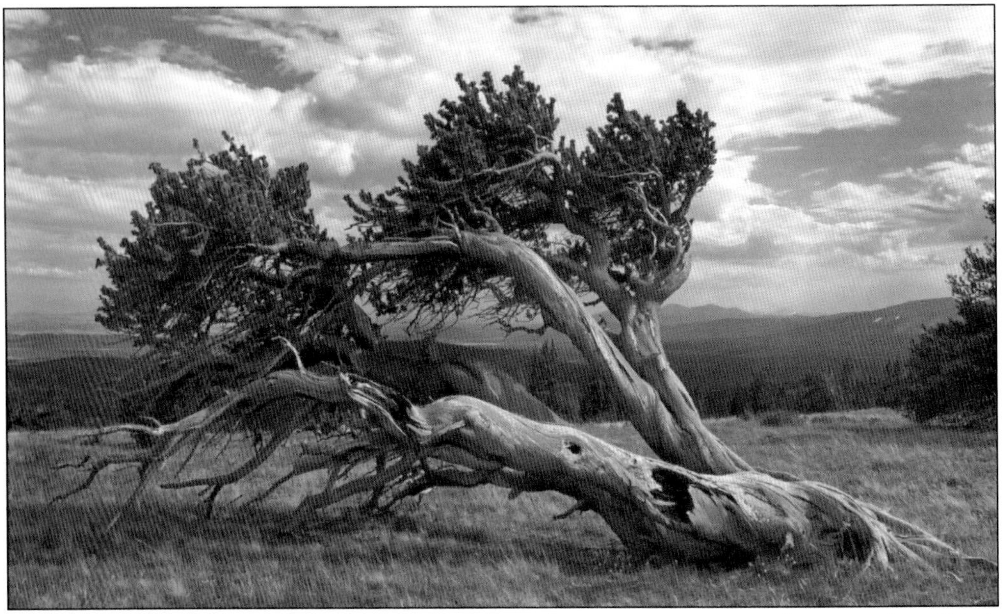

Nature photographers are constantly on the hunt for ever more spectacular examples of Park County's abundant supply of ancient pines. This bristlecone pine on Beaver Ridge, northwest of Fairplay, has bent before the wind, but it clings to life with astonishing tenacity. These trees are estimated to be up to 2,500 years old. (Courtesy of Gary Nichols.)

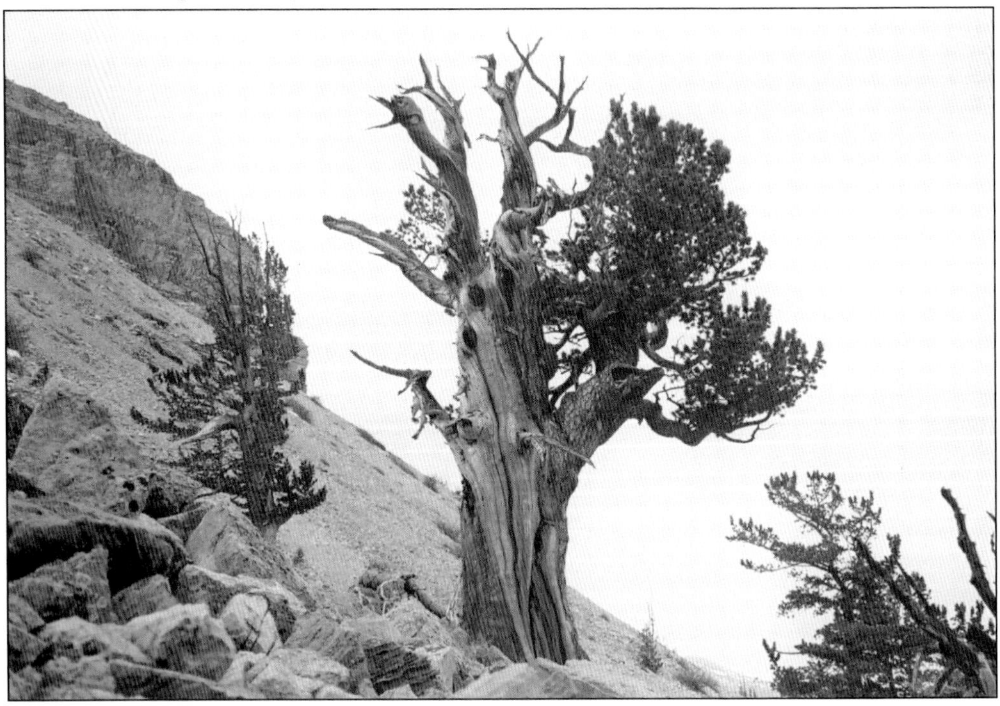

This limber pine in Limber Grove, west of Fairplay, has defied both the wind and Father Time. Lines of character have been etched by driving snow into its barkless, windward side. With their striking appeal, such "character trees" can be found throughout Park County by those willing to seek them out in the high, harsh places they call home. (Courtesy of Jerry Davis.)

Five

Towns and Settlements

For millennia worldwide, people have grouped together in settlements small and large, for many reasons. So it has been in Park County, with actual cities a notable absence here. As a result of the boom-and-bust mining era, about half of the settlements highlighted in this chapter are now inhabited by ghosts of the past rather than by the living. The following images offer glimpses into history, albeit exclusive of Native American settlements, which predated widespread photography.

The first Euro-American settlements were established in 1859, springing up around placer gold deposits. Those were Tarryall, Fairplay, and Buckskin Joe (Laurette). The early 1860s gave rise to many more, and this process continued in fits and starts, even up to the birth of an agricultural hamlet named Trump in the 1930s. Most of the highlighted settlements (with a few exceptions) were within a quarter mile or less of a live, year-round stream. This chapter features only places that had some economic diversity, as opposed to populations at a given mine or logging camp, which sometimes held more people than some of the very small towns.

Apart from mining, other economic factors caused or contributed to the creation of settlements. Among those were animal-based transportation including staging and freighting, railroads, ranching and farming, logging, government offices and services, ice-harvesting, and recreation, including resort hotels.

Most of the towns had post offices. Sometimes, a name was changed by the Post Office Department if the submission was already in use elsewhere. Developers would change a settlement's name if they sought one that they thought more prestigious. That has led to some confusion over the years. Examples are Buckskin Joe/Laurette, Fairplay/South Park City, Mosquito/Sterling, Leavick/Horseshoe/Doran, East Leadville/Horseshoe, Idaville/Freshwater/Guffey, Puma City/Tarryall, Gold City/Conrad, Jasper City/Hayman, Slaghts/Fairview, and Kaiserheim/Grousemont. A number of Park County post office names did not indicate towns, but rather were located at ranches, depots, and even a mine.

Fairplay, Alma, Horseshoe, Como, Guffey, and Jefferson were all once incorporated towns. Only Fairplay and Alma retain formal, functioning governance. Incorporated or not, Park County's communities remain a source of pride and, often, nostalgic longing.

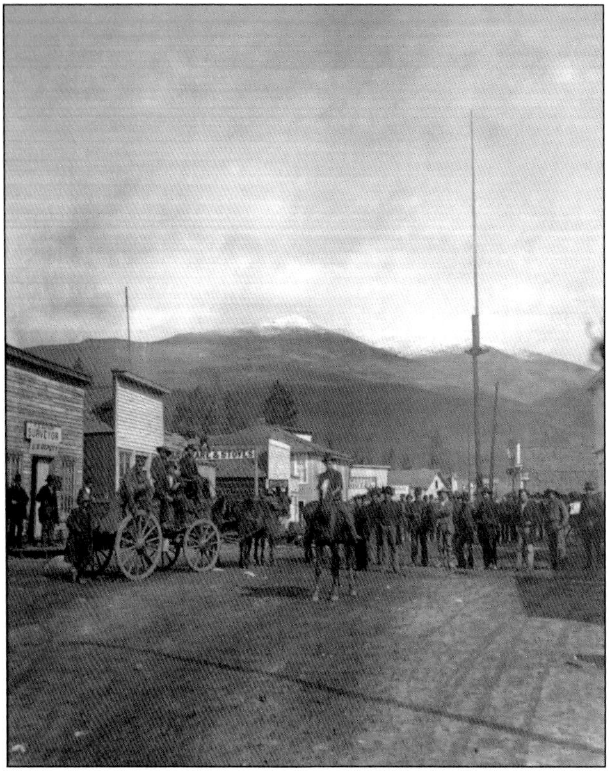

The burgeoning town of Alma is shown here in the late 19th century. Established in 1872 as a supply hub for the Mosquito Range mines, the town has seen many booms and busts. Through good times and bad, Alma has outlasted many a nearby ghost town.

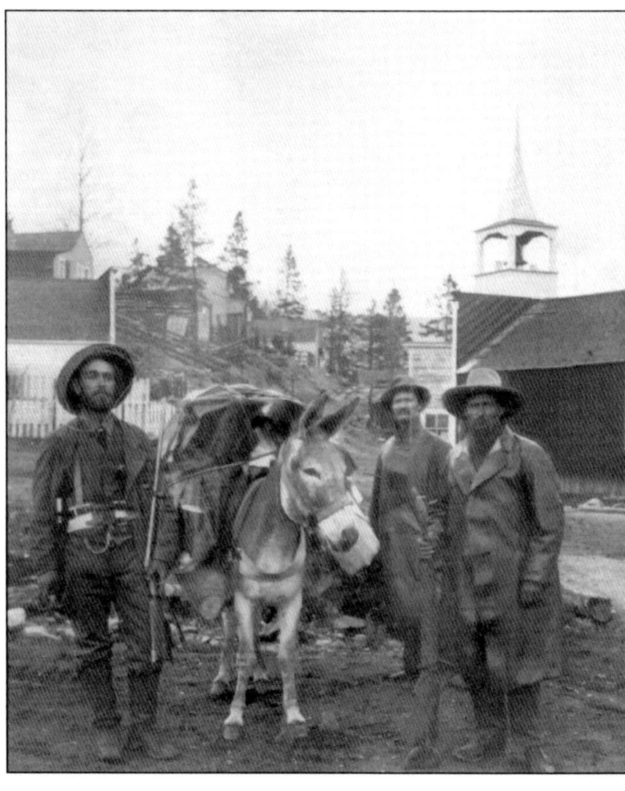

This photograph of Alma, taken between 1880 and 1882, is worth a thousand words. It portrays the astonishing load-bearing capacity of the ever-dependable burro. They were a highly respected animal, but the earsplitting, wee-hours serenade of the "Rocky Mountain canary" sure could test one's patience. The belfry of Alma's Methodist Church rises on the right.

Bailey is barely a wide spot in the road, as revealed in this early 1870s photograph. The town developed around the 1864 Bailey's Ranch (very likely shown at center), a roadside hostelry serving the busy wagon road to South Park. Since the railroad arrived in 1878, bustling Bailey has never looked back.

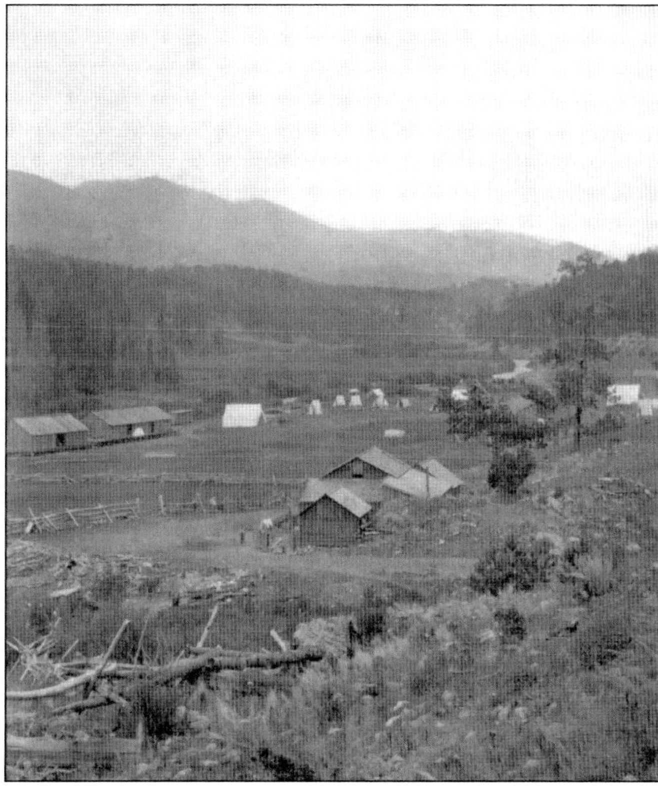

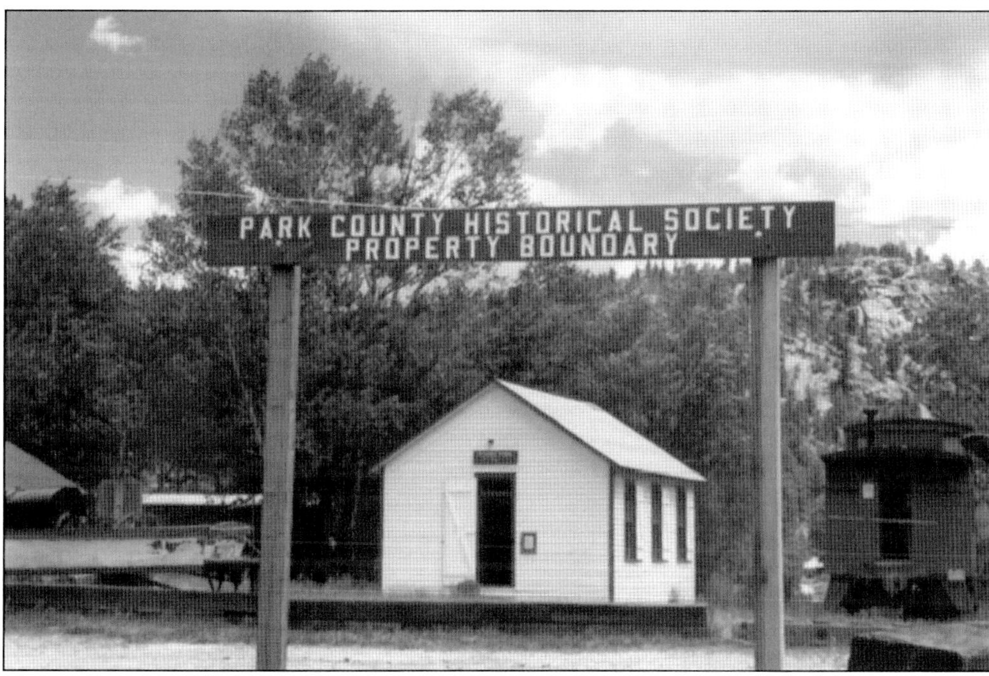

A staple in the town of Bailey is McGraw Park, named after Helen McGraw Tatum, who donated 20 acres to the Park County Historical Society in 1969. Her grandparents were local pioneers who owned a grocery store. The park, open to the public, includes a variety of historic area buildings.

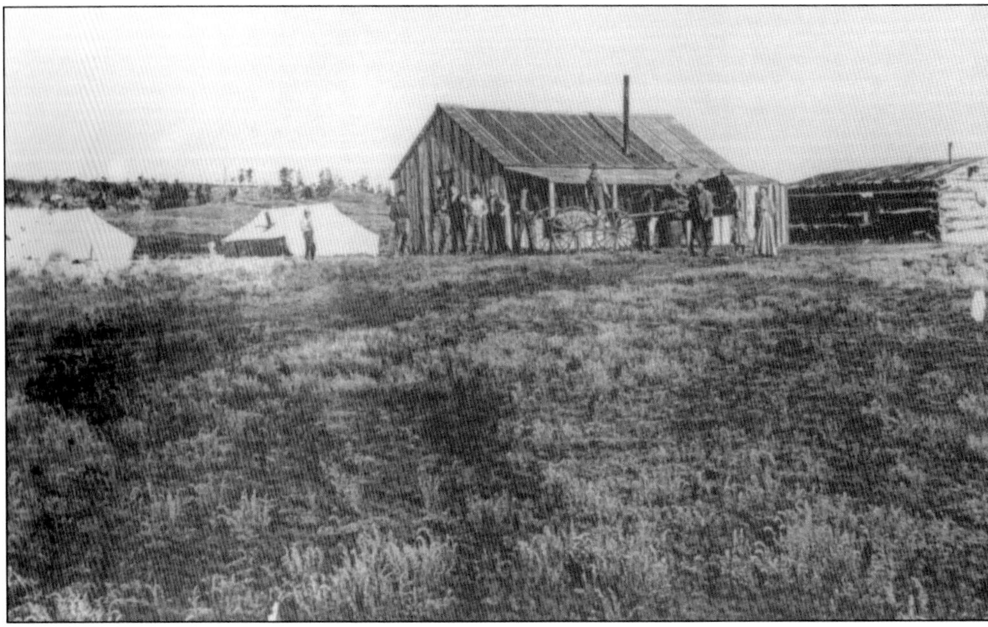

South of Hartsel, the town of Balfour sprang up almost overnight upon the rumors of gold. It is shown here in the latter part of 1893. The gold was an illusion, and Balfour's flame was short-lived. Balfour, Freshwater, Alhambra, and Puma City could all be considered spinoffs of the Cripple Creek boom. Only Puma City (Tarryall) and Freshwater (Guffey) survive.

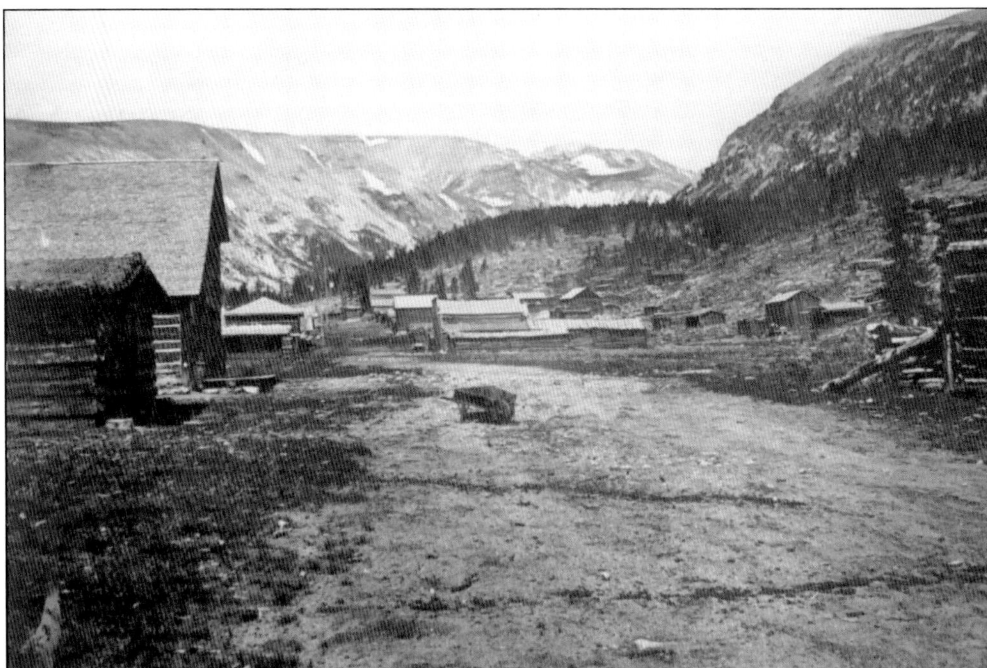

Buckskin Joe, platted in 1861 as Laurette, is shown here in 1864. It was first settled in 1859, but most settlers left by 1865 after the "easy," near-surface gold diminished. Later revivals never equaled the early 1860s boom. Park County's largest town in 1861, Buckskin was the county seat from 1862 to 1867.

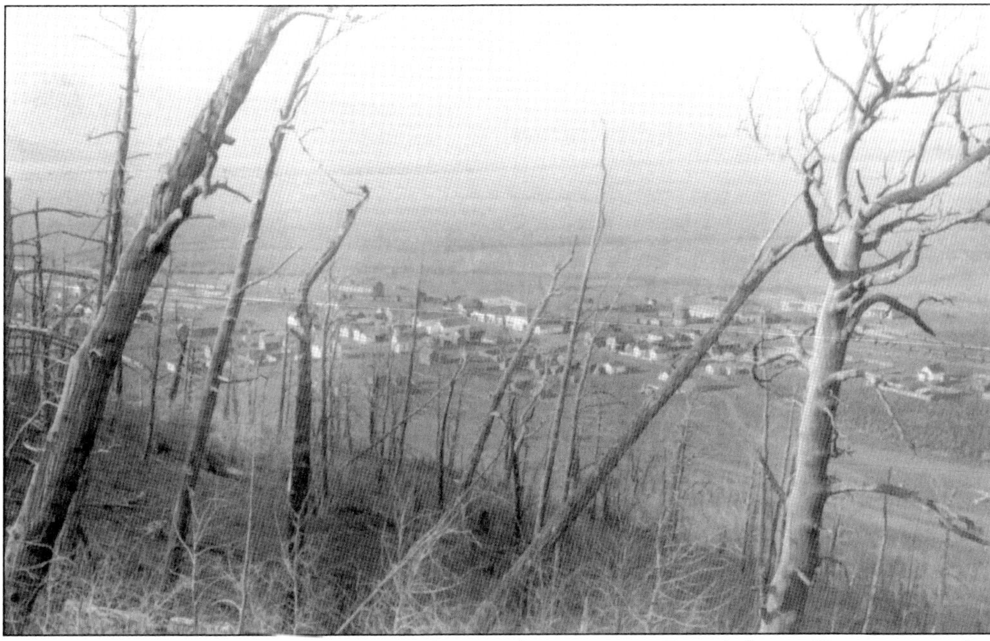

Como, shown here in the 1890s, was a substantial community. Founded in 1879 upon arrival of the railroad, it was an important division and equipment-maintenance headquarters. Dispatchers and controllers, skilled mechanics, and engineers were among the talented railroad employees who made Como equivalent to a regional airport today. The railroad shut down in 1937.

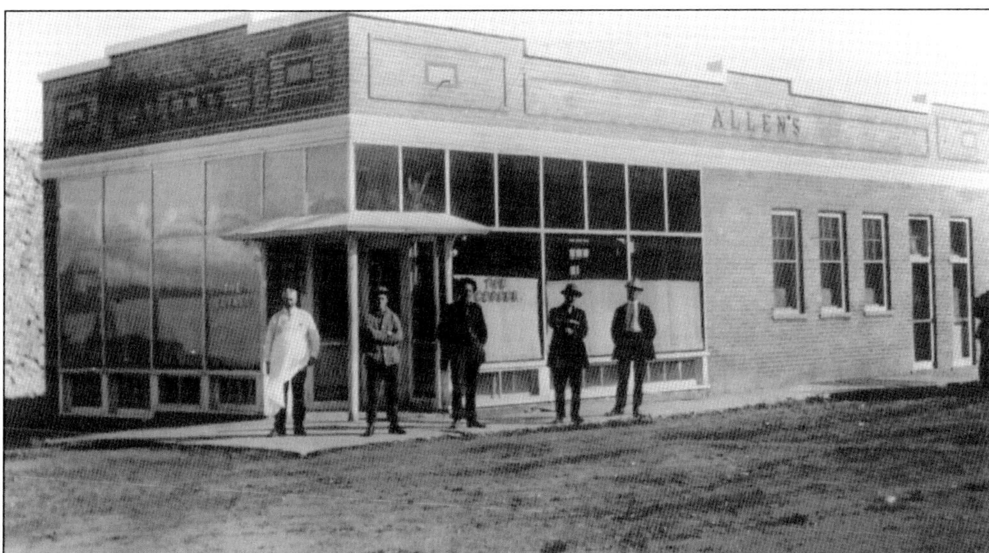

Como development continued in the 20th century. Shown here is a prosperous Allen's saloon. There were a number of other saloons in town in the 19th century. Allen's later became the Como General Store. The town's population (475) dwindled after the railroad began laying off workers in 1910.

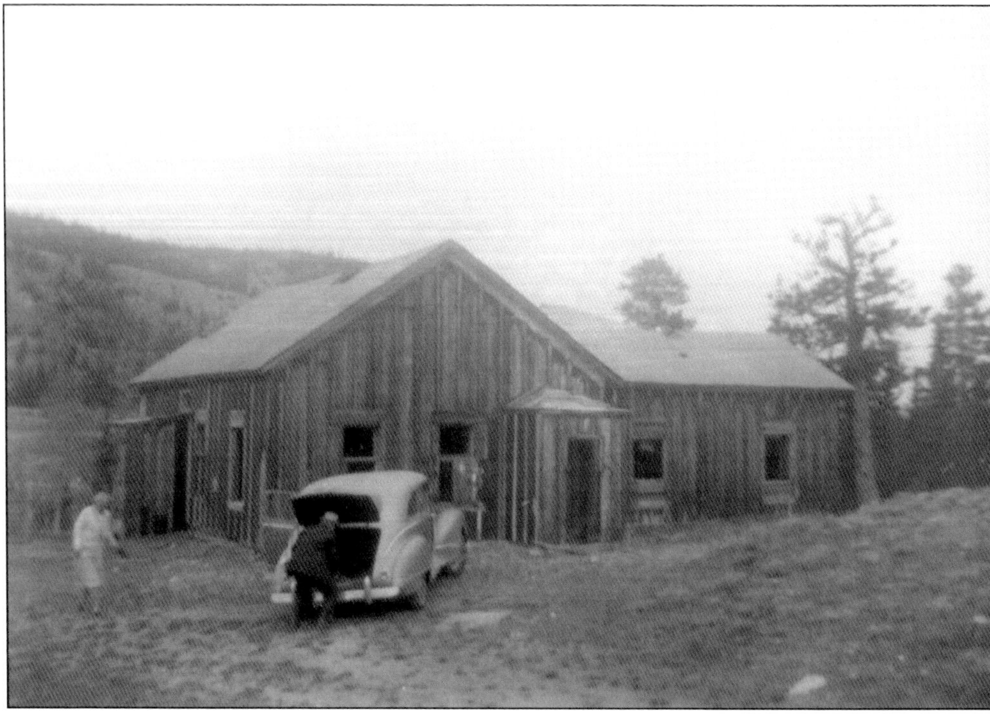

The abandoned Moose Mine office at Dudley is shown probably in the latter 1940s. Just north of Alma, Dudley arose around the 1873 smelter complex, built to process silver ore from the Moose Mine, located near the 14,000-foot level on Mount Bross. Operating sporadically, the smelter was never a great success.

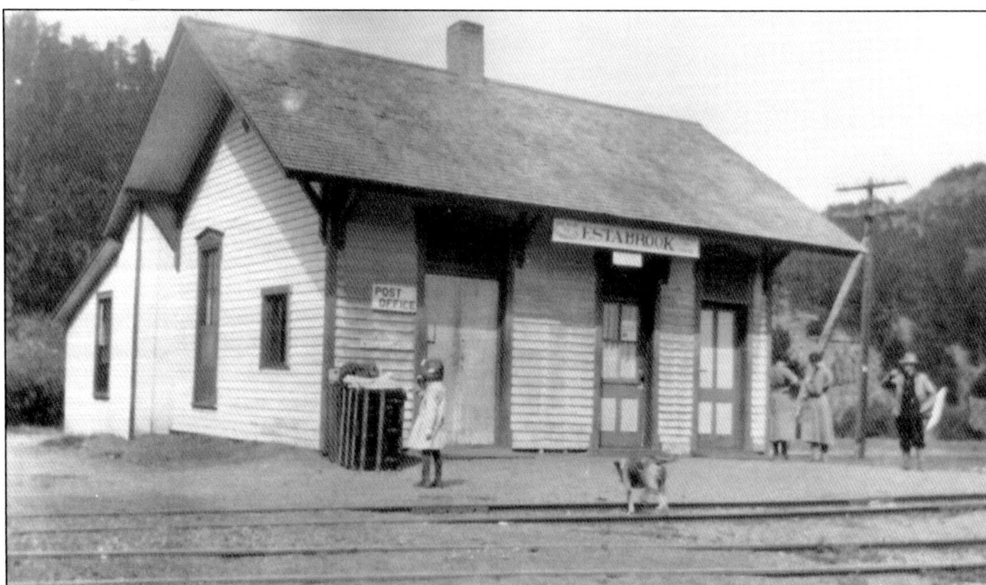

This 1920s photograph shows the dinky depot at Estabrook, with a local pooch perhaps en route to seek some affection from the little girl at center. The town, two miles downriver from Bailey, was largely a small, summer-home community. It had been formally platted in 1892. It supported a school and post office from 1880 to 1937.

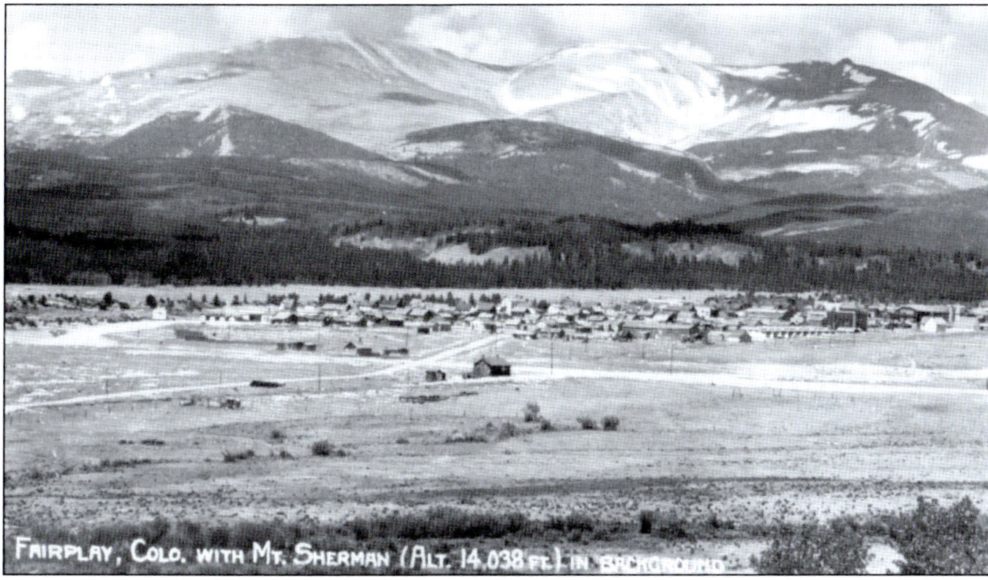

Feeling unwelcome at Tarryall Diggings, 1859 gold-seekers moved southwest, calling their new camp Fair Play, in contrast to what some derisively called "Grab-all." It has been the county seat since 1867. Retaining numerous historic structures, Fairplay, seen here in 1872, is a proud survivor of gold rush Colorado's earliest beginnings.

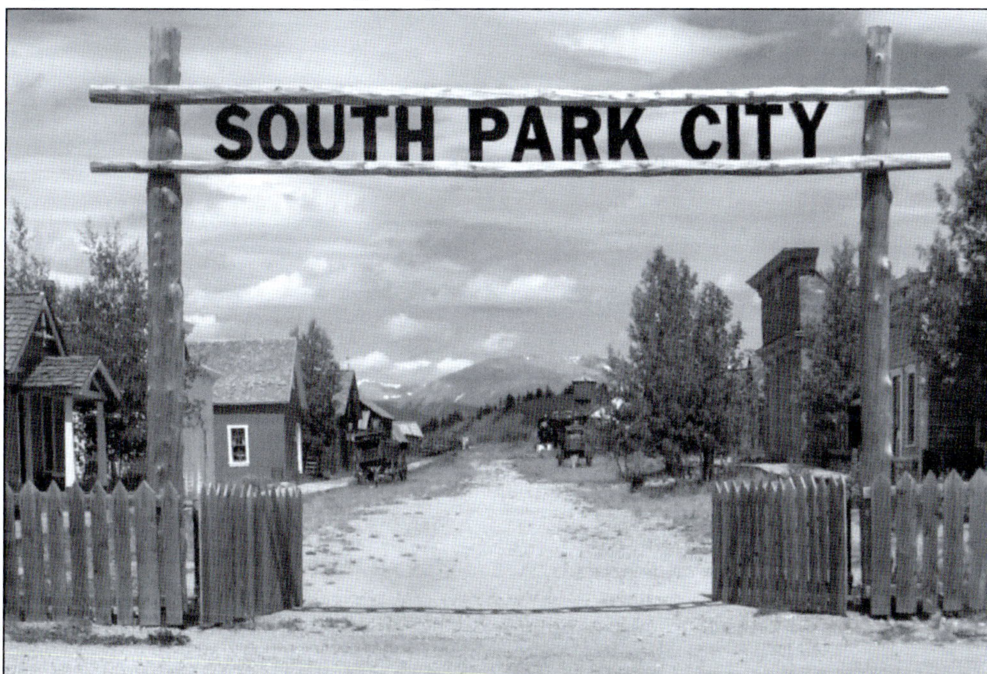

The South Park City Museum in Fairplay is the epitome of a living 1800s frontier town. Opened in 1959 to commemorate the 1859 Colorado gold rush, it houses 35 original historic buildings and their contents, gathered from around Park County. Visitors have the opportunity to experience the pioneer way of life. It was listed in the National Register of Historic Places in November 2014. (Courtesy of Jim Sapp.)

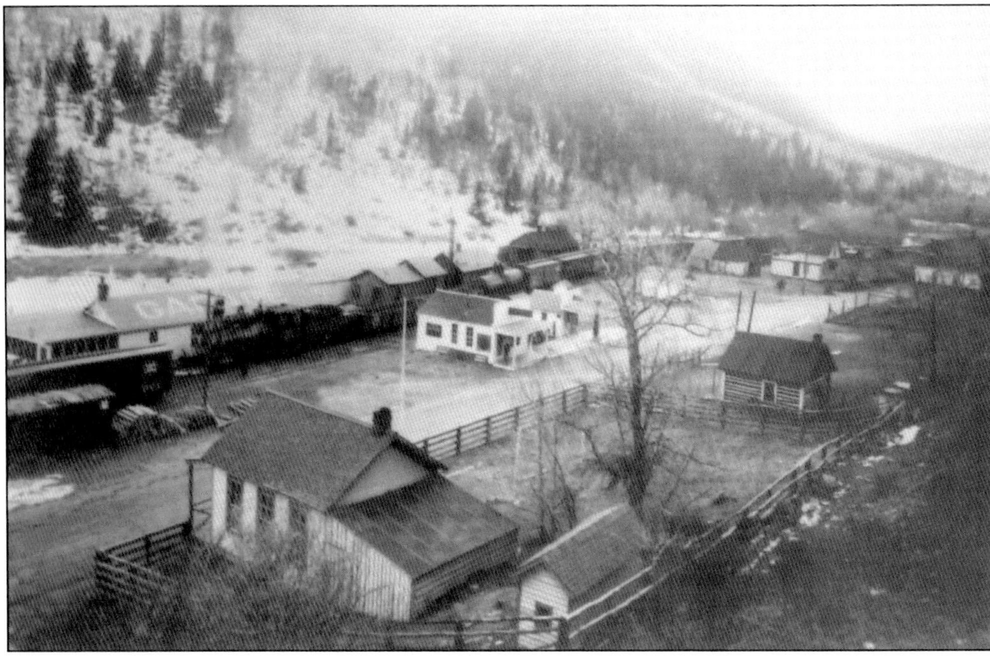

Early in the automotive age, a mixed freight train at Grant still fends off truck freighting. First settled in the 1870s, Grant became the shipping point for the mines, high on Geneva Creek. It featured the usual structures—school, post office, and small businesses—along with the Geneva Lodge.

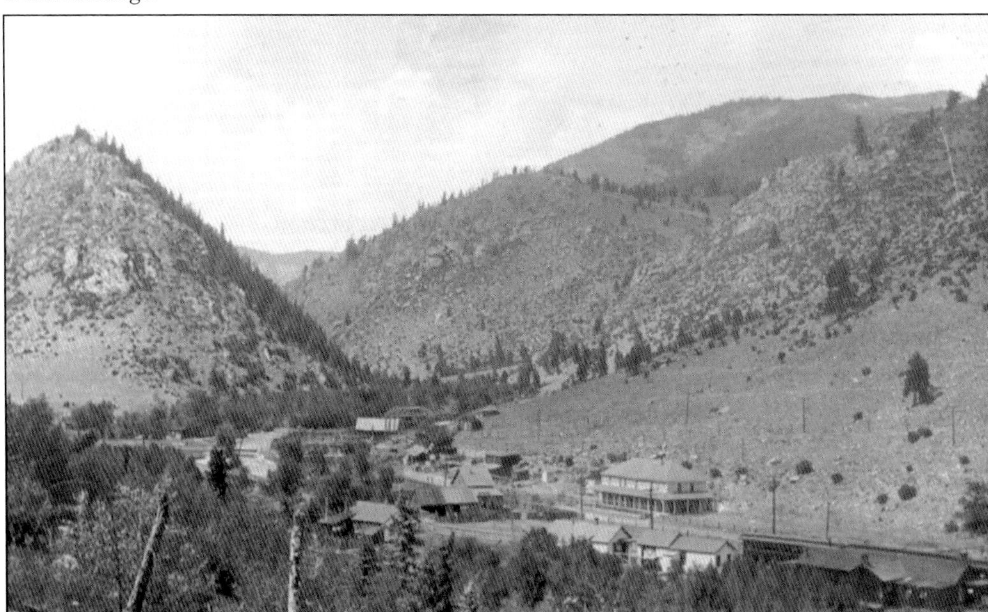

The Geneva Lodge, the large two-story white building in the right foreground, was constructed in the 1880s and was owned by the McFarland family. The builders adapted a common 1880s vernacular home design to a larger scale, adding a large wraparound veranda where guests could relax and enjoy the beautiful mountain scenery. The lodge was a popular stopping point for tourists and travelers in its time.

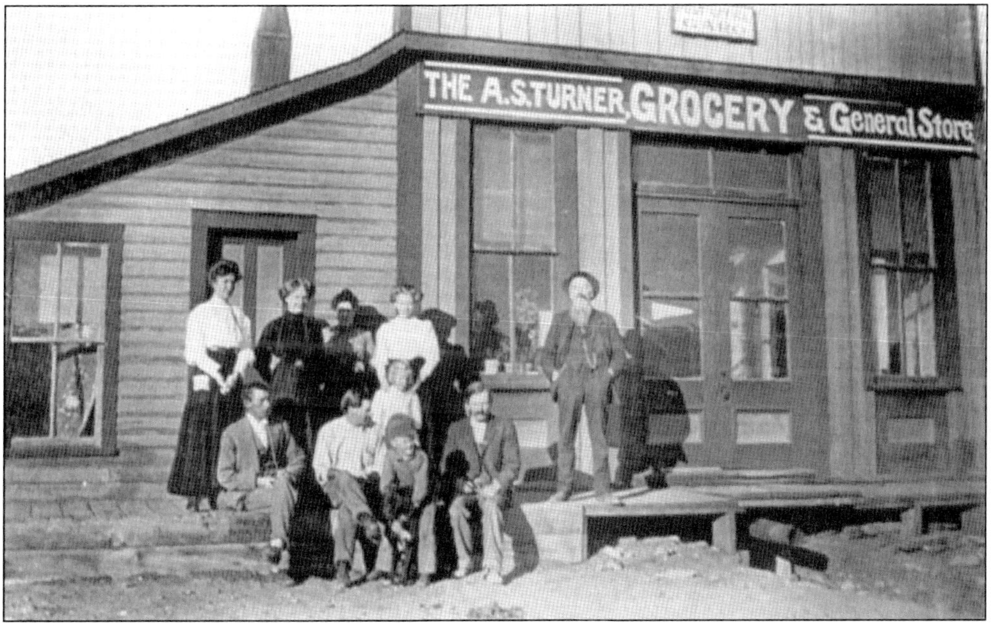

Local folks pose around 1900 at the Garo store and post office, which operated from about 1885 into the 1960s. The junction point for the railroad branch to Fairplay, Garo featured a school, saloons, slaughterhouse, and a petroleum bulk plant. Countless tons of hay, cattle, sheep, and wool were shipped from here. The town was named after an early pioneer family, the Guirauds from France, who amassed substantial ranch holdings.

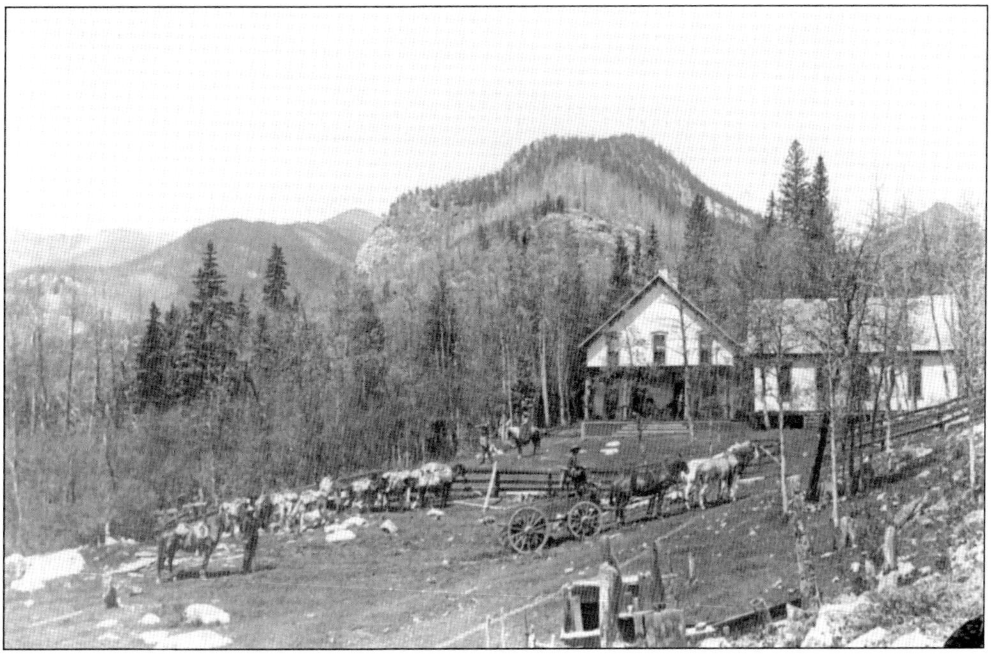

Hall Valley, also called Hallville and Hall City, is shown here in the 1870s. It was founded early that decade by English immigrant Col. Jairus W. Hall. His smelter was ultimately unsuccessful in serving Hall's silver mines high in Hall Gulch. The white house at right was Hall's residence. Hall Valley Campground is now located at the townsite.

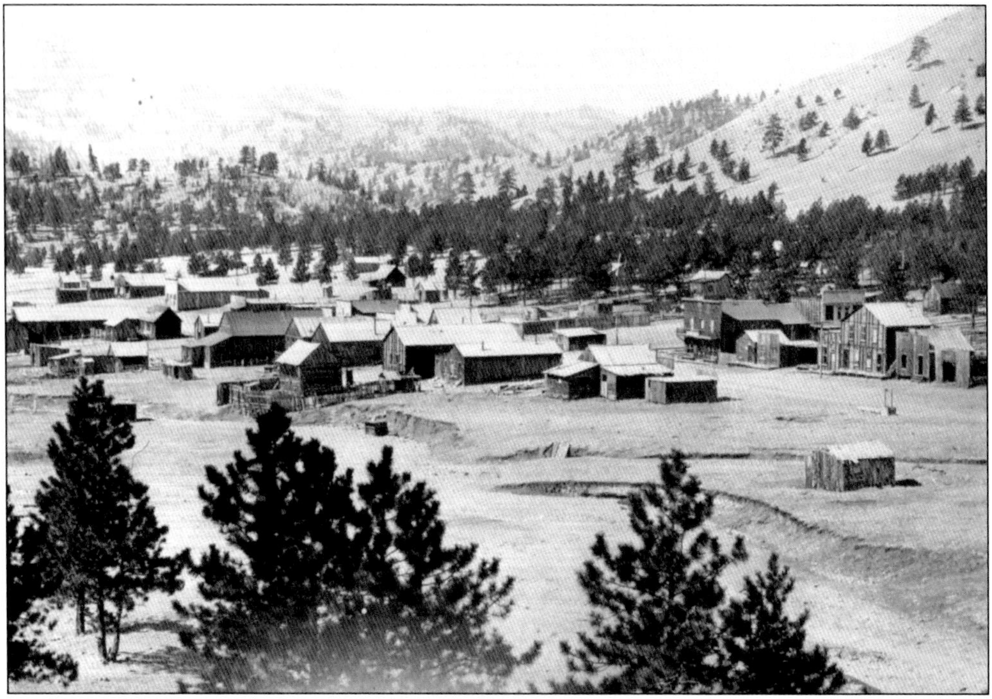

Guffey, also called Freshwater and Idaville, is seen here probably not long after 1900. It arose out of an 1895 mining phenomenon. The mining died out, but ranching, logging, and recreation sustained the little town, making it possible for it to support several businesses, along with a still-operating post office and school.

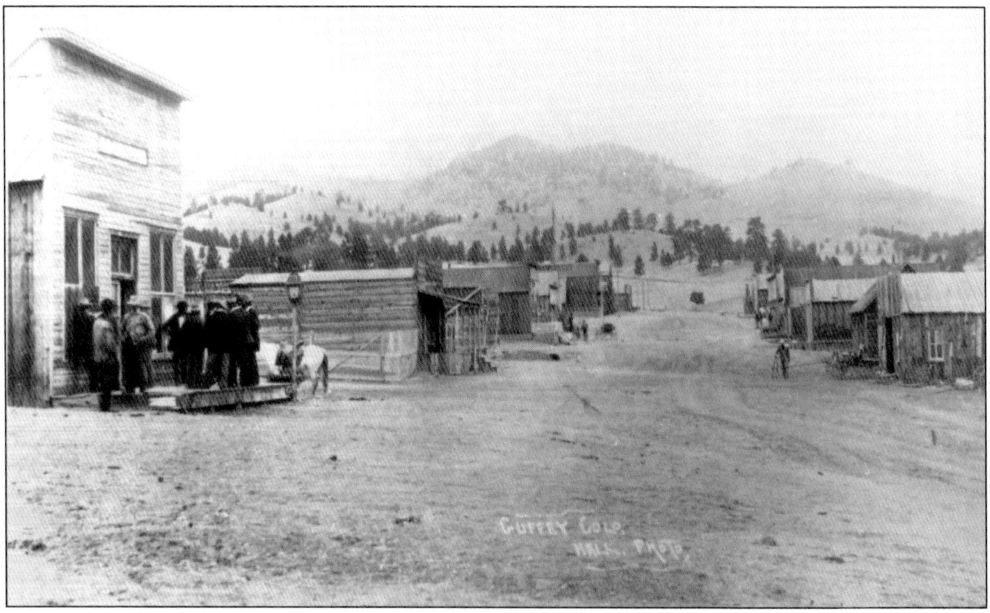

The Guffey Town Hall was built in 1896. Dances were frequently held here as well as many other community events. It has been refurbished as a museum and is chock full of memorabilia including old harnesses, pails, and frying pans hanging from the rafters. In spite of its remote location, it still attracts many visitors.

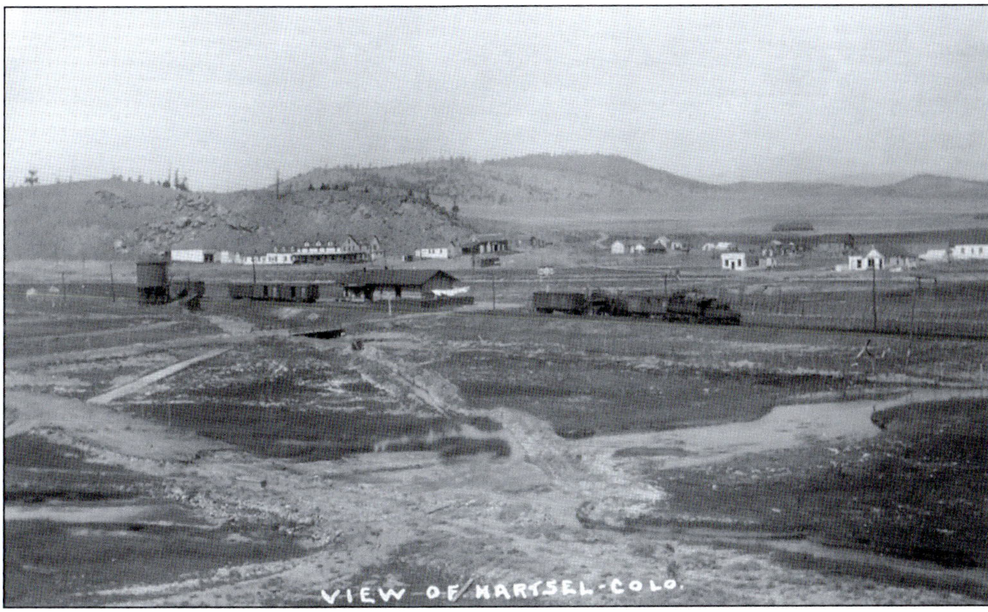

Shown here in the first decade of the 20th century, Hartsel is still very much alive. The gabled Hartsel Hotel is visible behind the Colorado Midland depot. The town sits at the junction of routes to Colorado Springs and Canon City. The area's first significant settlement took place when Sam Hartsel developed its hot spring and hotel/post office around 1878.

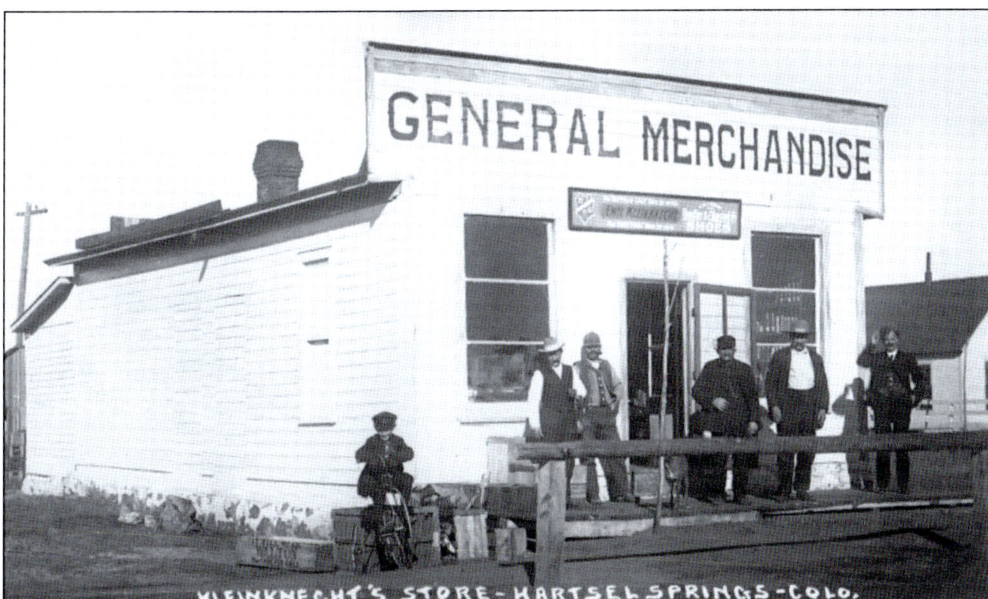

Shown here between 1905 and 1910, the Kleinknecht Store in Hartsel was a hub for locals to meet and visit with each other. Moving here from Puma City after that town's boom had largely expired, the Kleinknecht (Klein) family was active in business for many years, even maintaining a Chrysler-Plymouth dealership into the 1950s.

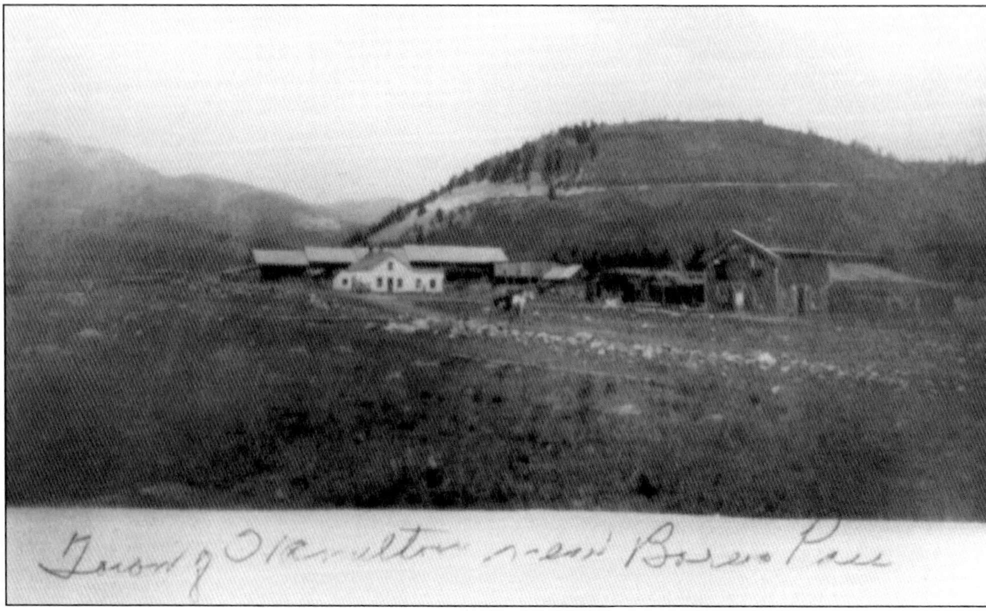

Dated 1894, this photograph shows a few of Hamilton's remaining buildings (right) and those of the Peabody Ranch (left). All succumbed to dredging around 1940. The Tarryall Diggings were first settled in 1859, with the competing townsites of Hamilton and Tarryall City established in 1860. The former was a much more successful settlement.

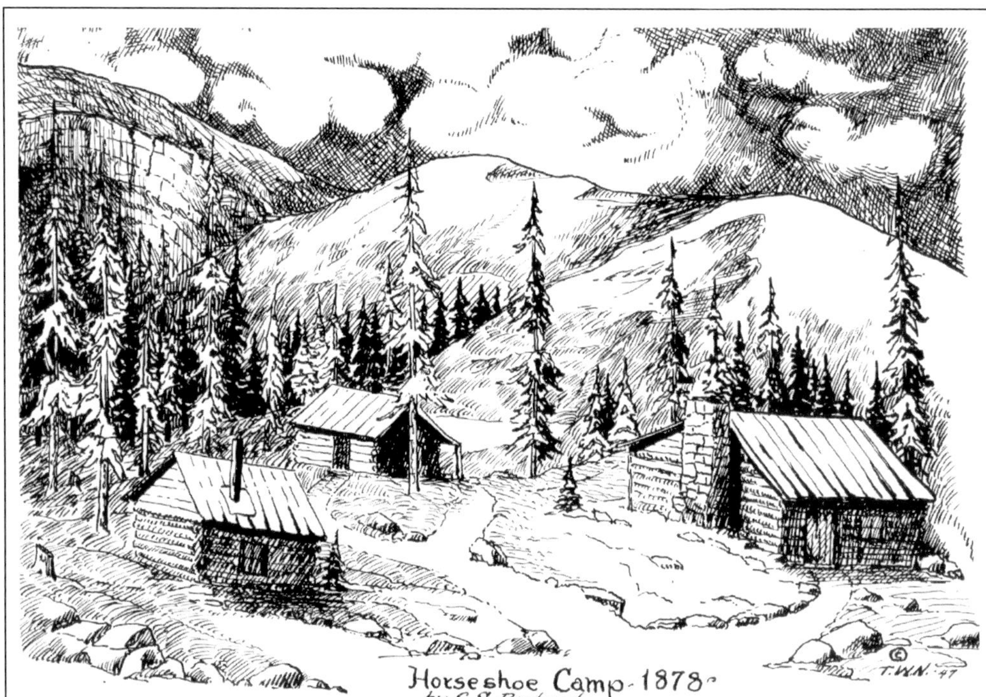

This 1878 sketch shows the mining town of Horseshoe, a profitable mining area in the Mosquito Range. It was originally named East Leadville but the town was incorporated as Horseshoe in 1881. By 1886, the miners had moved on and the post office was closed.

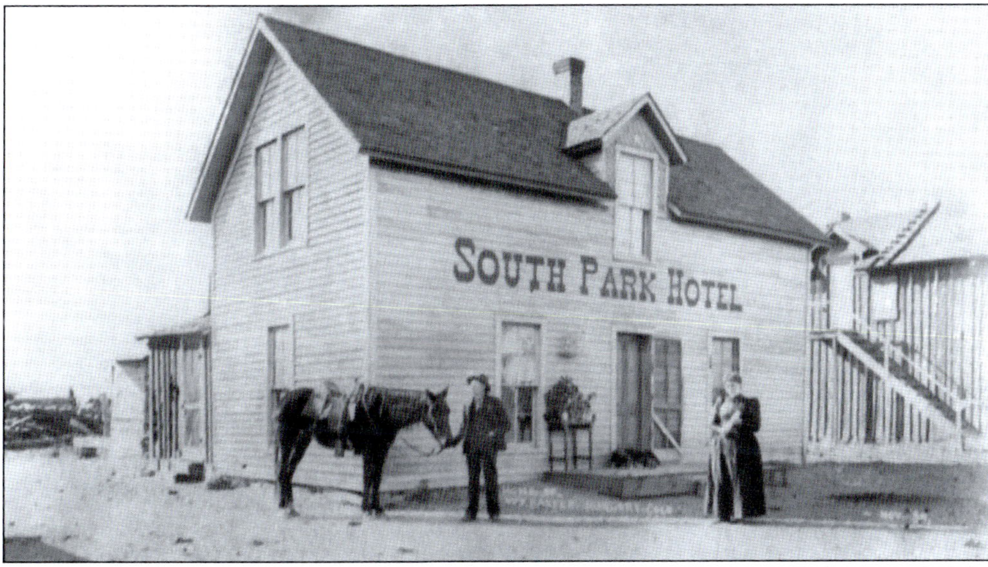

The South Park Hotel at Howbert is shown in 1894. Howbert sprang up with the arrival of the Colorado Midland Railroad in 1887, becoming a shipping point for hay, livestock, and lumber. The hotel later became the Epperson family home. Soon after 1930, the townsite was covered by Eleven Mile Reservoir.

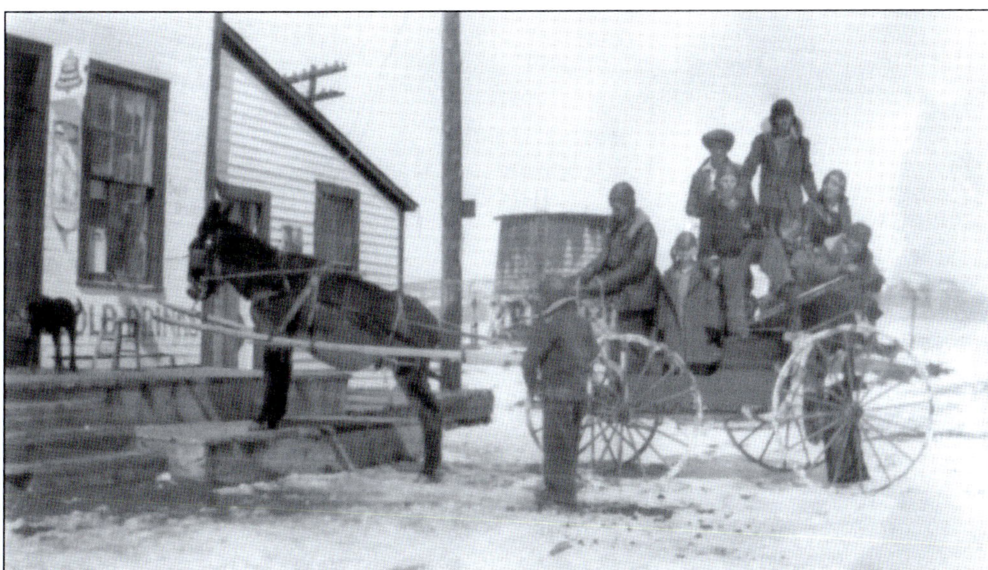

Burro power provided dependable transit in wintry Jefferson in 1926. Founded when the railroad arrived in 1879, Jefferson was a shipping center and a business hub for nearby ranchers, travelers, and recreationists. It is not to be confused with the 1860–1863 settlement of Jefferson City, located several miles to the northwest.

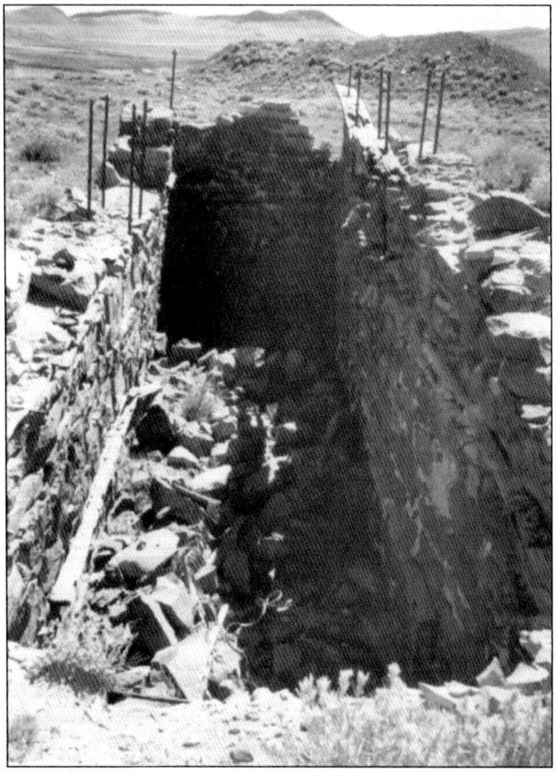

This is the crumbling foundation of the huge fan that pumped air into the gassy, railroad-owned coal mines at King. Located more than two miles southeast of Como, King was a true company town, with small tenement housing dotting the landscape. After a tragic 1893 explosion, the mines finally closed altogether in 1896.

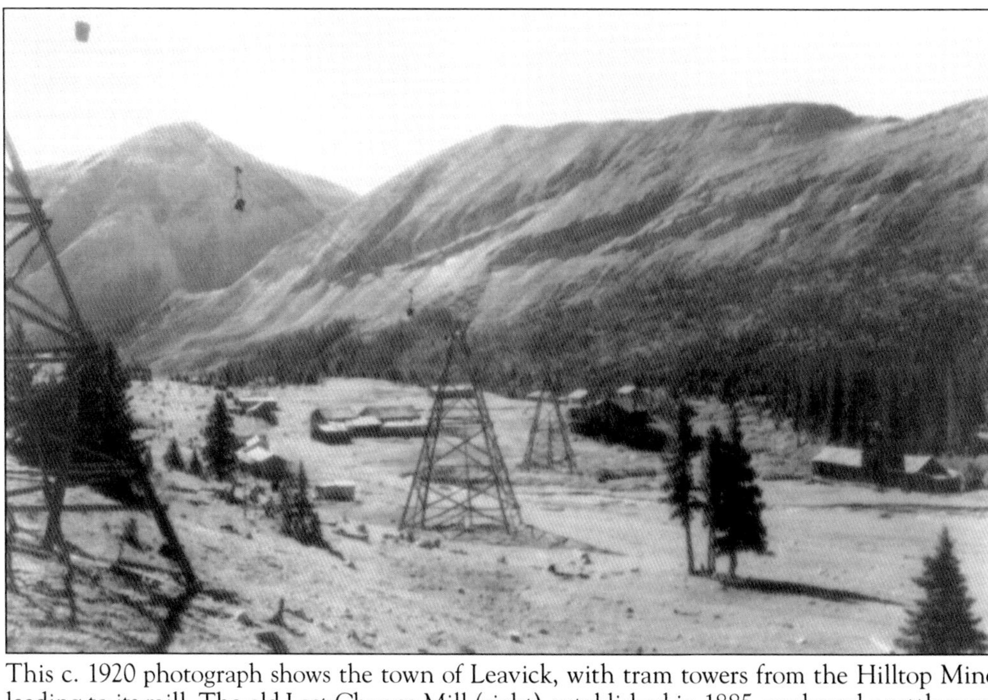

This c. 1920 photograph shows the town of Leavick, with tram towers from the Hilltop Mine leading to its mill. The old Last Chance Mill (right), established in 1885, anchored a settlement called Double Cabins. It expanded to become Leavick in 1896–1897. The post office here was also named Doran and Horseshoe.

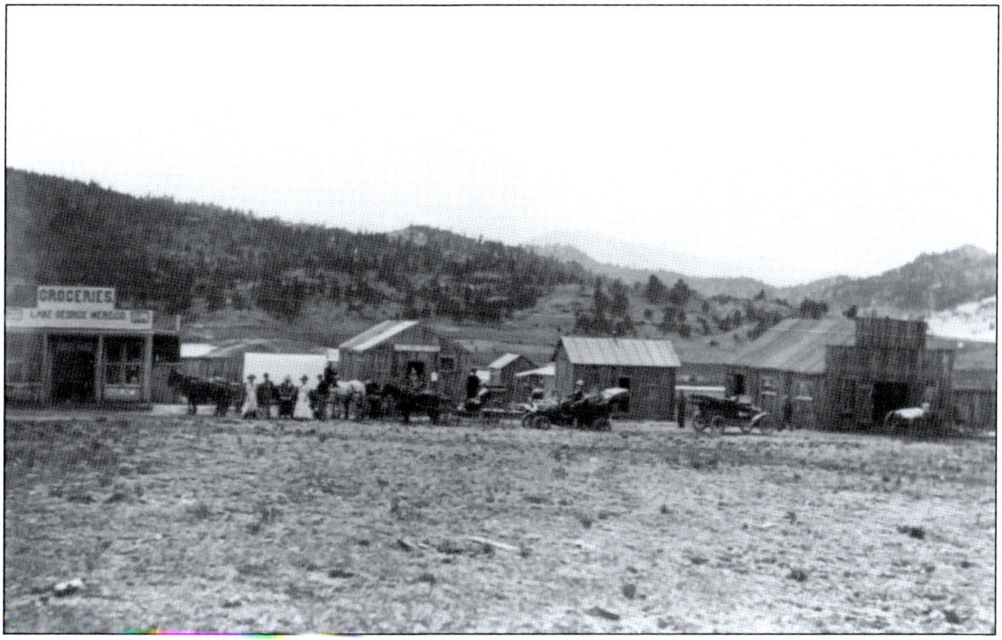

In this c. 1912 photograph of Lake George, the lake's surface is visible beyond the well-dressed ladies. This settlement coincided with construction of the dam and lake in 1891. A large ice-harvesting operation here shipped via the nearby Colorado Midland Railroad. A larger town plat in 1909 saw more settlement that outlasted the railroad's demise.

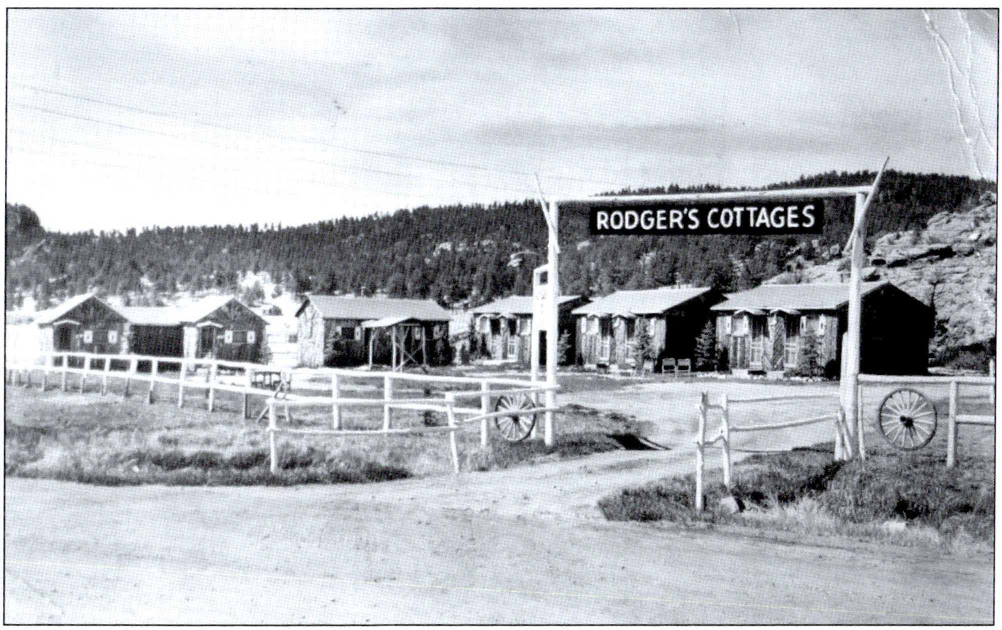

In the 1930s, Lake George increasingly became known as a tourist destination. Cottage camps like Rodger's Cottages, pictured here around 1950, provided lodging for travelers eager to experience the beauty of Eleven Mile Canyon and the Tarryall Valley. Today, National Forest and State Parks recreation bring great activity to the area, which has also seen development of many residential and second-home subdivisions.

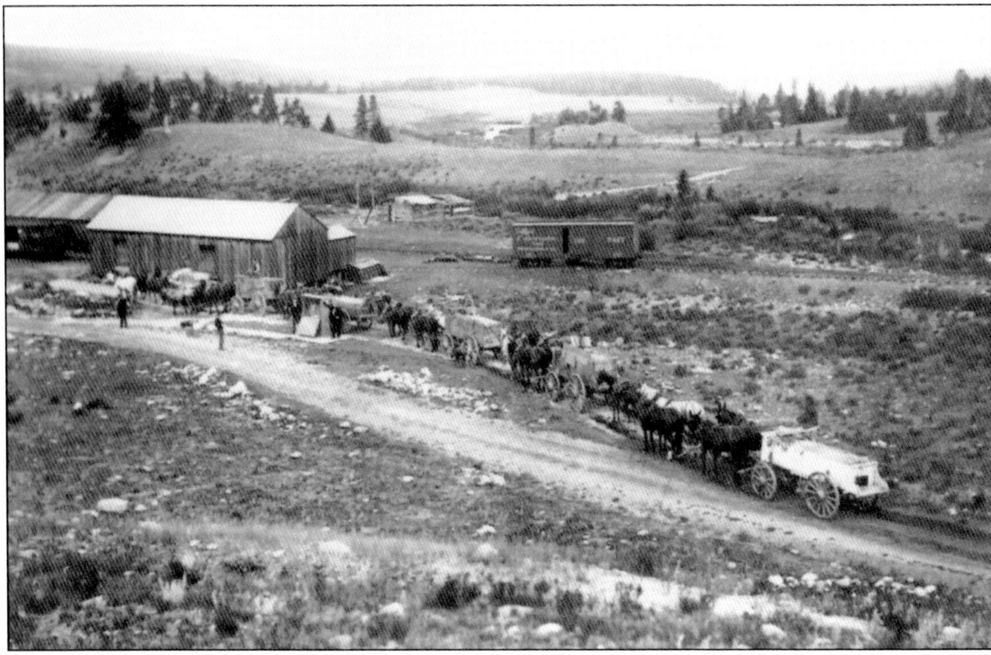

Freight wagons line up at the London Junction depot scale; the town was also called Alma Junction. Here ended the main railroad branch. A smaller branch extended up Mosquito Gulch. This depot served Alma and a large mining area to the west and northwest. The railroad and a large ore mill anchored the 1883 townsite.

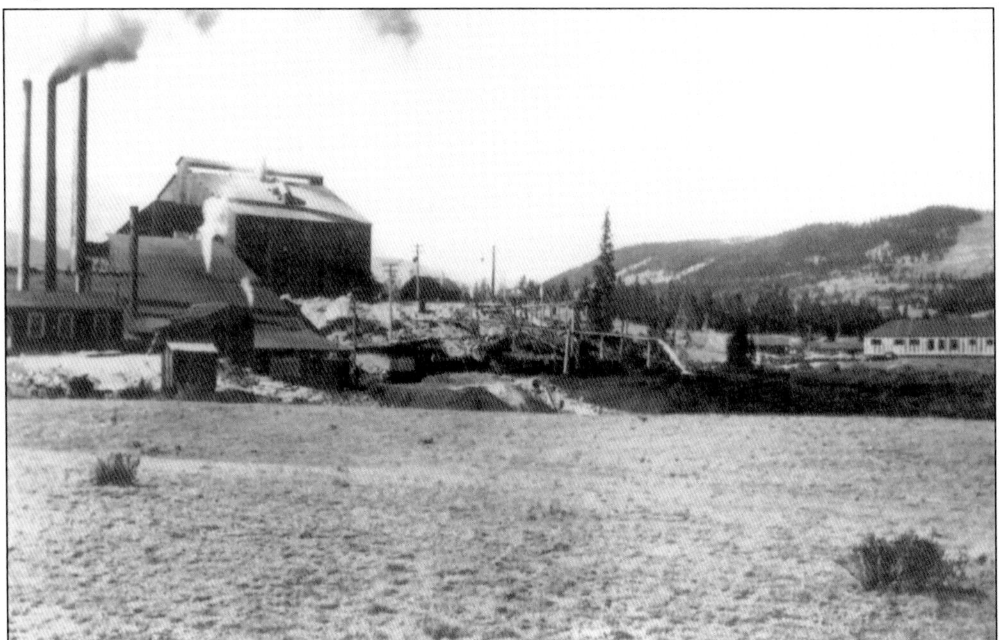

The short-lived smelter at London Junction is shown here between 1910 and 1912. It closed after the 1912 death of financial patron George Moe. An 1880s ore mill serving the celebrated London Mine had occupied the same site, accompanied by a smaller reduction works, which also had a short, unsuccessful tenure doing custom work.

Abandoned buildings and machinery are evident in this photograph of Montgomery from the early 1880s. Platted in 1861 and now lying beneath Montgomery Reservoir, it was very active in the early 1860s. Later, sporadic revivals centered largely on ore mills and some nearby mines that came and went with the boom-and-bust mining economy.

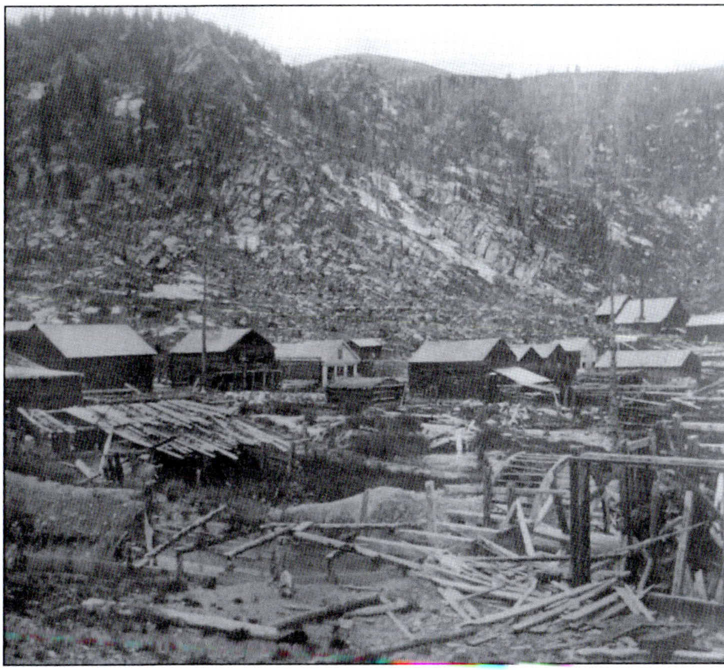

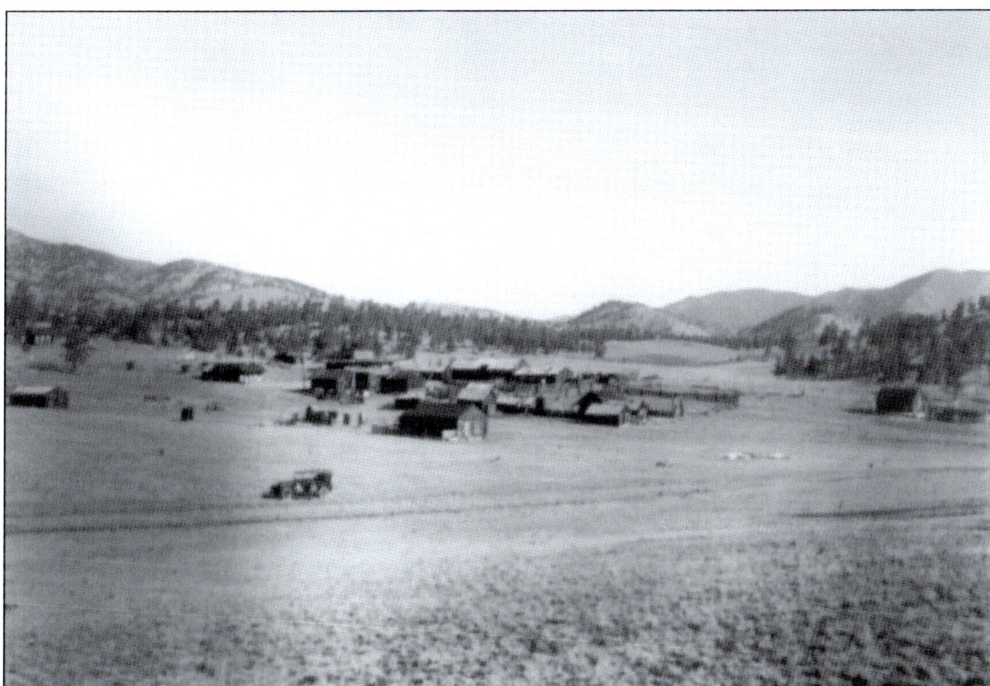

Boom-and-bust Puma City (now called Tarryall) is shown in 1920. A Cripple Creek spinoff in 1896, Puma listed some 40 businesses and 1,000 people in 1897. In 1899, those figures had been reduced to 8 and 50. The town is still home to a small group of hardy souls and a National Register one-room schoolhouse.

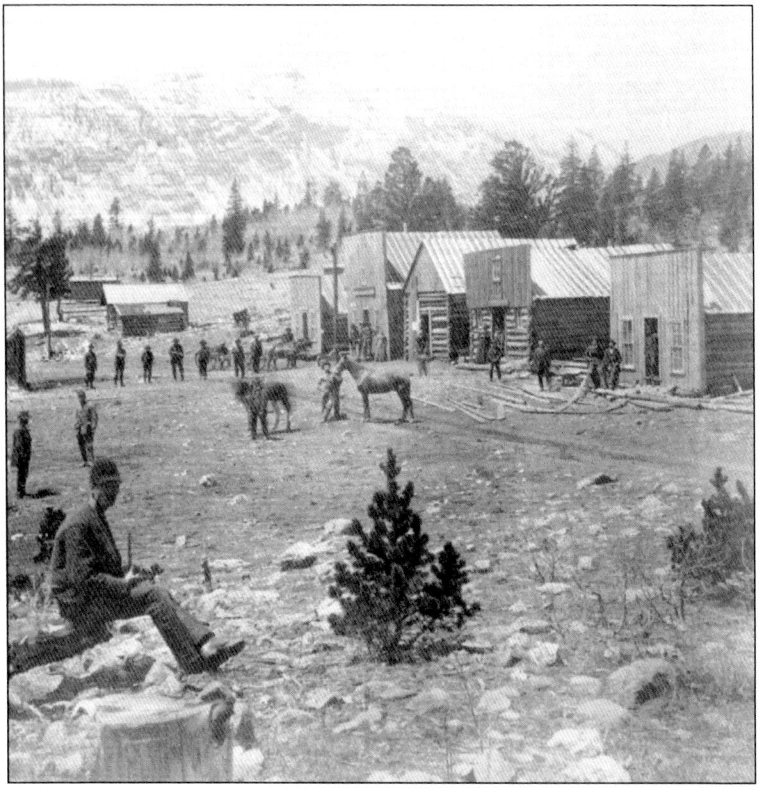

Platted in 1882, Park City was on a more hospitable, flat site just east of the 1861 Sterling/Mosquito townsite. It served a nearby mining area that included the prominent Orphan Boy, Hock Hocking, and Mascotte Mines. Park City was the last business center on the Mosquito Pass Road, which accessed the famed London Mine and other mines high in Mosquito Gulch.

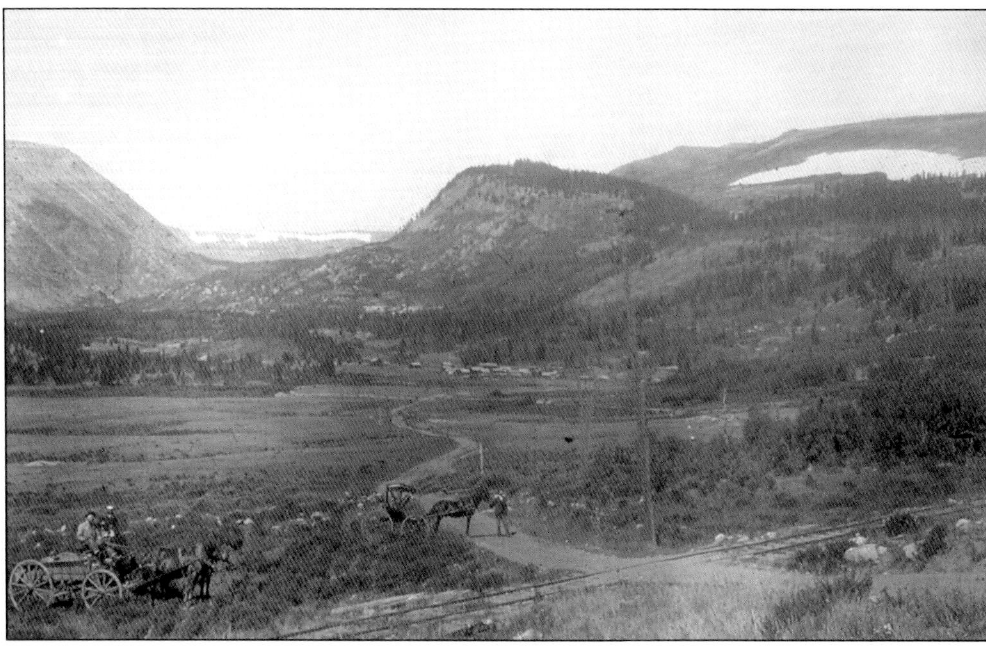

This late 1880s panoramic photograph shows Park City (center) and its surroundings. The railroad to the North London Mine is in the foreground. Some of the town's old buildings survive here in what is sometimes described as a ghost town. A number of current residents would dispute that label.

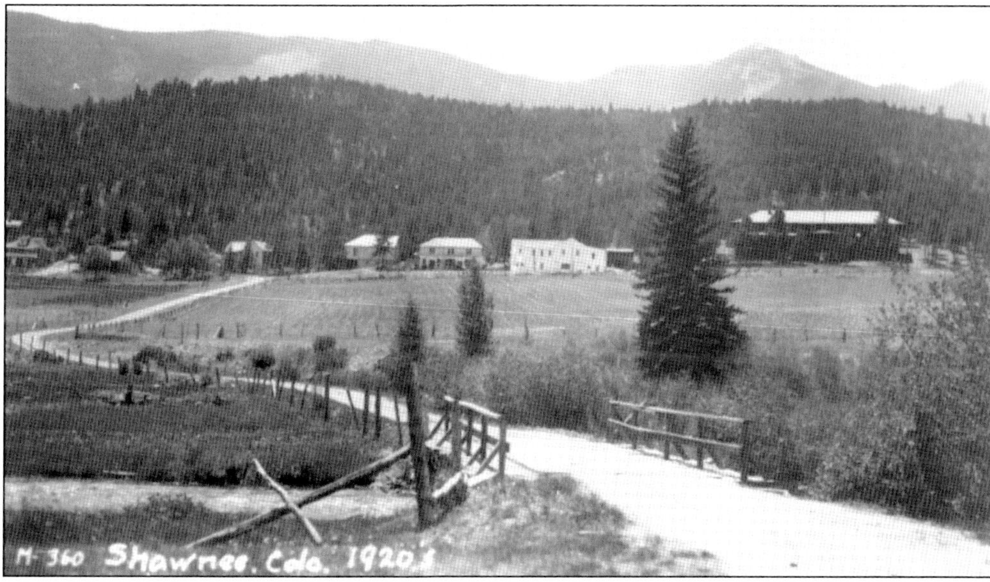

Developed in 1900 by the Colorado & Southern Railroad, Shawnee is shown here in the 1920s. It essentially replaced the nearby settlement of Slaghts/Fairville (1863). Intended largely as a summer-home community, Shawnee also included the railroad-owned Shawnee Lodge (right), which burned down in 1929. Shawnee is now a National Historic District with many permanent residents.

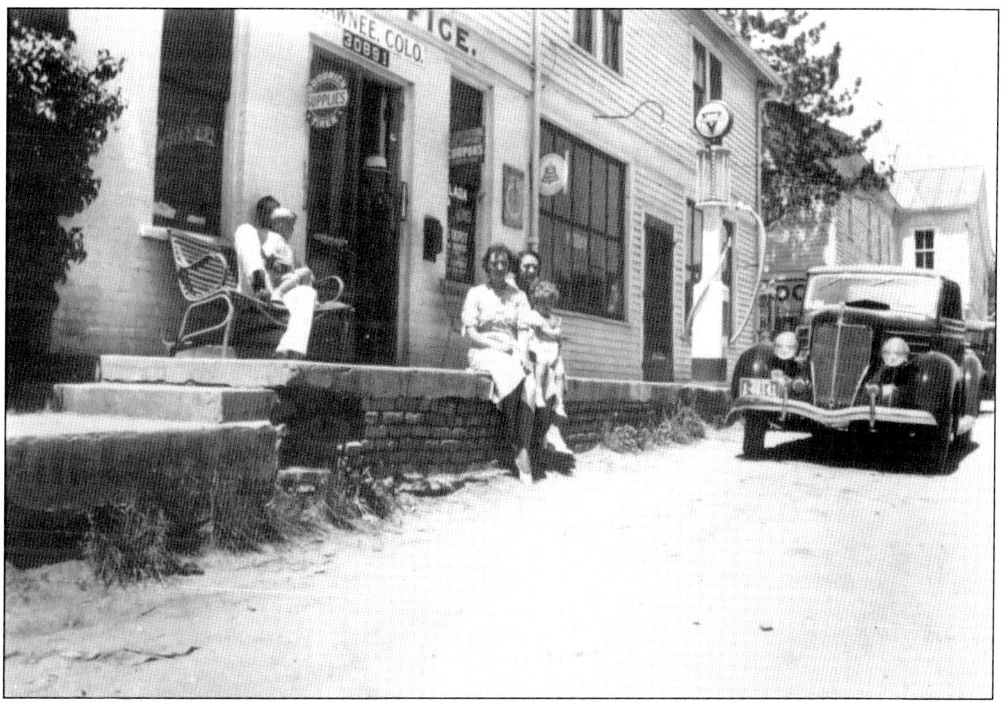

Shawnee's post office and store, a popular gathering place, is shown in 1936. A spiffy 1936 Ford convertible shares the scene. When the railroad shut down in 1937, the impact was tempered by the paving of US Highway 285 within a year. In 2014, Shawnee still retains its post office.

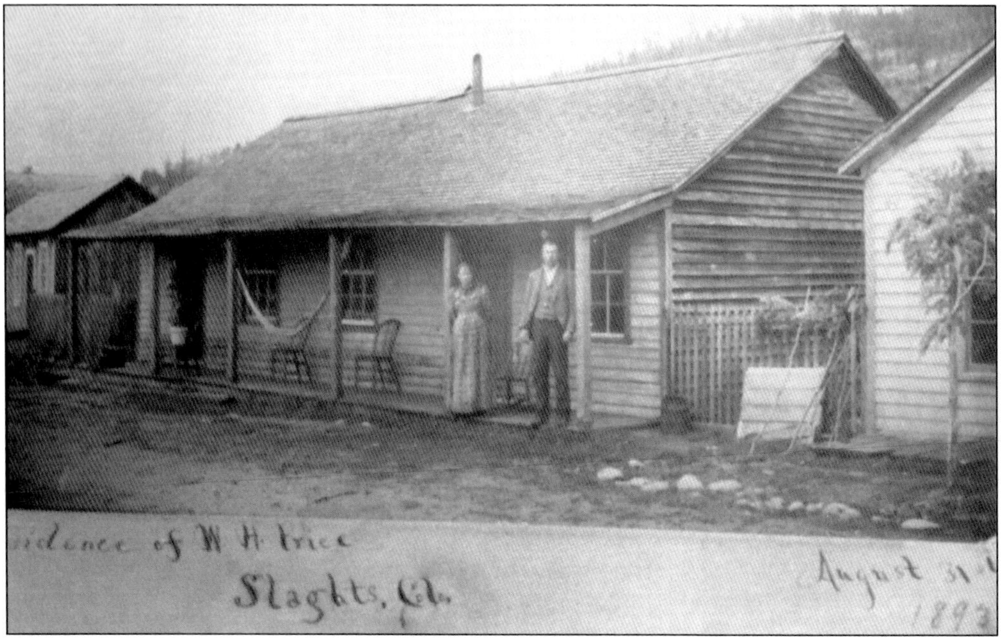

Storekeepers W.H. and Maud Price are shown in 1893 at home in Slaghts, founded in 1863 by Azel Slaght. The settlement was also known as Granite Vale and Fairville. As did many roadside ranchers, Slaght carried on sideline businesses to supplement his income. Those enterprises included a hotel/stage stop/post office and blacksmith services.

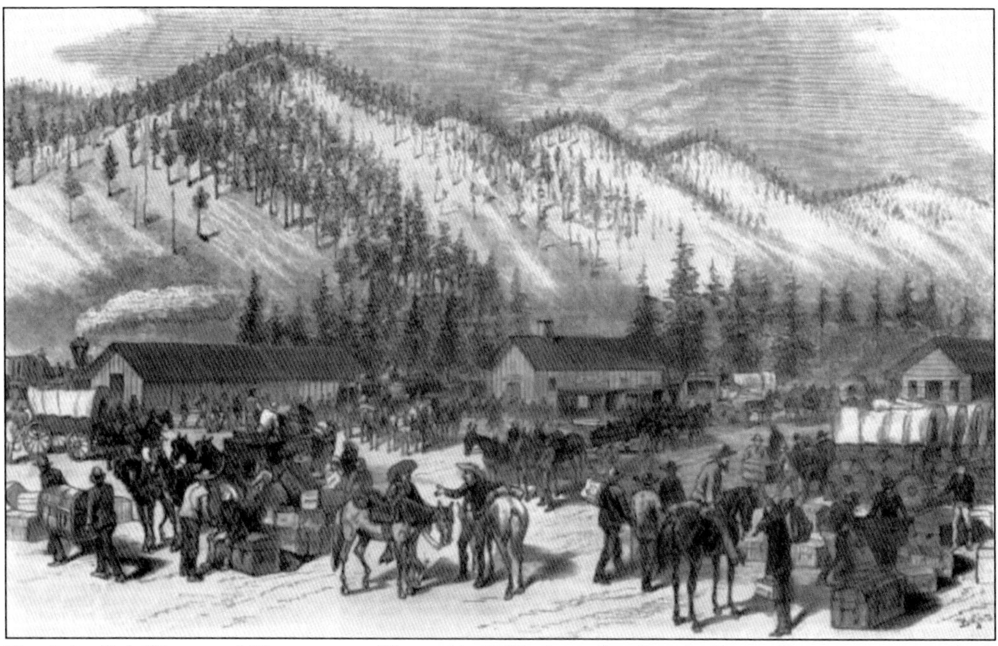

Frank Leslie's Illustrated Newspaper of June 21, 1879, describes Leadville traffic swarming end-of-track Webster in Platte Canyon: "The pine-clad bluffs, the rude station, the stages packed full as sardine-boxes, the teams, the wagons, the newly-arrived silver-seekers panting to push on at any cost and in any mode, the freight, the successful miners returning to civilization, the haggard questioners, the yelling freighters, the bustle, hurry, turmoil and excitement."

Six

Schools and Churches

Schools and churches in Park County provided the needed education, religious training, and social outlets for its early population, as they still do today.

One of the earliest schools, established in the raucous mining camp of Buckskin Joe in 1862, was headed by a teacher named Esther Mann. From 1866 through 1867, silver king "HAW" Tabor was the county's school superintendent prior to making his fortune in adjoining Lake County. Park County boasted at least two female superintendents, one being Sadie Maxey, one of only 26 female county superintendents in the late 1800s.

Outlying ranches often hosted on-site schools, providing living quarters and classroom space for a teacher. Such was the case of the Hammond ranch school in 1906, located in central South Park.

The buildings were typically constructed from available materials, the most prominent being logs in the mid-1800s. Dimensional lumber was adopted as building methods and financing improved. The classic one-room schoolhouse typically sported two or three windows on each side and included all grades. The interior consisted of a stove for heat, desks, chalkboards, and other utilitarian features. Schoolhouses were often the only public building within miles, providing a central point for social events such as dances and political meetings, as well as religious events, including weddings and church services.

A 1950s federal mandate requiring small school districts to consolidate prompted many one-room schoolhouses to merge with nearby districts, leaving many vacant buildings. The Hall Valley District claimed only two students in 1894, showing the need to combine buildings and students.

Churches were constructed after the discovery of gold in 1859 in the county. A variety of denominations, both Catholic and Protestant, ministered to the burgeoning mining population. The Methodists, active in the mid-1800s, had two well-known preachers, Father John L. Dyer and Irving Howbert. They spread the good word in Park County. Rev. Joseph P. Machebeuf was instrumental in establishing a number of Catholic churches during his tenure. These also flourished in Colorado's fledging towns, including Georgetown, Boulder, Golden, and Oro City (Leadville).

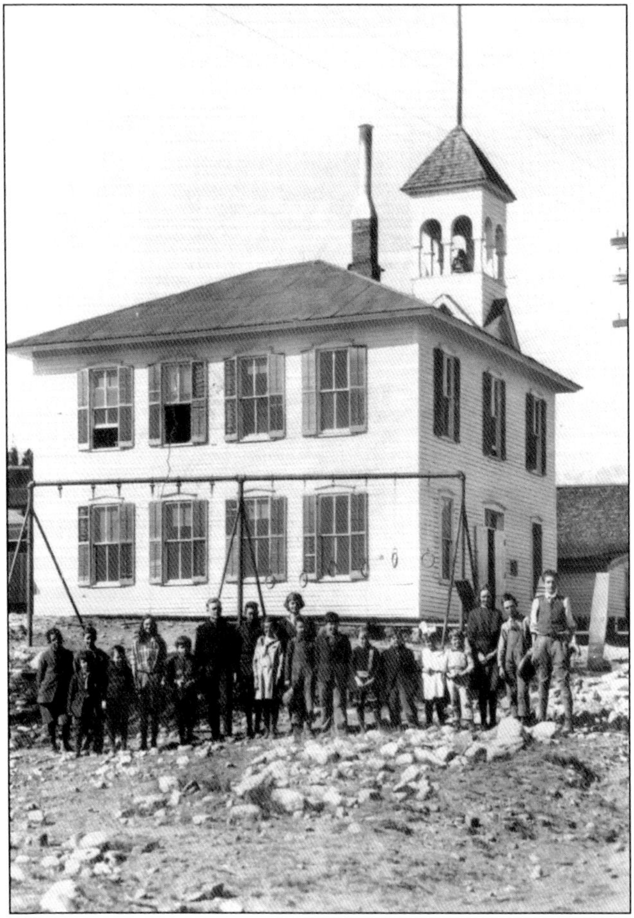

The town of Alma was established in 1872 as a result of the rich silver mines in the nearby Mosquito Range mountains. This two-story wood schoolhouse was built in 1887 to accommodate the many mining families that moved into the area.

The school burned to the ground on May 15, 1928. By that fall, a new building had been erected in an entirely different style. The Mission-style structure is still in use today as the town of Alma's offices and town hall.

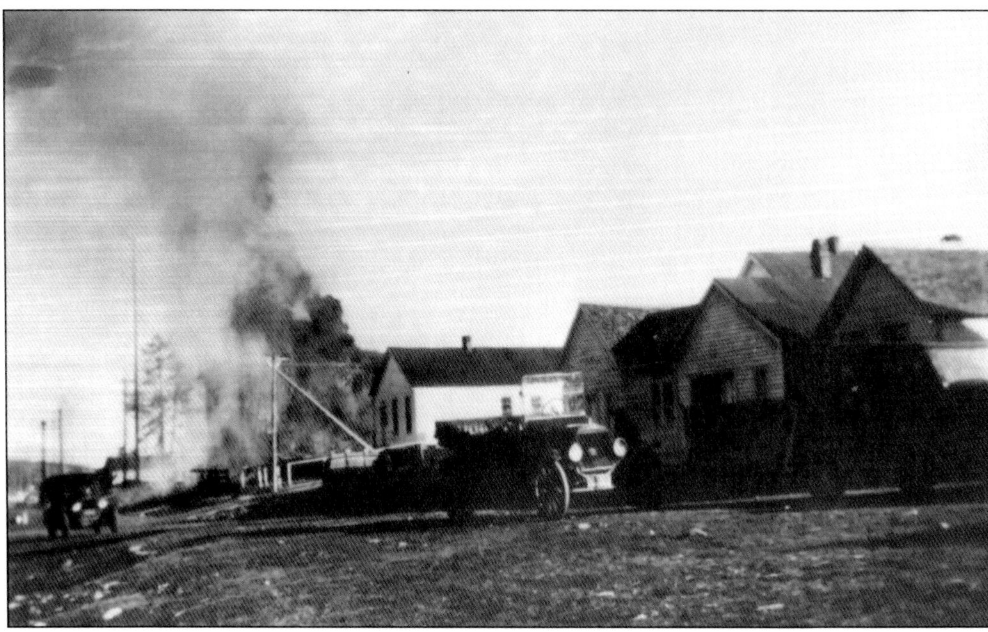

This 1881 photograph of the Union Chapel in Alma shows the interior of a popular church during Christmas. In addition to regular services, the chapel served as a meeting place. By the turn of the 20th century, repairs were needed, so various fundraisers, including an art show, were successfully held there as well.

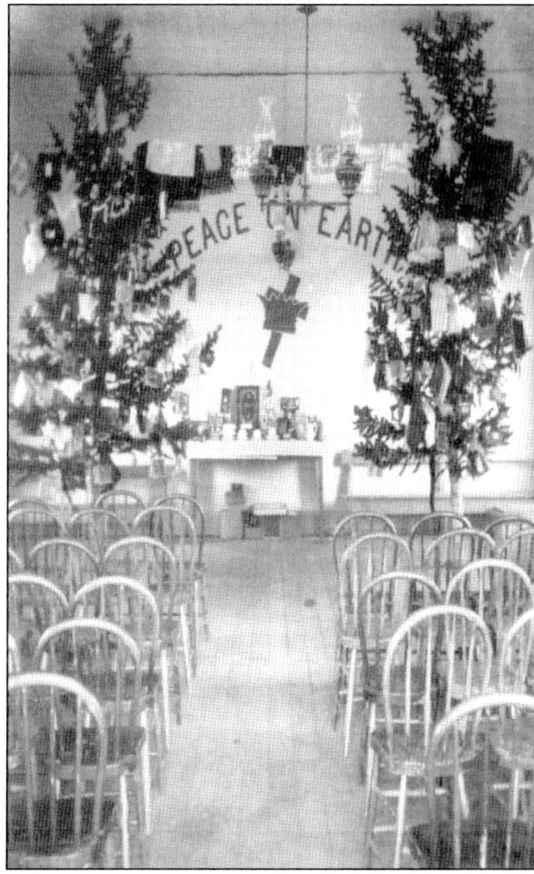

This Catholic church was located near the corner of US Highway 285 and County Road 68. Monsignor Monahan was the priest assigned to the parish in the 1960s. The building, later called White Eagle Lodge, was at one point owned by an order of nuns and used as a summertime destination.

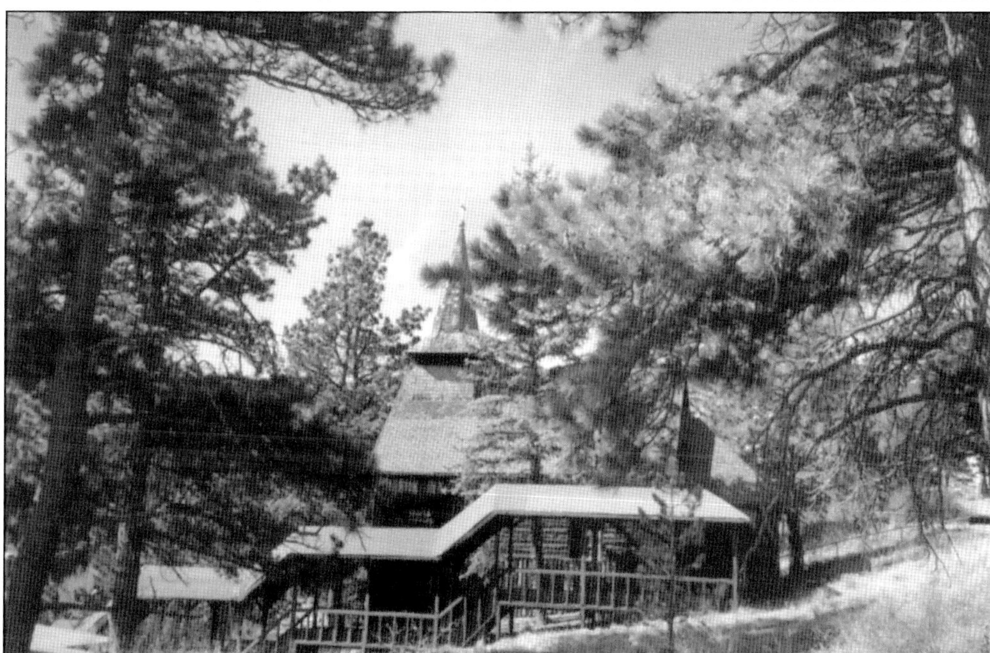

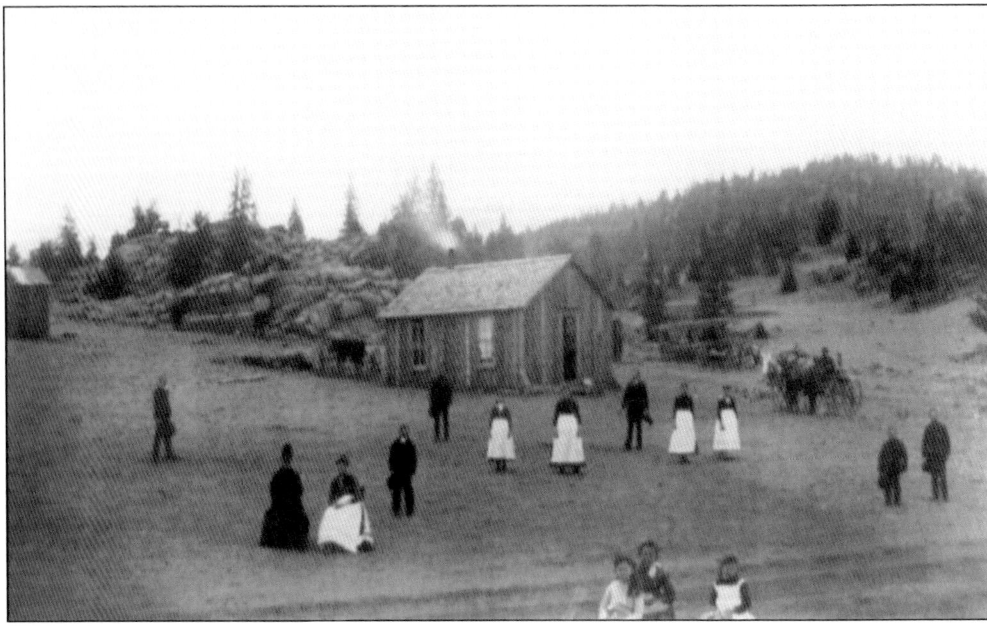

The Bordenville school, located along the Tarryall River east of Jefferson, boasted 10 students in 1886. In this photograph, smoke curls from the schoolhouse chimney on a chilly morning. Mary Borden is seated in the foreground at left, wearing a white apron. Her husband, Olney Borden, was one of the town's founders and a prominent rancher.

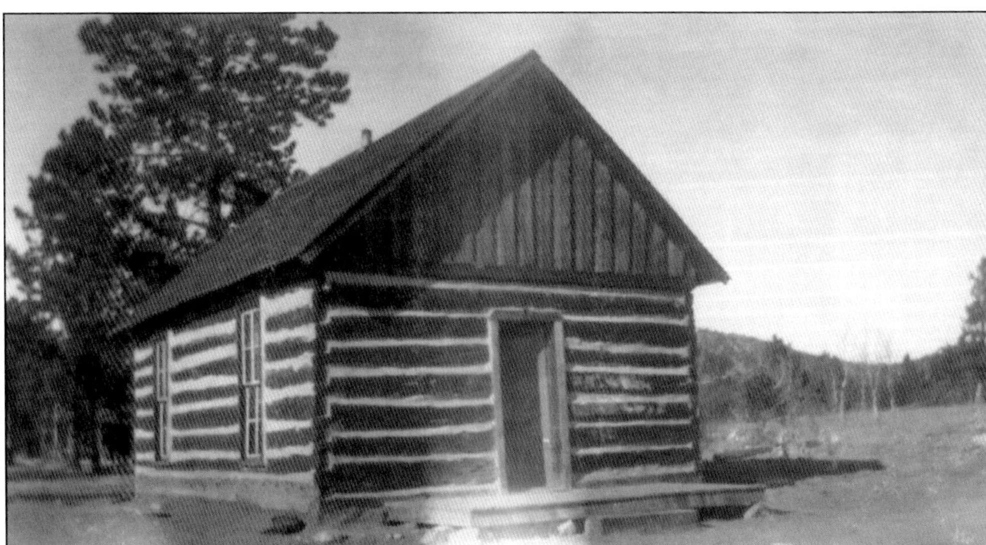

The Crow Hill school, in use in the early 1880s, was probably built by a local resident named Robert Kelso. Located at the top of the hill near County Road 72, the site is now vacant, but it is surrounded by a neighborhood of dispersed mountain homes.

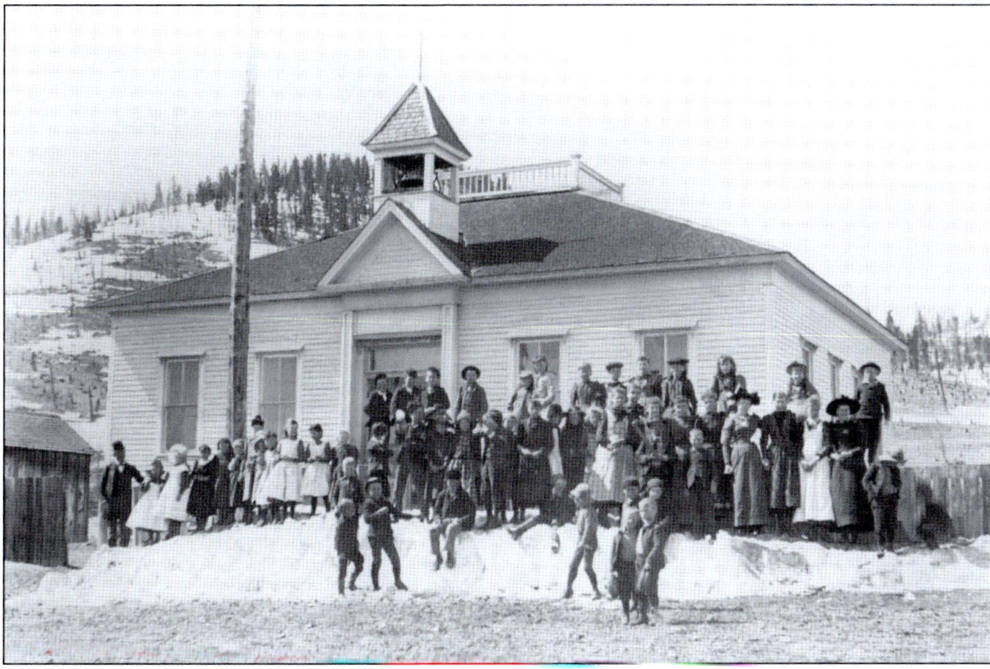

The town of Como was a thriving community in the 1800s, as evidenced by the large number of students seen here frolicking in the snow. The building still stands and is listed in the National Register of Historic Places. Last used as a school in 1948, it is owned by the Como Civic Association and serves as a town hall and meeting place.

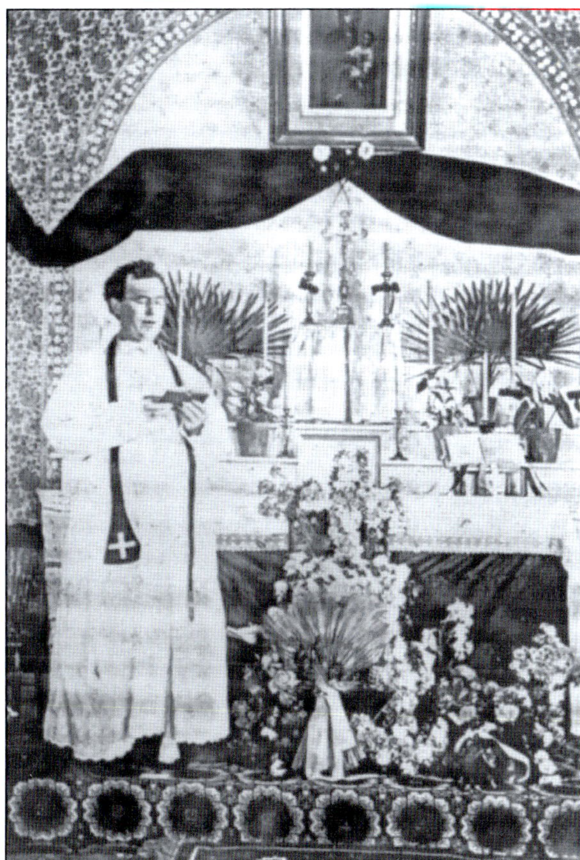

The Como Catholic Church, built in 1881, also had an adjacent rectory. Construction was probably completed by local Italian stonemasons and miners. The building was converted to a private home in the 1950s and remains a living symbol of the important Italian presence in Como's early days. Here, Father Robertson officiates at a 1901 funeral.

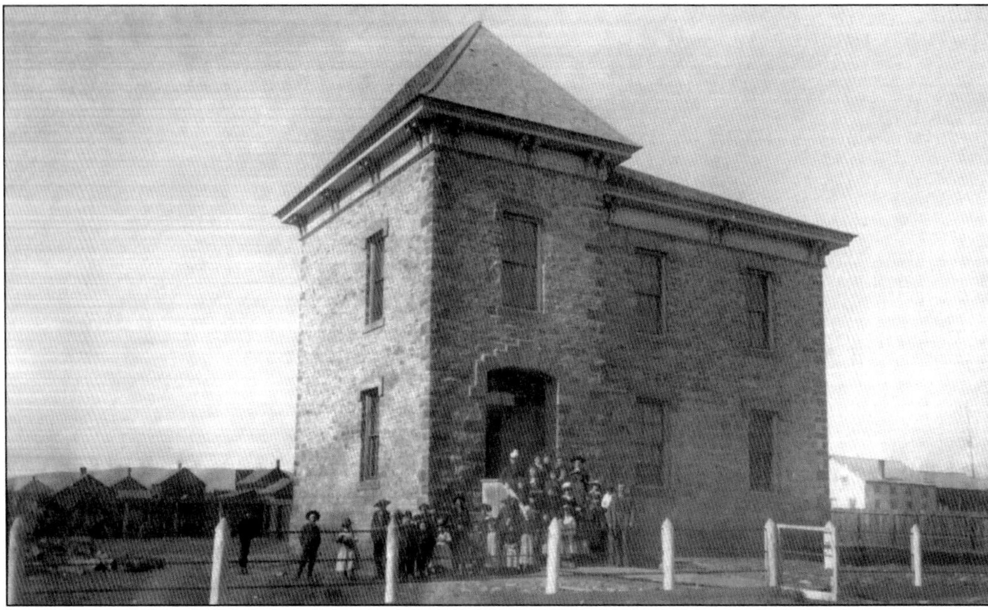

The Edith Teter Elementary school, built in 1880, was constructed of local red sandstone, similar to that used for the nearby original courthouse. The school was named after a well-known teacher who served the area for many years. One of the oldest Colorado schools, it is listed in the Colorado State Register of Historic Properties and is also a Park County Historic Landmark.

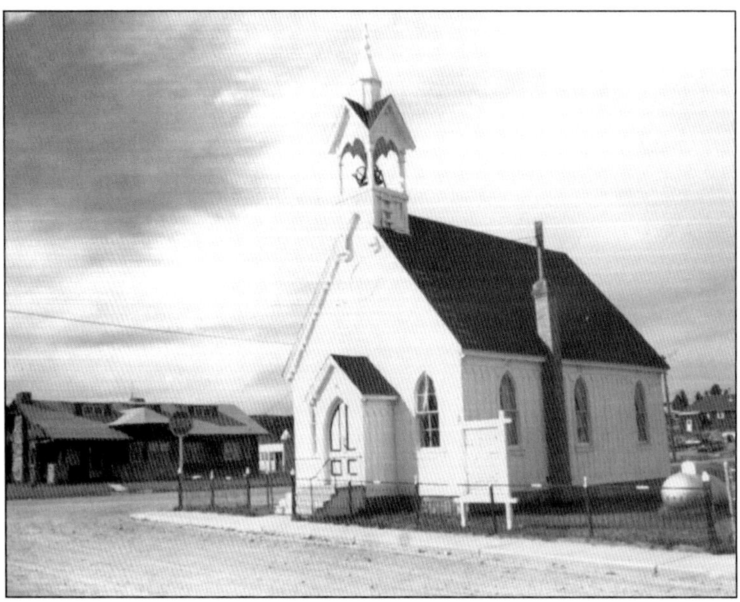

Built in 1874, the Sheldon Jackson Memorial Chapel stands in Fairplay and is still in use as a Presbyterian church by the South Park Community Church. Jackson was a colorful frontier character and a prolific church-builder, having constructed at least 22 churches in Colorado alone and over 100 in the western United States in the mid-1800s.

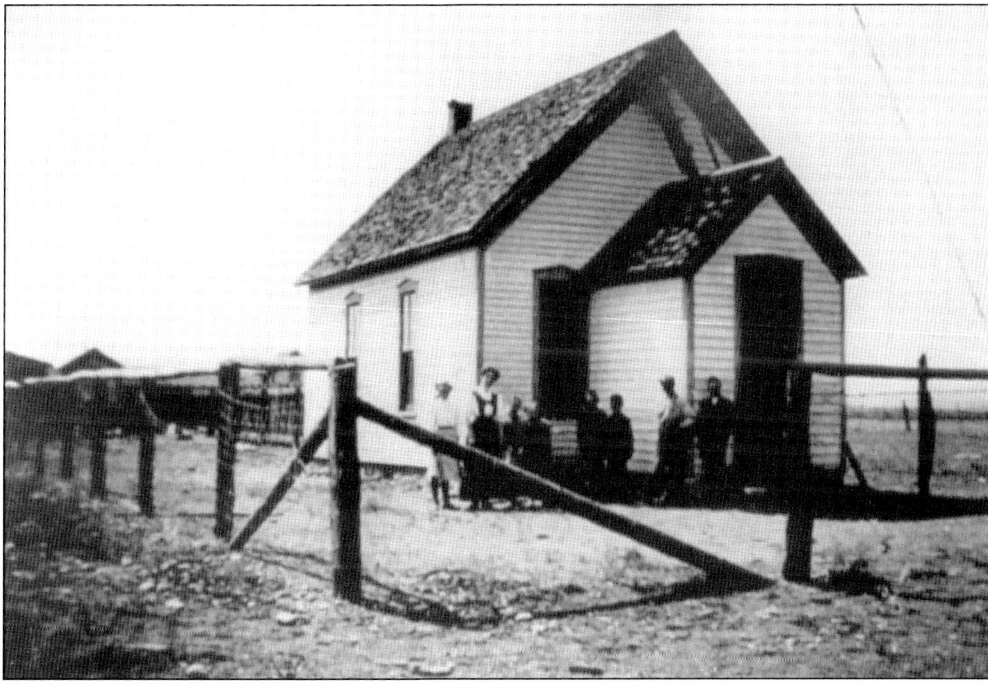

The town of Garo, located nine miles east of Fairplay, was named after an early homestead family from France, the Guirauds. The Garo school, constructed in 1879, initially sported red siding with white trim before it was repainted, as seen here around 1900. The Garo teacher earned $60 per month. The building was moved to the South Park City Museum in 1960.

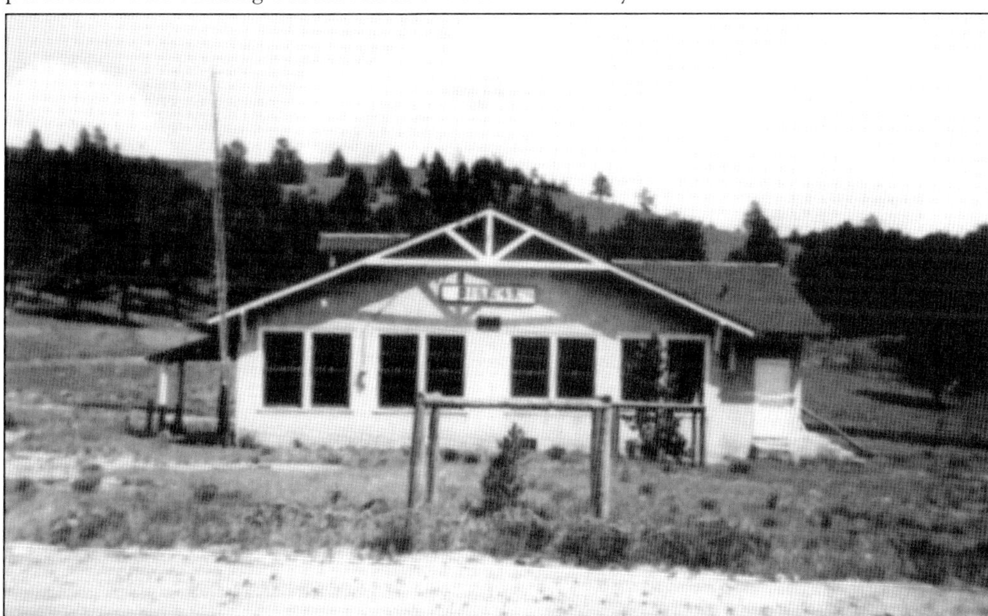

The Guffey school/community center is shown here in the 1950s. The sparsely populated school district struggled to finance it, but the building was largely completed in 1918. The building's use as a school later had a hiatus of over 20 years before it resumed in 1981. As of 2014, the modified and expanded building houses a public charter school.

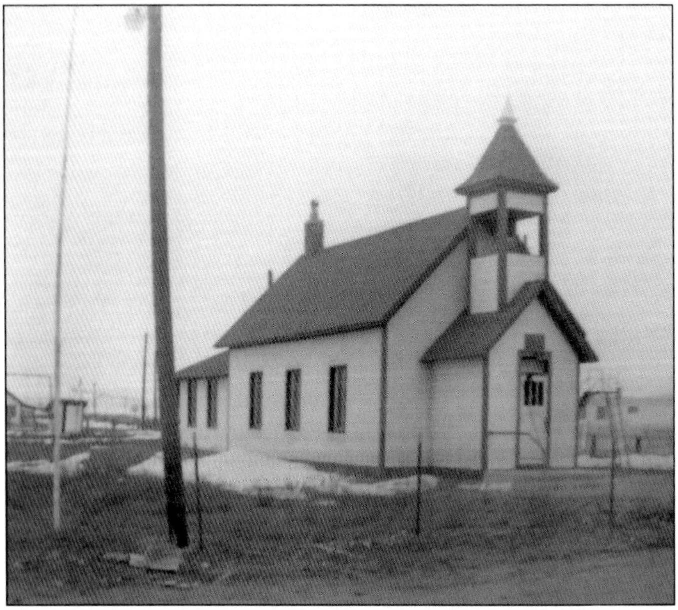

Although currently located in the town of Hartsel proper, the school building was moved just one block away in the mid-1940s after a land survey determined it was sitting on private property. The school closed in the 1960s, and students were bused to Fairplay. The schoolhouse is now used as the Hartsel Community Center.

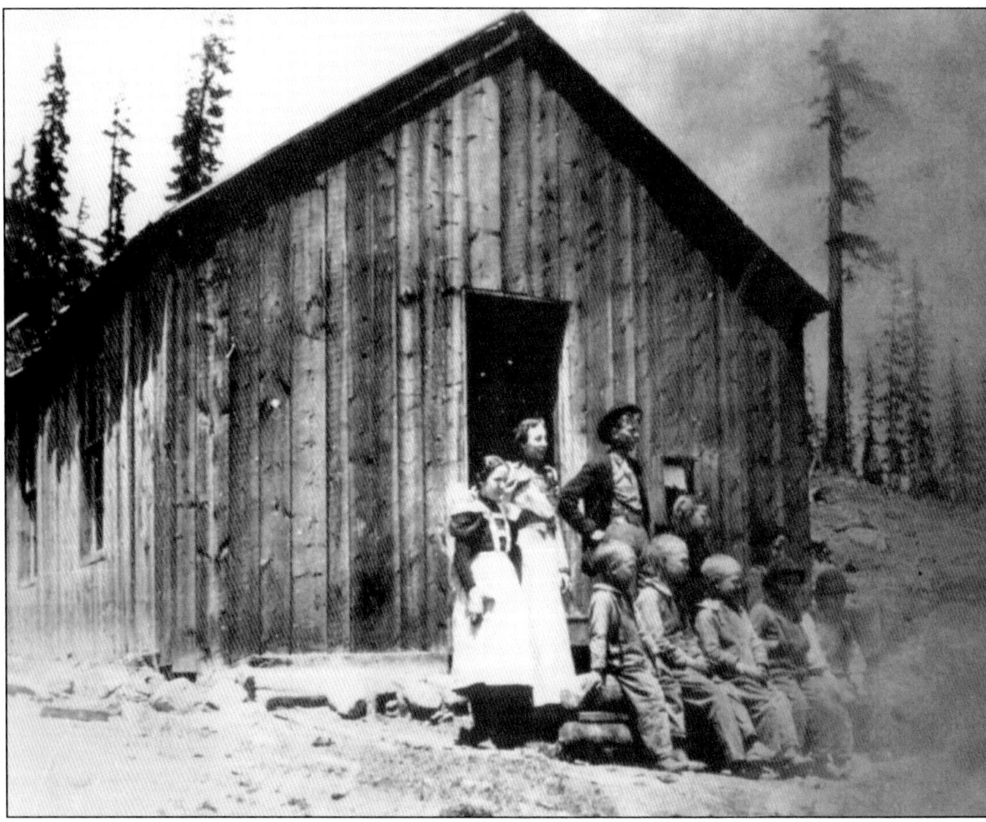

Students of the Leavick school, located on a hill, often used snowshoes to get to class. The mining camp was established in 1873 after the Last Chance and Hilltop mines were discovered. The town is located on County Road 18, or the Four Mile Road, which leads up to Horseshoe Gulch. The camp was named after 19th-century miner Felix Leavick.

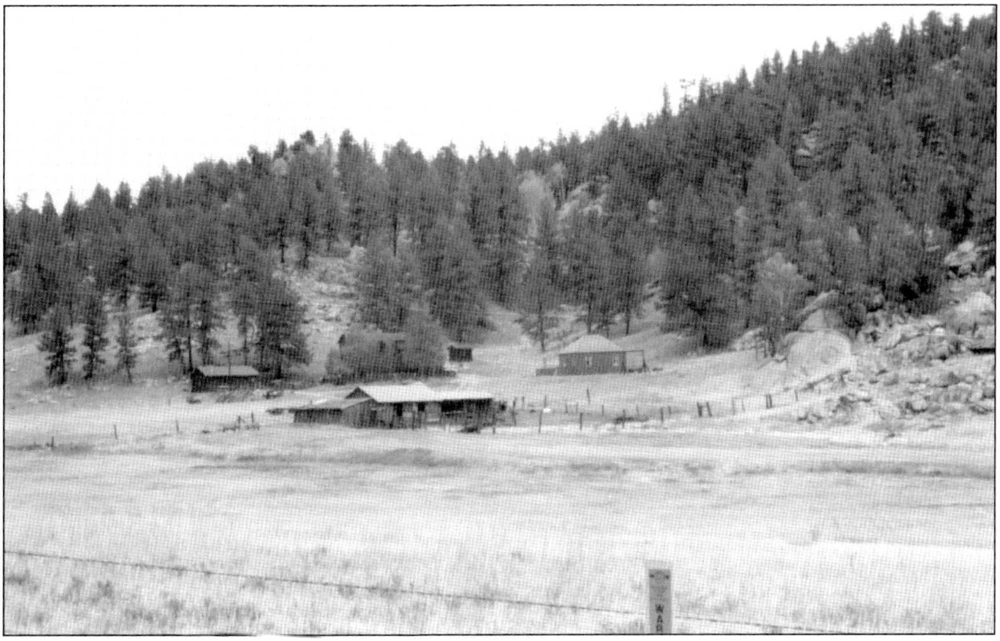

The town of Hayman was platted in 1898 to serve the mining, logging, and ranching community located near the Tarryall River. The school was built the same year. However, with a town population of only 40, business declined by 1911. The building was moved in 1917 along the Tarryall Road and is now on private ranch property.

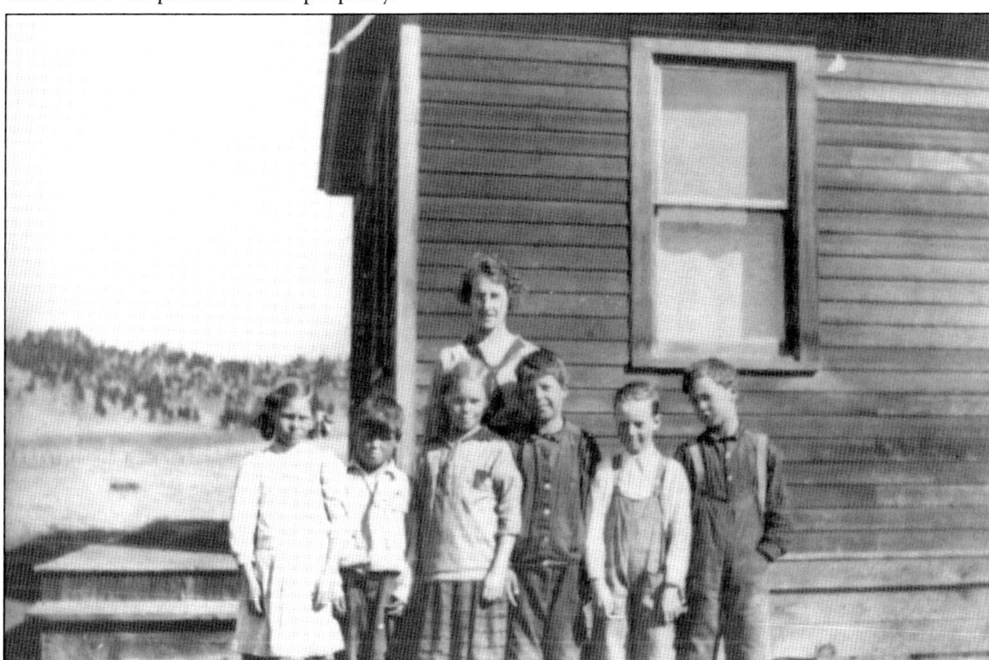

Children of the Warling, Thorn, and Loud families pose at the Hayman school around 1920. The teacher may be Marian Norton. Built by Fred Warling, this schoolhouse was located on the Tarryall Road about a mile east of the old Hayman townsite. The building is preserved on a nearby ranch.

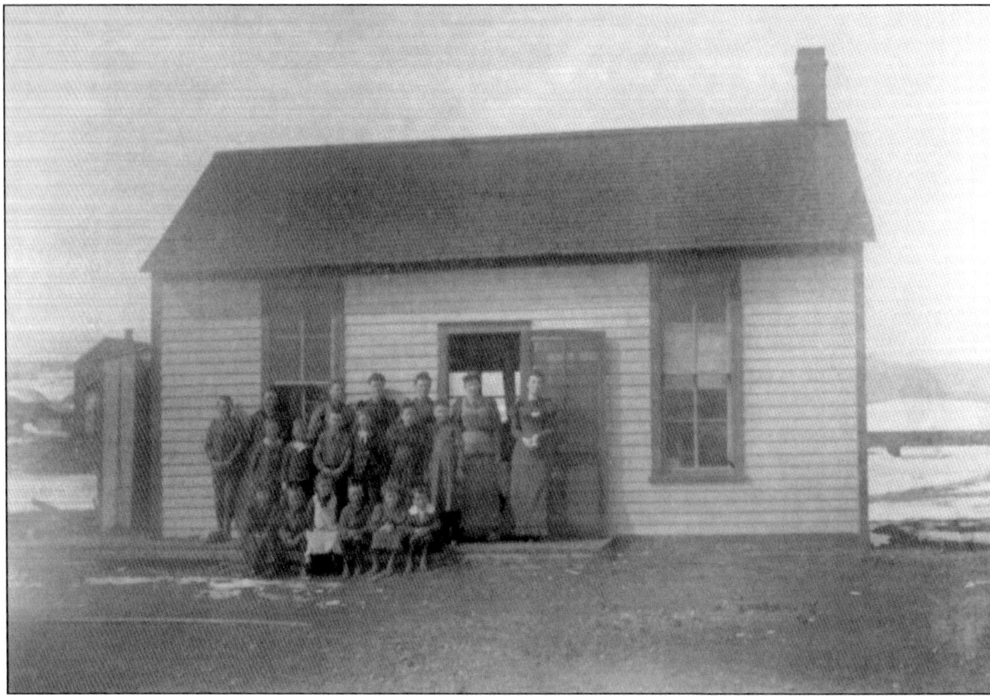

The original Jefferson school was built prior to 1895. The town of Jefferson was founded by Willard Head about the same time the railroad came through the area in 1879. Head ran a hotel out of his house and established a store, livery stable, and freighting business. The school no longer exists.

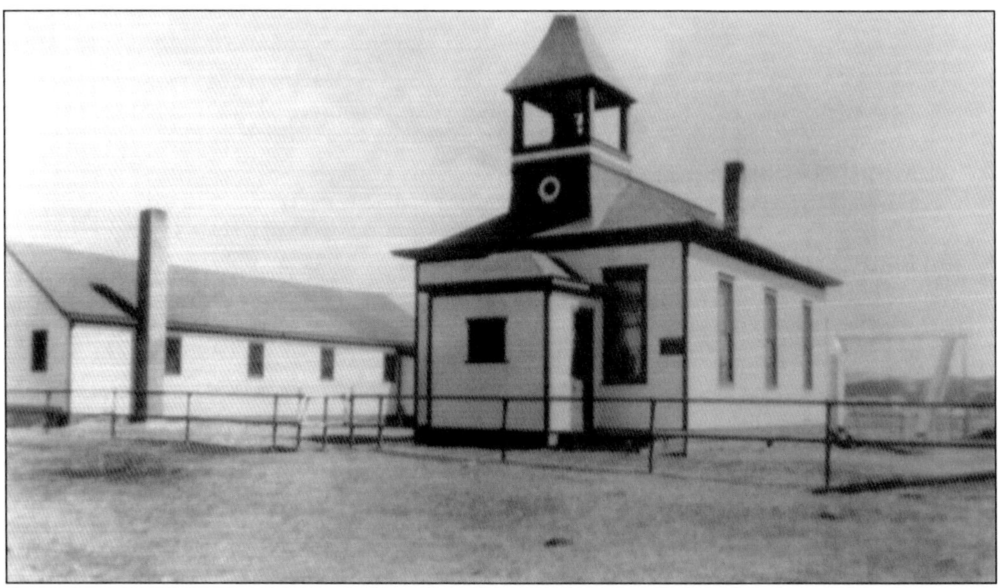

The Jefferson school, built in 1901, featured a bell tower. The building is now used for church services. The building adjacent was constructed in 1936 as a gymnasium. It also hosted other recreational activities. Today, it is used as a community building. A kitchen and indoor bathrooms were added in the 1990s to facilitate hosting a variety of meetings and events.

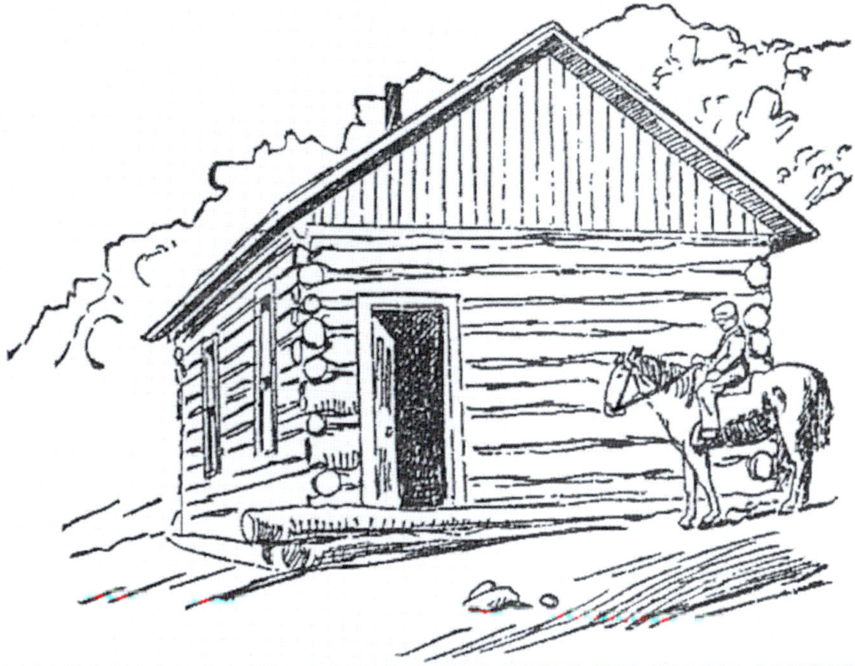

SCHOOL HOUSE ON THE DUNBAR RANCH WHERE THE KILLING OCCURRED.

The Michigan Creek school, located along the Tarryall Road, was sometimes referred to as the Dunbar school, because it was located on Charles Dunbar's ranch. Sadly, it was the scene of a triple homicide in 1895, when rancher Benjamin Ratcliff shot three members of the school board here after one of them spread untrue gossip about his handicapped teenage daughter.

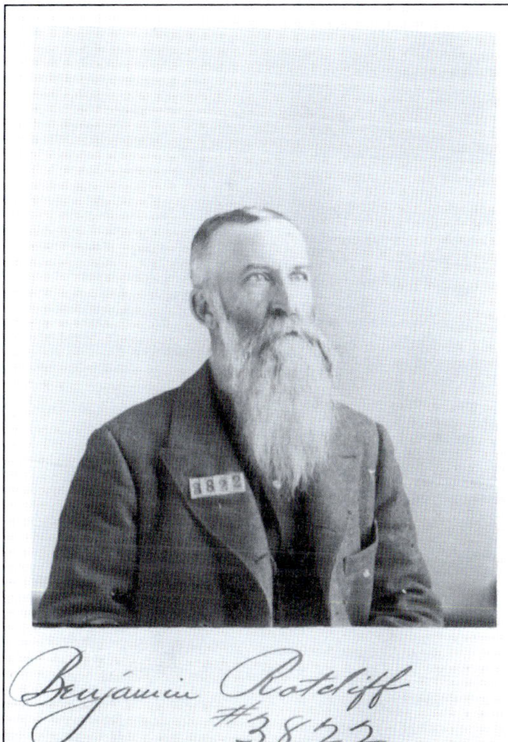

Benjamin Ratcliff's mug shot was probably taken on July 25, 1895, the day he was transported to the Colorado Territorial Prison in Canon City after he was found guilty at jury trial of three counts of first-degree murder. Executed on February 7, 1896, Ratcliff was the only Park County citizen to be legally executed by the state in the 19th century.

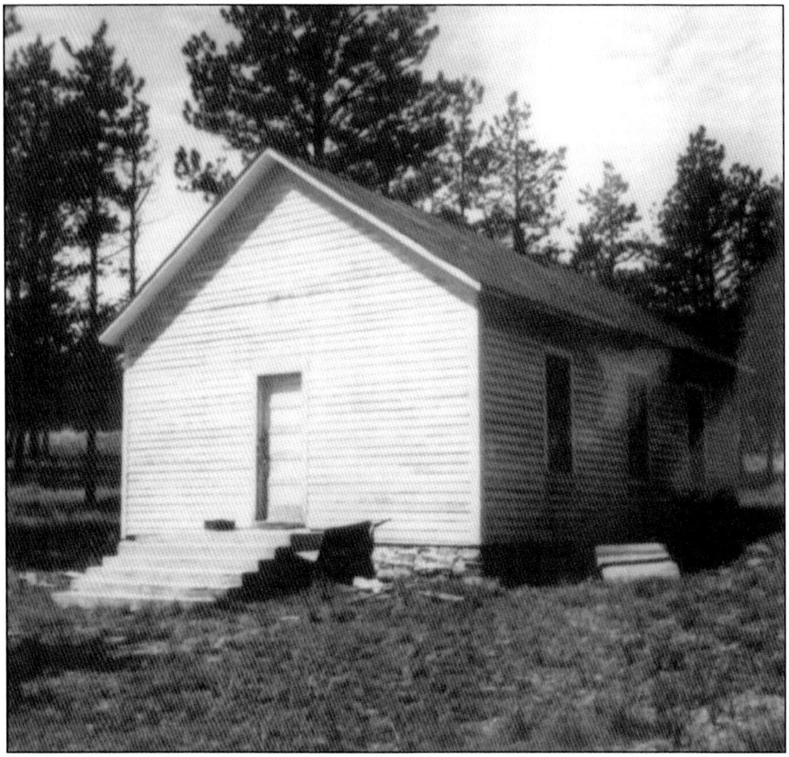

The settlement of Rocky, located near scenic Park County Road 90, west of Lake George, was rich ranchland as well as a brief mining locale. In 1894, up to 30 miners were working in the area, prompting the need for a schoolhouse for the children of local ranchers and miners.

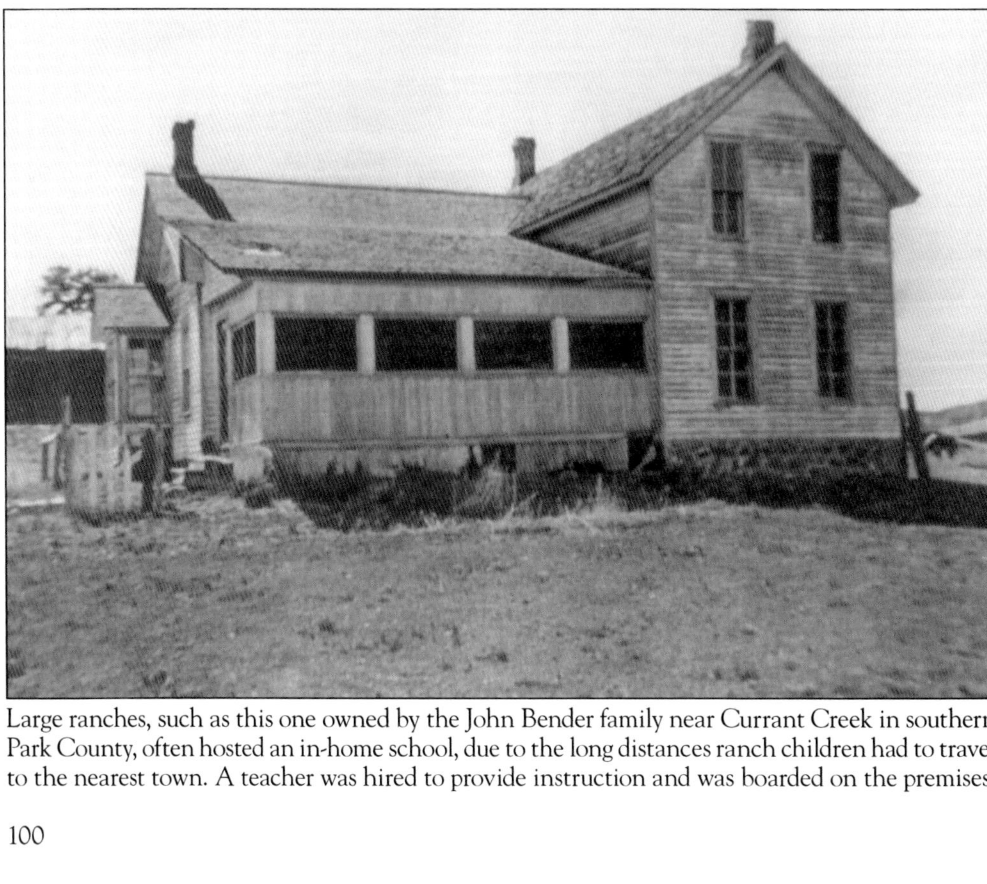

Large ranches, such as this one owned by the John Bender family near Currant Creek in southern Park County, often hosted an in-home school, due to the long distances ranch children had to travel to the nearest town. A teacher was hired to provide instruction and was boarded on the premises.

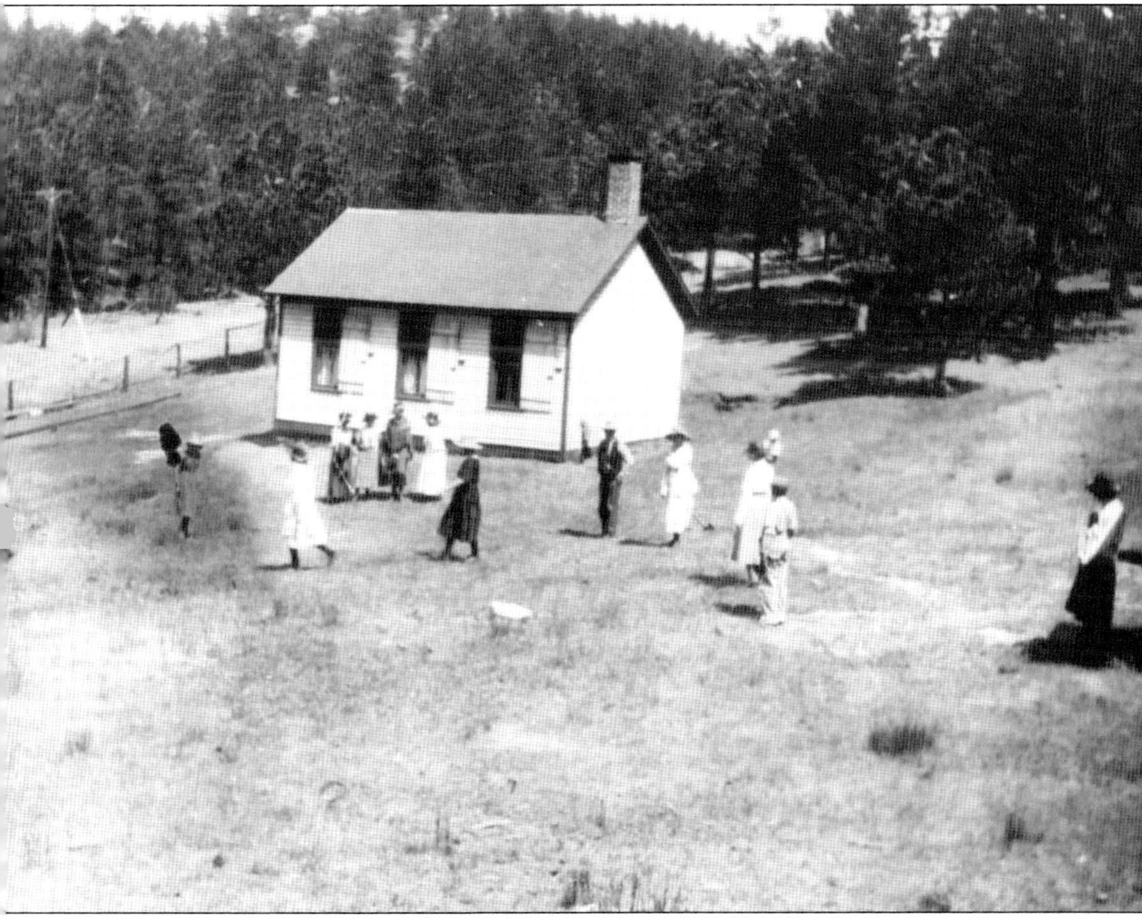

In 1897, the Slaghts school was built one-half mile from Shawnee on Park County Road 64. Because Shawnee became a more prominent community, the name was changed to the Shawnee School in 1899. This school contained grades one through eight. It was used until 1943, when it closed. The school reopened from 1946 to 1948, when it was permanently closed. The building was moved next to the community center in Shawnee in 1953 and was used as a Sunday school. In 1983, the Park County Historical Society moved the school to its present location in McGraw Park in Bailey. The building is a good example of the one-room schoolhouses in this area from the late 1800s until the 1940s. A rectangular building with tall, narrow windows, a front gable, and narrow boards for siding were typical features of these one-room schools.

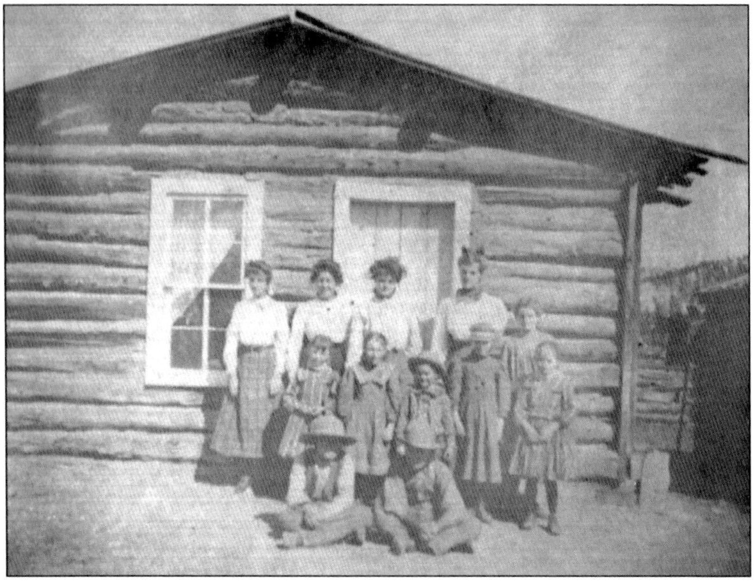

The first Tarryall schoolhouse was built 14 miles northwest of the town of Lake George around 1880. The small log cabin served the needs of the Tarryall valley's children at the time. A mining boom toward the end of the 1890s necessitated a larger building for the influx of families, as the population reached 1,000 in 1897.

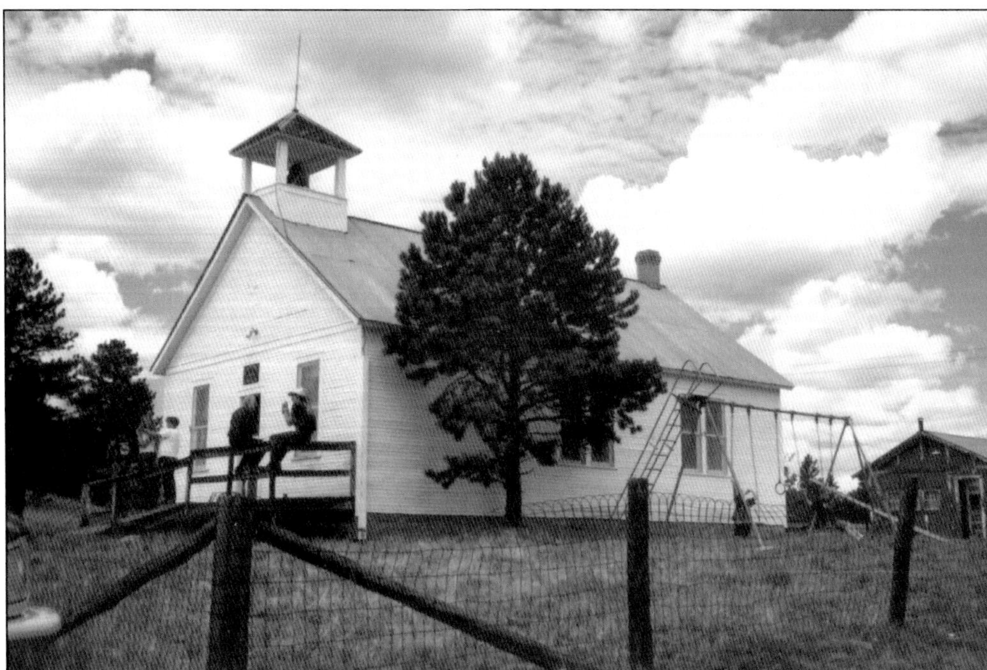

The present schoolhouse was constructed in 1898, one mile north of the original cabin. Built entirely by local residents, the one-room structure utilized lumber from a local sawmill. The interior included all-wood flooring (still intact), a cloakroom, a small kitchen, and one large classroom. The two blackboards were installed from the original cabin.

Seven

WATER

"Whiskey's for drinkin'; water's for fightin' over." That old adage has long applied to arid Park County. Beyond water's necessity in sustaining life, the fightin' arose as demand came to exceed supply. Following Euro-American settlement, water was developed for utilitarian purposes in mining/milling, enhanced domestic uses, agriculture, forest industries, transportation, manufacturing, recreation, and, eventually, complex municipal uses in thirsty downstream cities.

Early mining development gave rise to disputes among water claimants. Park County's earliest attempts at resolving those disputes took place within the context of 1860s laws and courts established by early mining districts.

When state and local government became established in Colorado, water law evolved to become such a complex thicket that, no matter the dispute, the invariable winners were "the blasted lawyers." The first adjudication of irrigation water in Park County took place in 1889, with other uses not adjudicated until 1913.

Colorado water law springs from the "prior appropriation" doctrine. To wit, a downstream 1875 appropriator on the plains could shut down an 1880 Park County appropriator, even if the stream in question might flow directly through the latter's ranch. This proved a bitter pill for some. The 1889–1890 State Engineer's Report references South Park irrigators thus: "The Superintendent . . . found that in the excited condition of the people it would require the State Militia to enforce his orders." Water-law administration eventually calmed; but it is not unknown even now to find a junior-right ditch flowing in the dark of night.

Denver water interests began eyeing Park County water sources well before 1900. Through a combination of money (to which water often flows uphill) and superior legal firepower, most of Park County's irrigation water eventually was gobbled up by downstream municipalities.

Even within the last 20 years, downstream water interests have tried to undermine the seniority of water rights in Platte Canyon and to obtain rights to suck great amounts of groundwater from beneath South Park. Such efforts have so far been repulsed by way of determined, expensive legal battles. Park County's remaining water is very much worth "fightin' over."

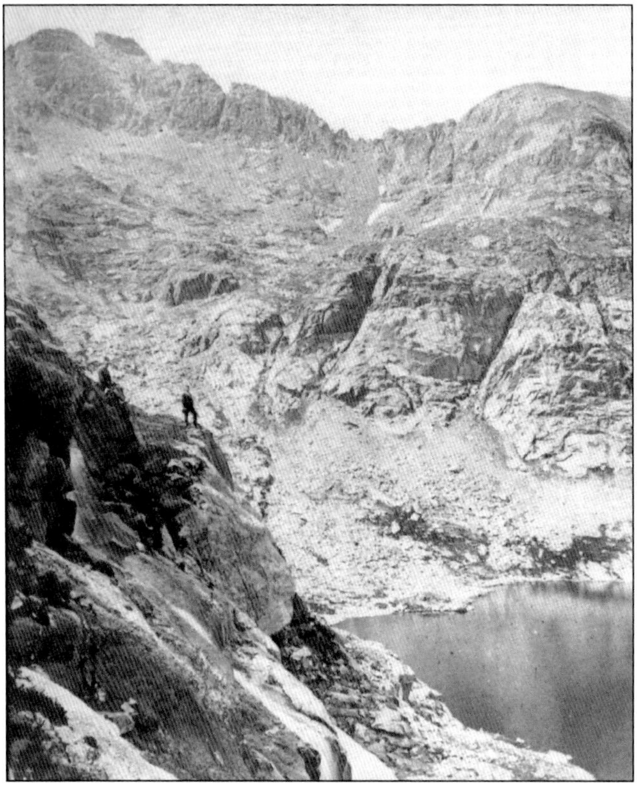

This c. 1880 photograph shows part of Wheeler Lake, with the 13,000-foot-plus Continental Divide in the background. This harsh landscape is the birthplace of the Middle Fork of the South Platte River. The melting snows from here have served thirsty animals and people, mining, agriculture, and industry in Park County for millennia.

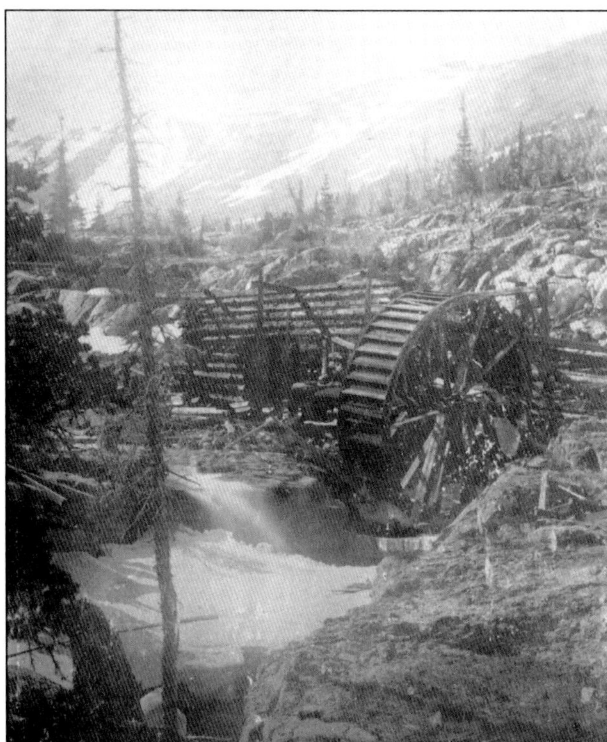

Abandoned and slightly askew around 1882, this Montgomery Gulch waterwheel was an ore-mill power source probably in the early 1860s. The Montgomery falls provided enough elevation drop to allow use of waterpower in the days before steam replaced these machines and their dependence on nonfreezing streams and sufficient water quantity.

Water-powered arrastras were common, as shown here in Montgomery in the early 1870s. Along with his gold pan and sluice box (right), this miner has three ore-processing methods near at hand. Use of water abounds, as shown by the water spurting from pressure boxes above. The flume at left carries water to some other processing site.

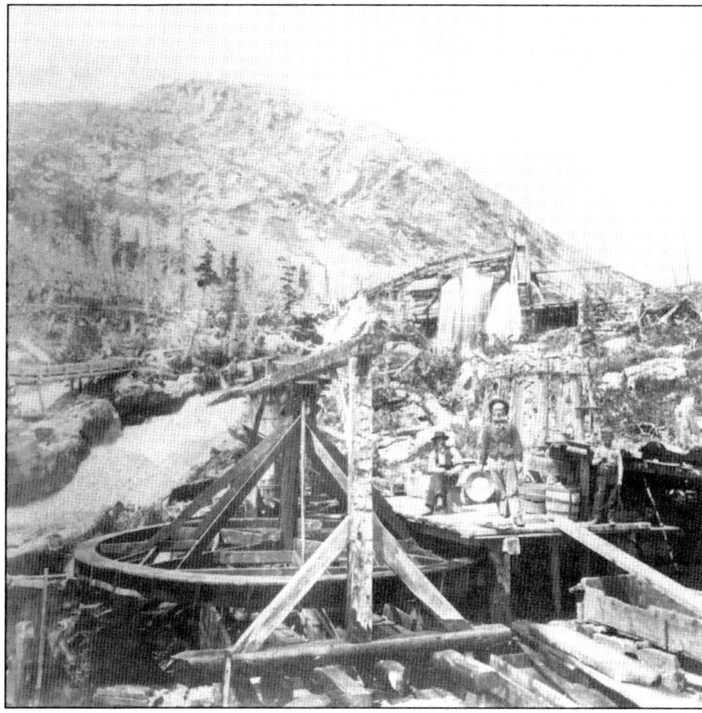

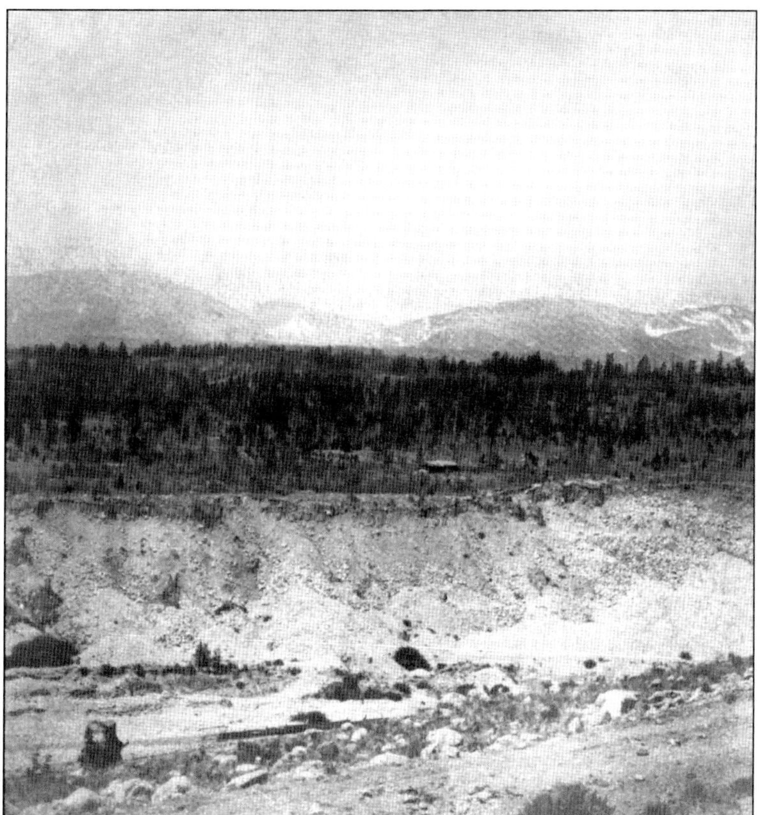

Shown here in the early 1870s is the aftermath of extensive, water-intensive placer mining along the South Platte River at Fairplay. Much of this backbreaking labor was performed by Chinese miners. Often disrespected and mistreated, the Chinese nonetheless contributed much to the local economy, whether mining, running laundries, or manually hauling cans of domestic-use water to town from the river.

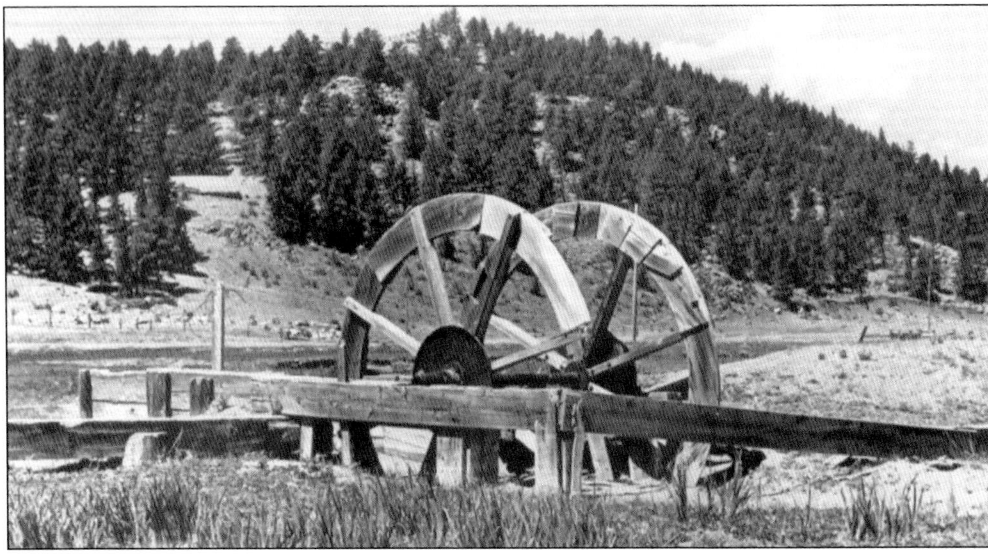

This undated photograph shows a deteriorated waterwheel at Hartsel, part of the system Sam Hartsel used to conduct water some two miles from his hot spring to his ranch. Hartsel, an early Colorado cattleman, successfully increased his original homestead size and cattle herds to prominence.

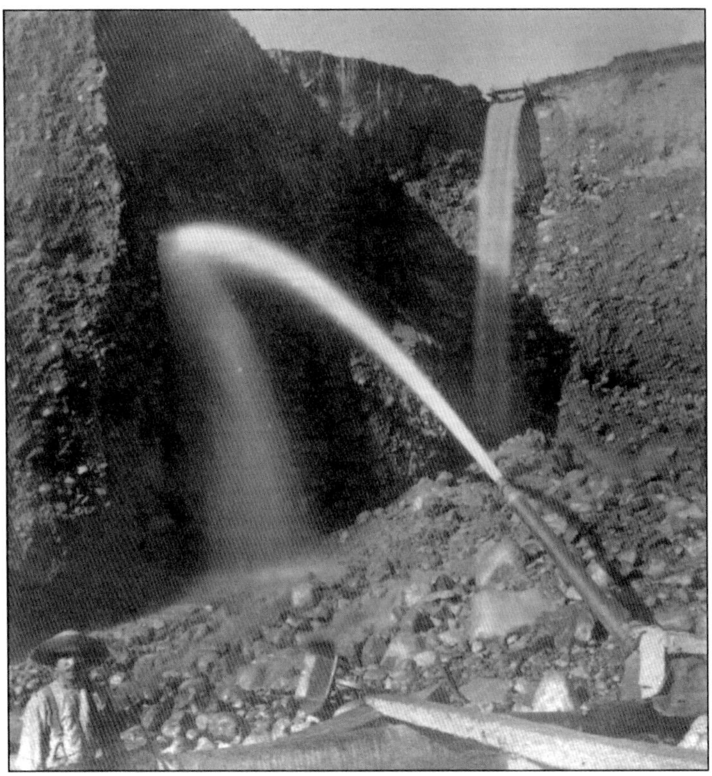

A giant nozzle, usually called simply a "giant," is seen carving away a bank of alluvial soil and rock in this 1880s scene near Alma. Ditches often had to be miles long in order to supply enough pressure to operate the giants. Cheaper than mechanical excavation, hydraulic mining was no respecter of the environment. Greatly dependent upon the water season, placering slowed or halted as runoff declined.

This 1885 photograph shows two large slurry tanks in the recently completed Sovereign Mill at Montgomery. Sufficient water was crucial to ore processing proper and to the steam engines that ran the mills, even after they no longer depended upon waterwheels to directly run machinery.

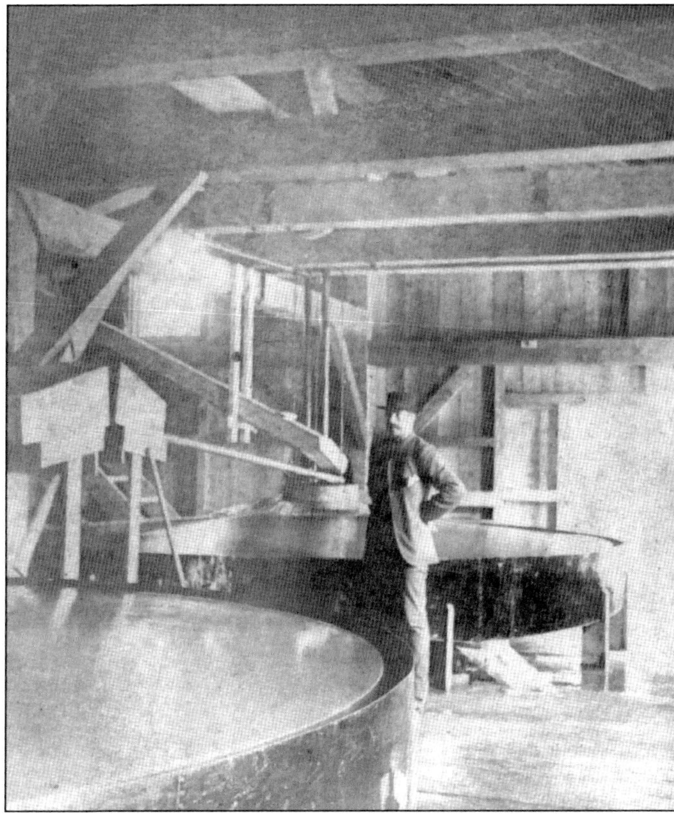

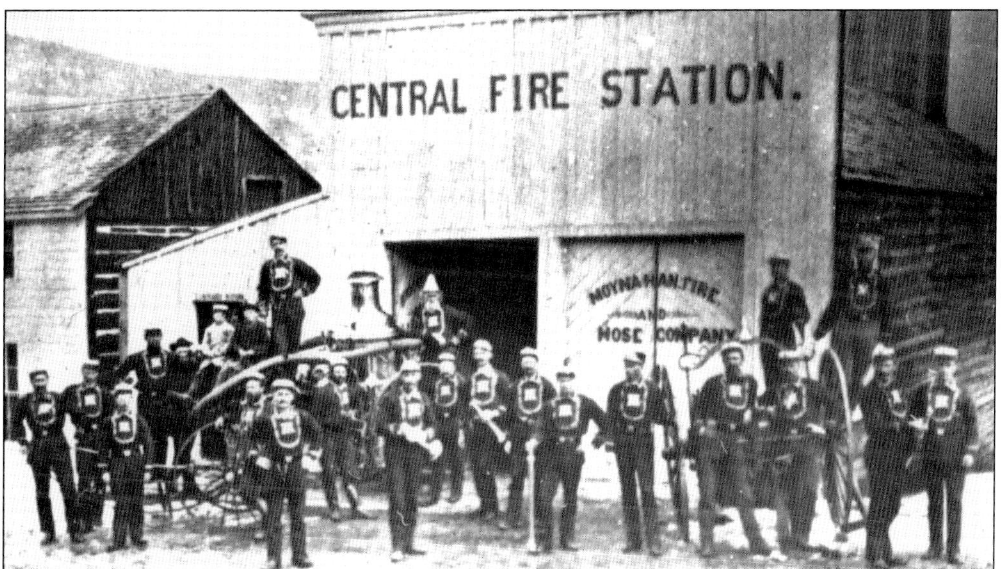

Dress uniforms adorn members of Alma's Moynihan Fire & Hose Company, shown here between 1882 and 1900 with their hose cart and 1882 steam fire pumper. The team would race to lay hose from a water source to fires, hoping to deliver sufficient water to the scene. Alma suffered several damaging fires for lack of a central water system. The steam pumper and Alma's first (1935 model) fire truck survive, the latter still operational.

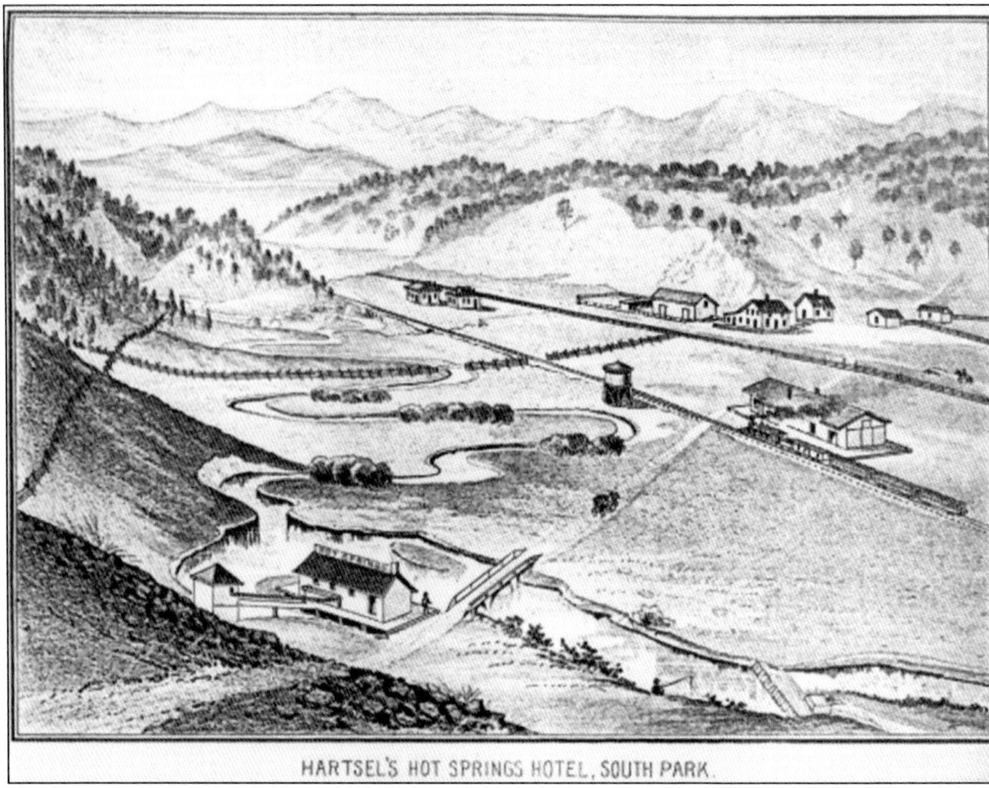

This 1888 drawing shows the Hartsel hot spring, along with its associated hotel and the Colorado Midland Railroad, which transported many of its health-seekers. Used for untold years by Native Americans, the spring was developed commercially by Samuel Hartsel, prominent rancher and entrepreneur. This was easily the most enduring among the five known attempts to develop hot and/or mineral springs in Park County.

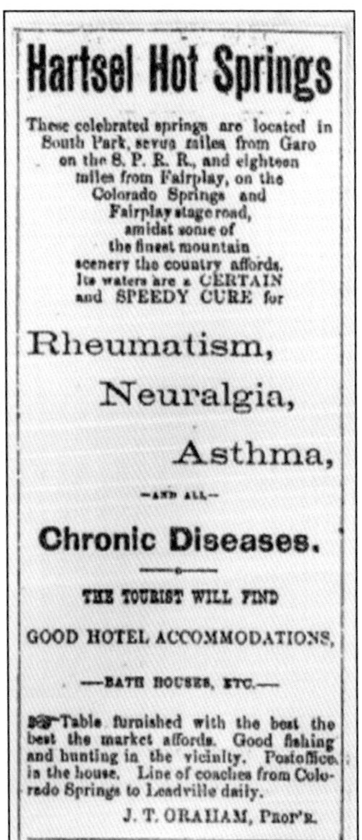

Early hot/mineral spring operators were not shy about claiming that their precious fluids could do wonders for those afflicted with ailments. This 1880 advertisement from the *Fairplay Flume* offers great hope to the suffering and less hope to advocates of truth in advertising. All those ailments, and various "magic water" hucksters, still survive. The past is indeed prologue.

This c. 1888 drawing of Fairplay's Summer Brewery, which later burned down and was rebuilt, and its ice pond to the rear depicts a very water-dependent industry. Leonhard Summer urged comparison of his South Park Lager Beer to all others on the market. In addition to beer, ice was later used to cool meat in Summer's postbrewery meat market (latter 1890s) in the brewery building.

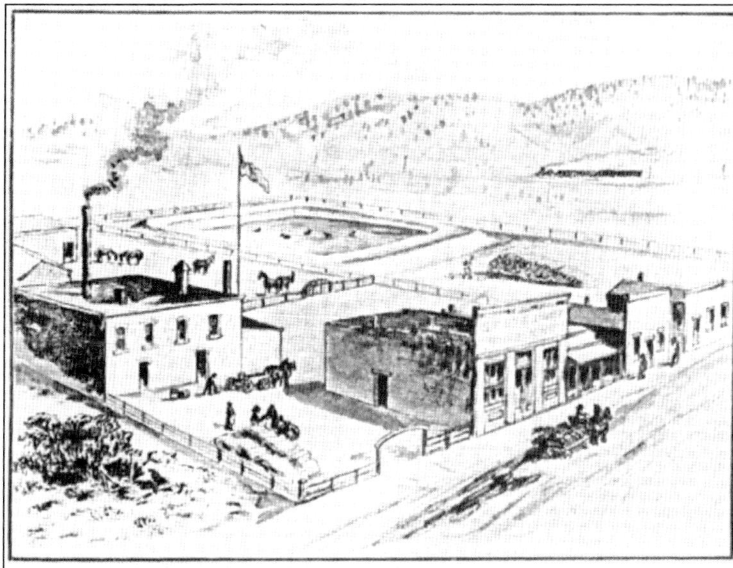

PROPERTY OF LEONARD SUMMER, FAIRPLAY.

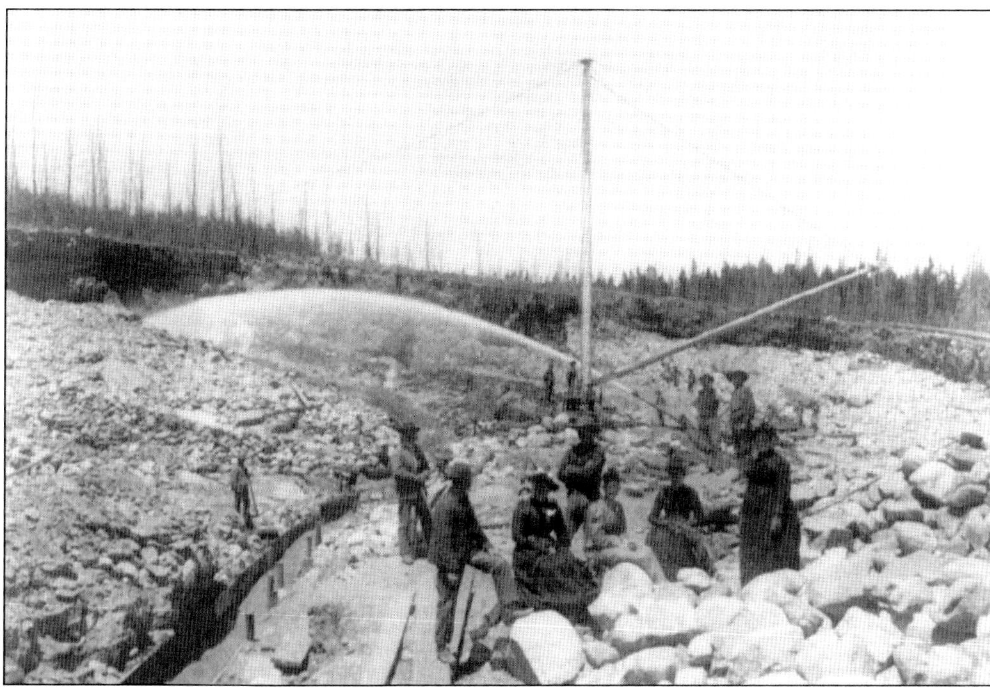

The Beaver Creek Placer, north of Fairplay, is shown on August 20, 1893, with a giant nozzle hard at work. Given the unusual presence of ladies, the miners may well have had to sanitize their language somewhat for the occasion. The ditch feeding the giant ran some six miles, all the way from Columbia Reservoir, north of Alma. The rotating derrick was used to move large rocks.

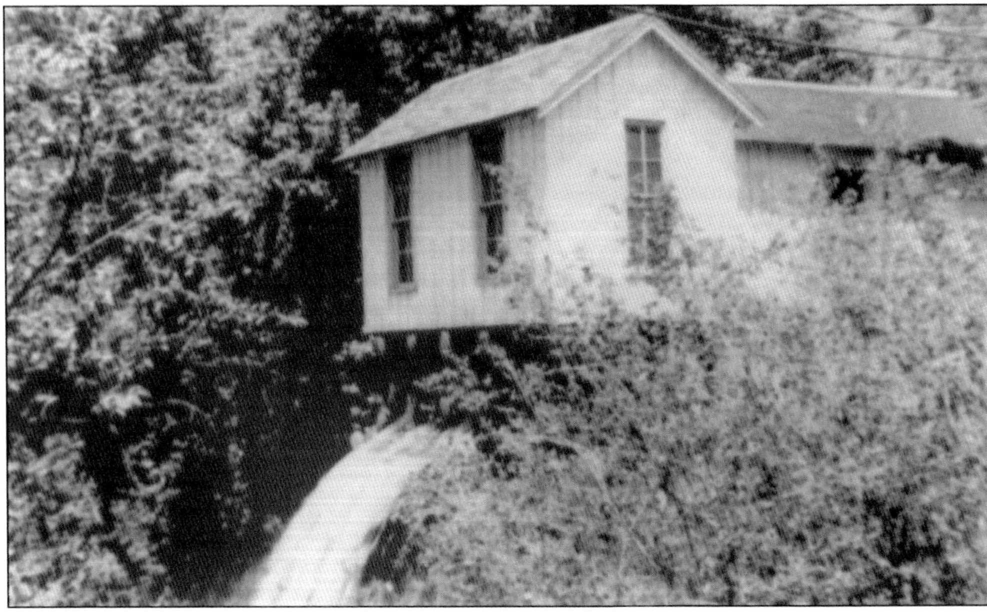

Tail water gushes from the hydroelectric plant at Cassells, a prominent resort, now Camp Santa Maria, near Shawnee. Installed in 1910, it reportedly served into the 1940s. This represented a bridge between early waterpower applied directly to machines and its newer and continuing generation of electricity. A small, little-noticed hydro plant west of Grant currently produces power from the Western Slope water flow at Denver's Roberts Tunnel.

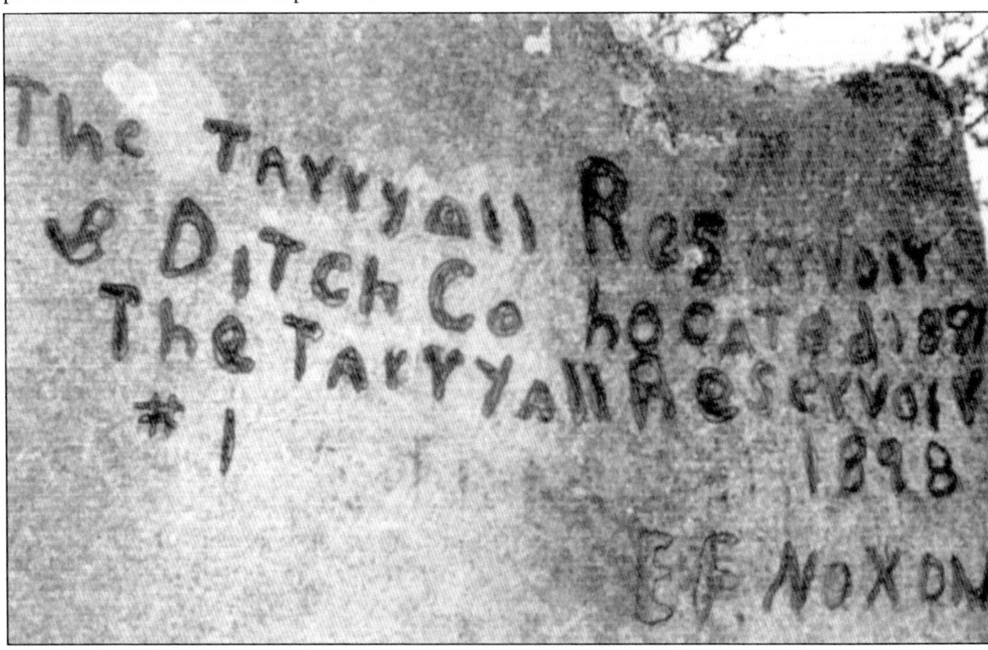

Originally called the Tarryall Water and Company, the Tarryall Reservoir had its beginnings in 1898 with financial backing from Eastern capitalists. By 1903, fifty local ranch owners sold their water rights to Colorado Springs for use in both irrigation water and power along the Front Range. Each rancher received approximately $25,000; they were given two years to vacate their land. This gave the company a 40-mile exclusive water rights region.

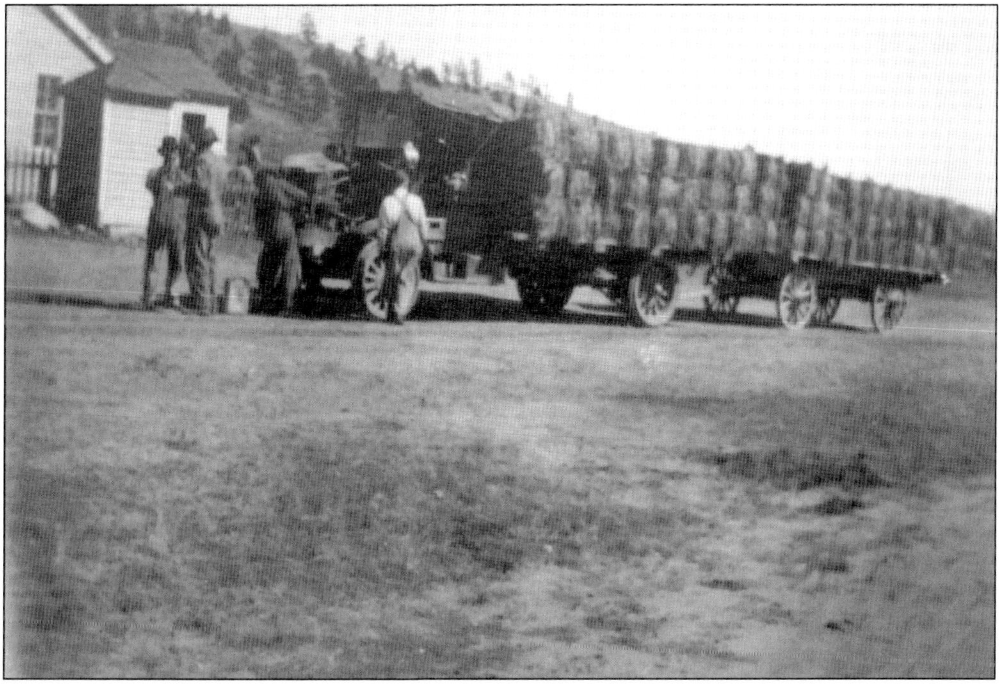

In this 1915 scene at the James (Badger Springs) Ranch, an overburdened motor truck may be asking for a drink of water or some other form of attention before resuming its labors. This ranch is an example of many located near valuable springs, which furnished livestock and domestic water. At one point, Tom James sold 100 tons of his irrigated hay in a single transaction.

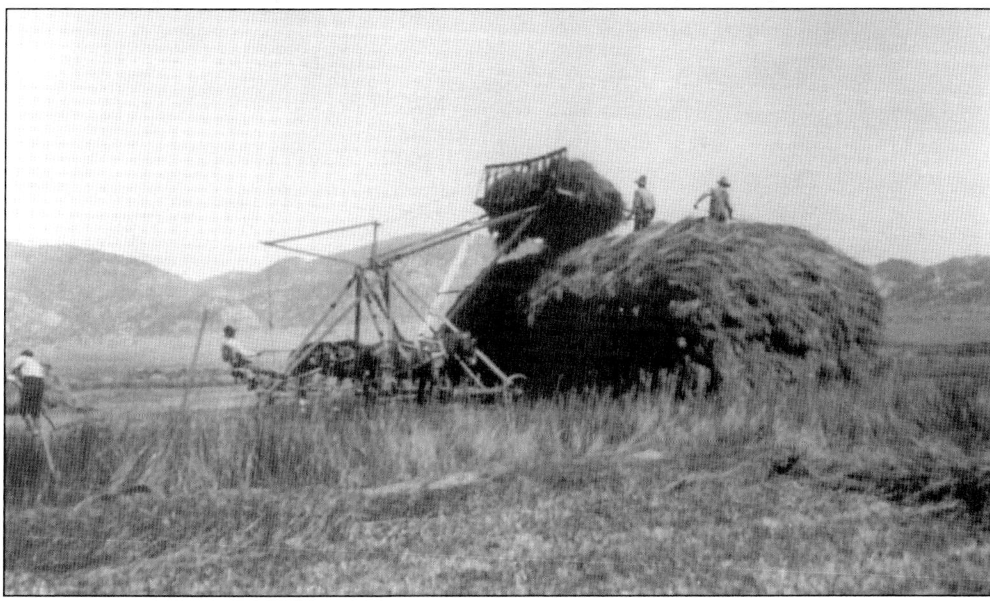

The Epperson family recorded the horse-team harvest and stacking of irrigated native hay. Ironically, their lush meadows now lie drowned beneath Denver's Eleven Mile Reservoir. Much of the water that once produced the celebrated South Park hay (over 200 tons annually on some ranches) now sprinkles thirsty urban lawns. Production of irrigated hay in Park County is currently at a small fraction of its former levels.

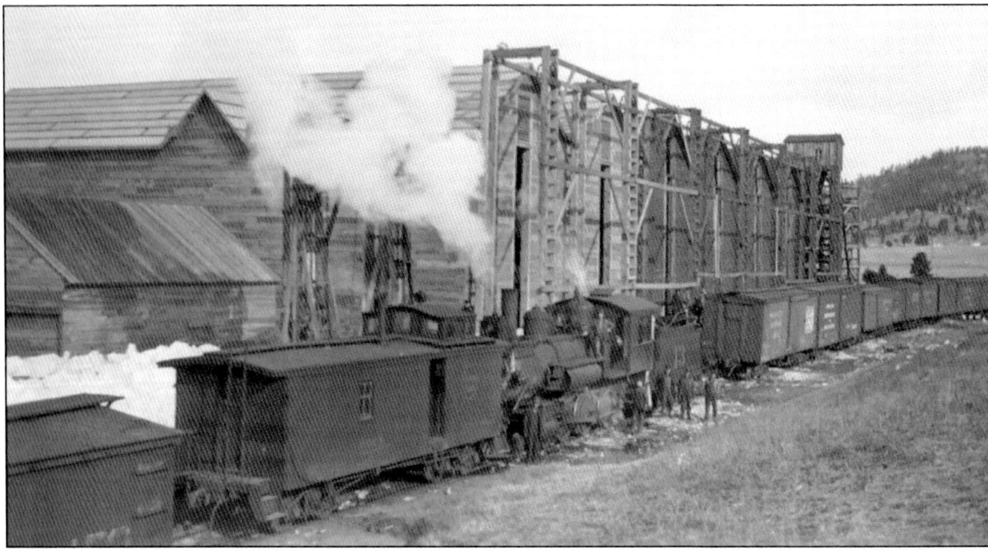

A Colorado Midland train is in position to load ice at the large icehouses of the Lake George Ice Company, whose ice was celebrated for its purity. Sold extensively for household use in Colorado Springs, it was shipped to railroad icehouses as far away as La Junta. The bumper ice crop of 1909 yielded over 100,000 tons. This photograph was taken around 1910.

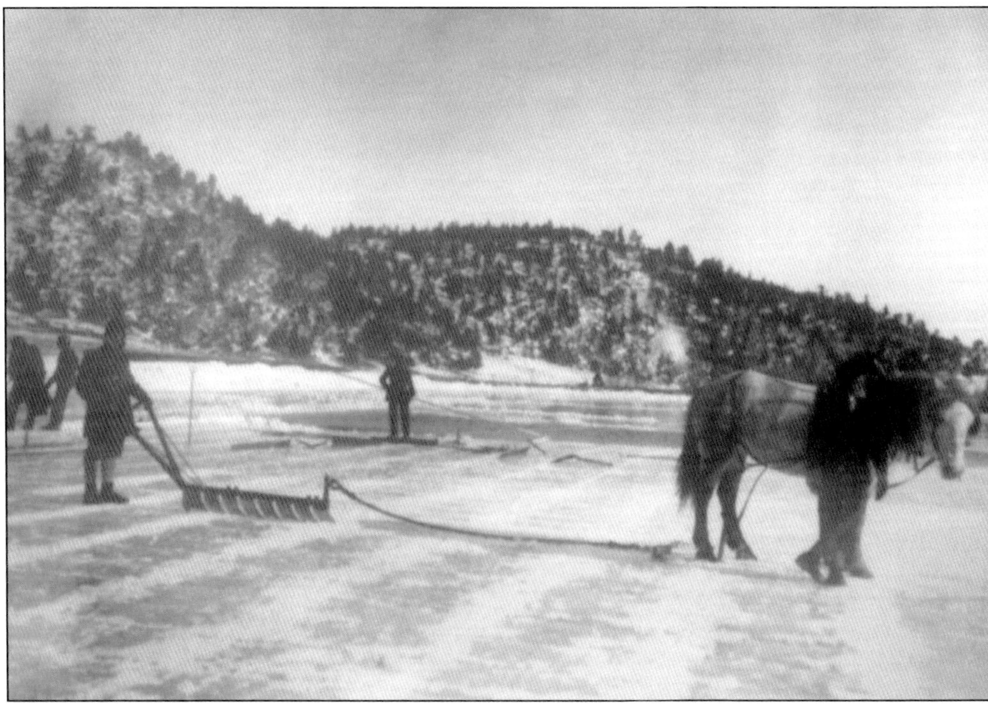

A horse-drawn ice-cutter is shown in the early 1900s at the Maddox Ice Company's pond, just east of Shawnee. For some years, this operation supplied Maddox's extensive sales of household and commercial-use ice in Denver. This cutter was used to score the ice, which was then cut into blocks of some 1,800 pounds, to be moved via conveyor into the icehouse and/or onto railroad cars.

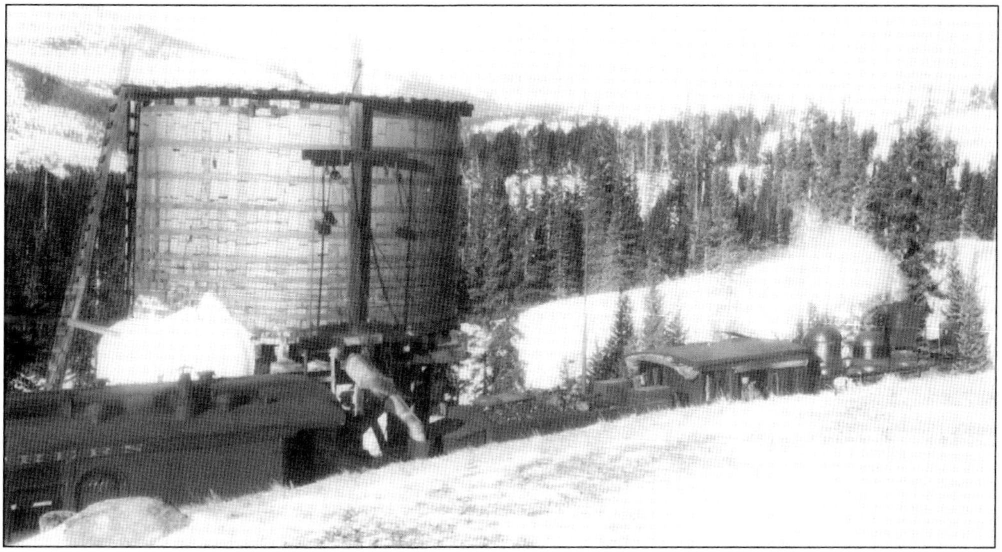

This undated photograph shows a train taking on water at Halfway tank on Boreas Pass. Water was the lifeblood of steam locomotives. These large tanks were located about every eight to ten miles. Care was taken regarding the water quality, to avoid clogging boilers. At one time, at least 15 such tanks were strategically located along Park County's two railroads. (Courtesy of DSP&PHS.)

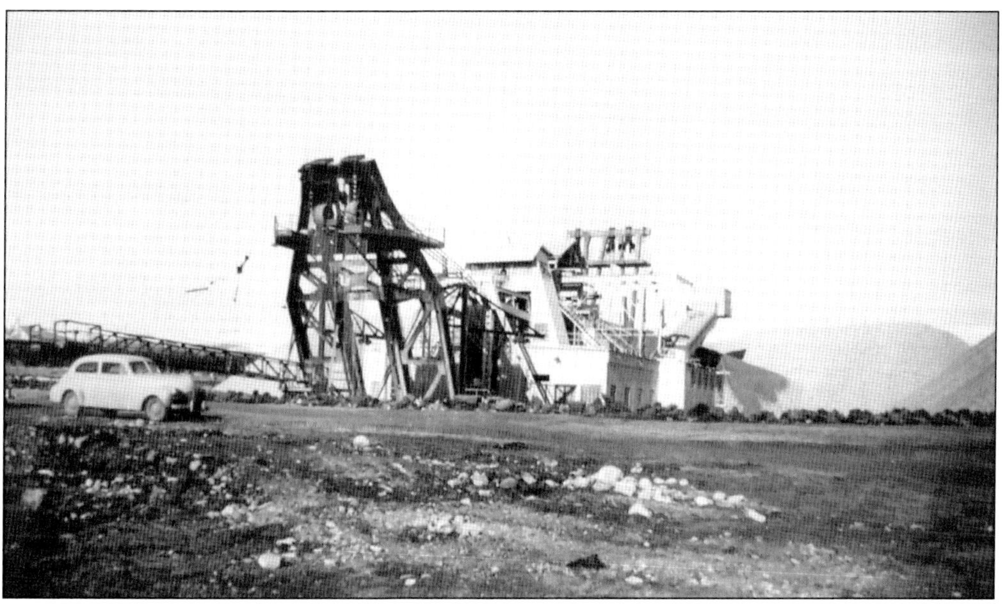

One of the largest in the world, this massive, electric-powered, floating gold dredge near Fairplay was completed in 1941. The 275-foot-by-300-foot dredge pond measured 15 feet deep and was fed by a tributary of the South Platte River. The buckets dug 70 feet below water level to scoop up the rich dirt. It operated until economics forced its shutdown in 1952. After sitting forlornly in its pond for decades, the dredge was dismantled and shipped to South America in the 1980s.

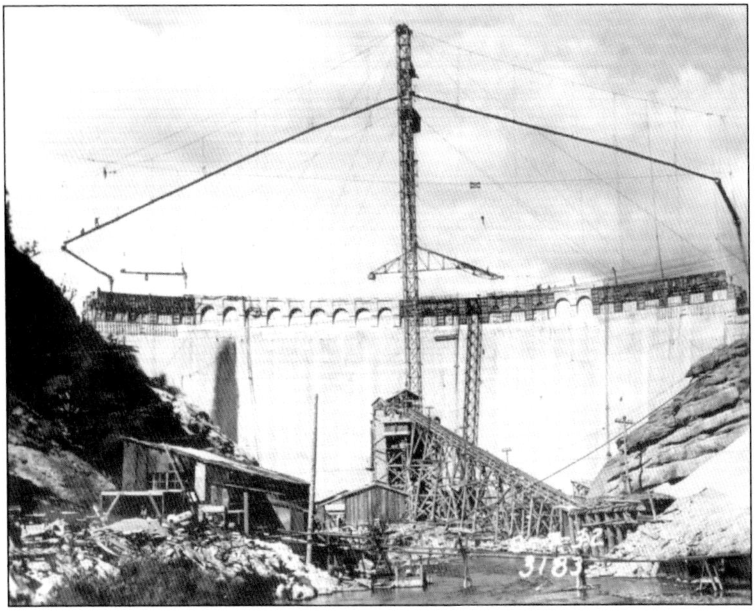

This photograph, taken on August 7, 1932, shows Eleven Mile Dam nearing completion. A web of guy wires secures what may have been a concrete-pumping apparatus. Apart from storing Denver water, Eleven Mile Reservoir is now a state park and favorite fishing spot. (Courtesy of Denver Water.)

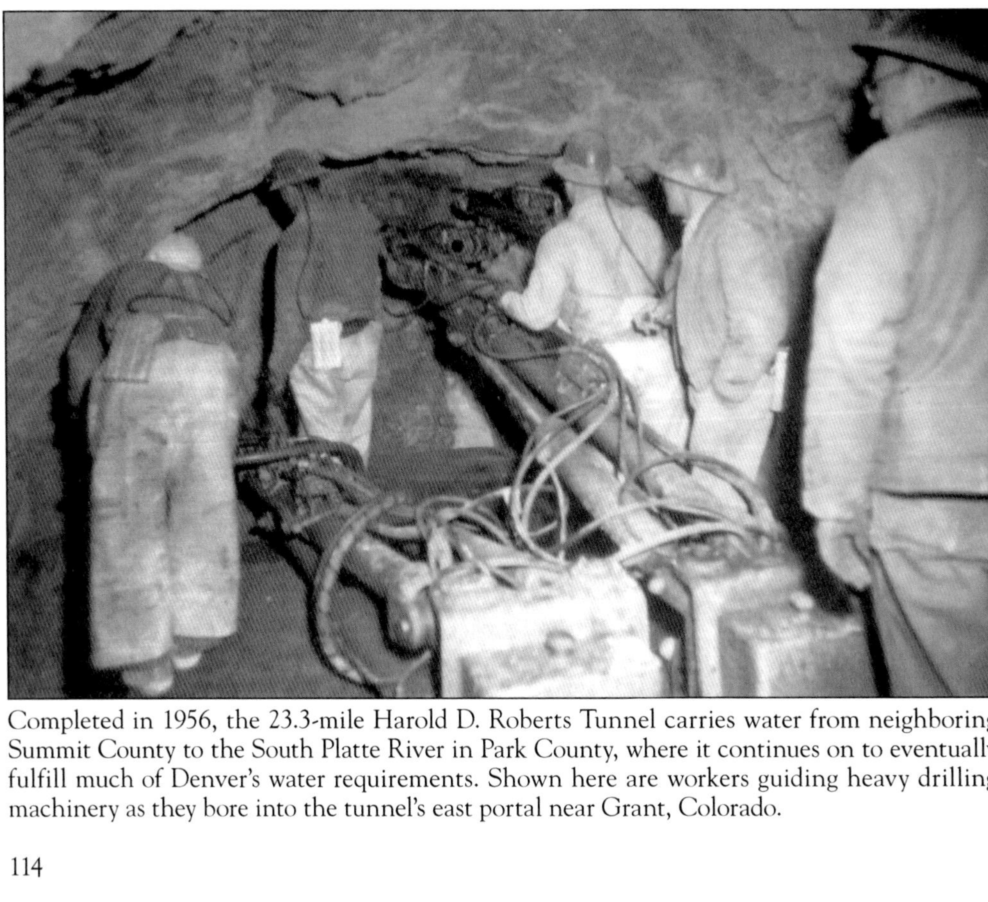

Completed in 1956, the 23.3-mile Harold D. Roberts Tunnel carries water from neighboring Summit County to the South Platte River in Park County, where it continues on to eventually fulfill much of Denver's water requirements. Shown here are workers guiding heavy drilling machinery as they bore into the tunnel's east portal near Grant, Colorado.

Eight

Recreation and Tourism

For early settlers, Park County's rugged mountains and high alpine plains offered both rich bounty and considerable hardship. The people who braved harsh conditions to make their living in the mines, ranches, and towns worked hard and played hard, embracing the opportunity to relieve the stress of daily life through recreation. Hunters and anglers sought the abundant game found throughout the county, while adventurous hikers chased the thrill of climbing majestic 14,000-foot peaks. Residents joined together in sport, cheering on their town baseball team or participating in community races and rodeos. Throughout the years, music concerts, dances, and theater performances played important roles in the social life of the community while providing outlets for creative aspirations.

After the railroad connected Park County with Colorado's Front Range in the late 1870s, visitors increasingly took advantage of the myriad outdoor recreational opportunities the county offered. Along the rail lines in Platte Canyon and South Park, spacious resort lodges catered to summer tourists seeking a taste of the rustic mountain lifestyle or simply a relaxing break from urban life. Visitors drawn by the natural beauty enjoyed fishing, golf, tennis, boating, picnicking, riding, and hiking. Similarly, summer camps operated by church groups, charities, and organizations such as the Boy Scouts provided children from all over Colorado a chance to experience the mountain wilderness.

After 1920, the automobile replaced the railroad as the preferred means of tourist travel. Visitors could now more easily access and enjoy recreational opportunities in the national forests and state wildlife areas, which constitute nearly 60 percent of the county. In the 1930s and 1940s, a number of local ranchers capitalized on increasing tourism by opening their ranches to visitors. These popular dude ranches promised an authentic Western ranch experience in addition to more refined amenities and activities.

With its local heritage very much intact, Park County remains a rugged and rustic place that offers both immense challenge and extraordinary beauty, where hard-working locals still play intensely and offer a friendly welcome to anyone looking for a taste of life in Colorado's high country.

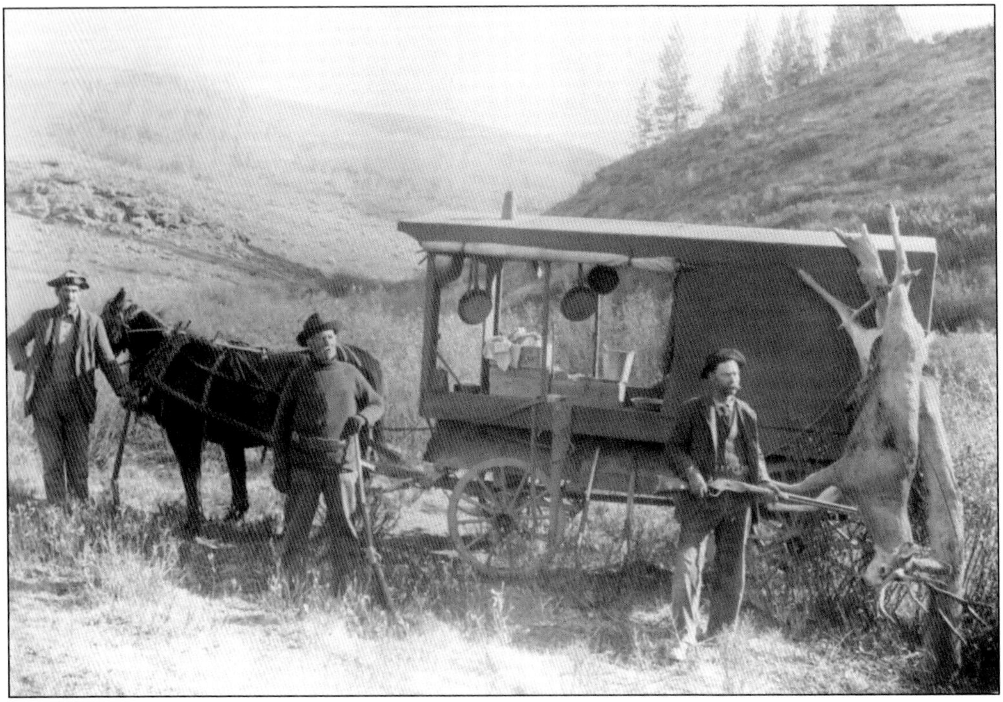

From left to right, Sam Carmichel, Sen. James Moynahan, and Jim Hamilton hunt in the mountain valleys near Alma around 1880. Moynahan operated one of the county's largest mercantile stores and was involved in a variety of successful mining ventures, most notably the Orphan Boy Mine. Arguably Park County's most prominent and politically active citizen, Moynahan was elected to the Colorado Senate in 1876 and held several local offices throughout his life.

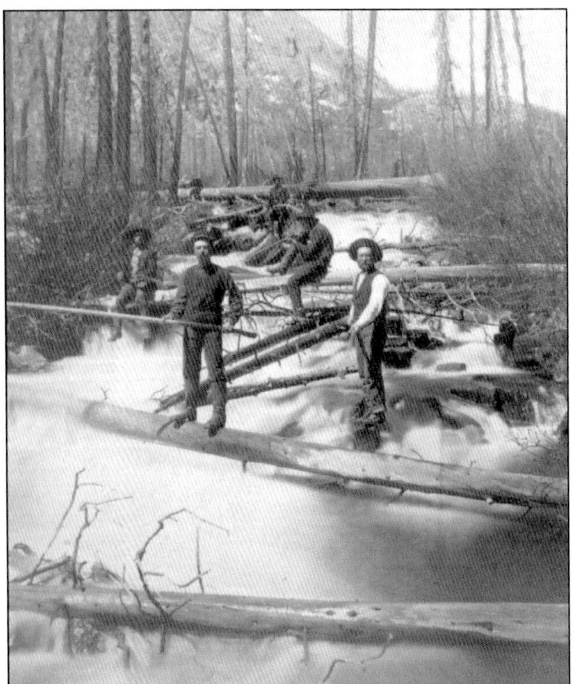

Early residents—presumably miners working the nearby gold and silver mines—fish for trout on Mosquito Creek near Alma in the 1880s. Home to a wide variety of trout species, including rainbow, brown, native cutthroat, and brook trout, Park County's mountain streams have drawn recreational fishermen to their banks since the mid-1800s.

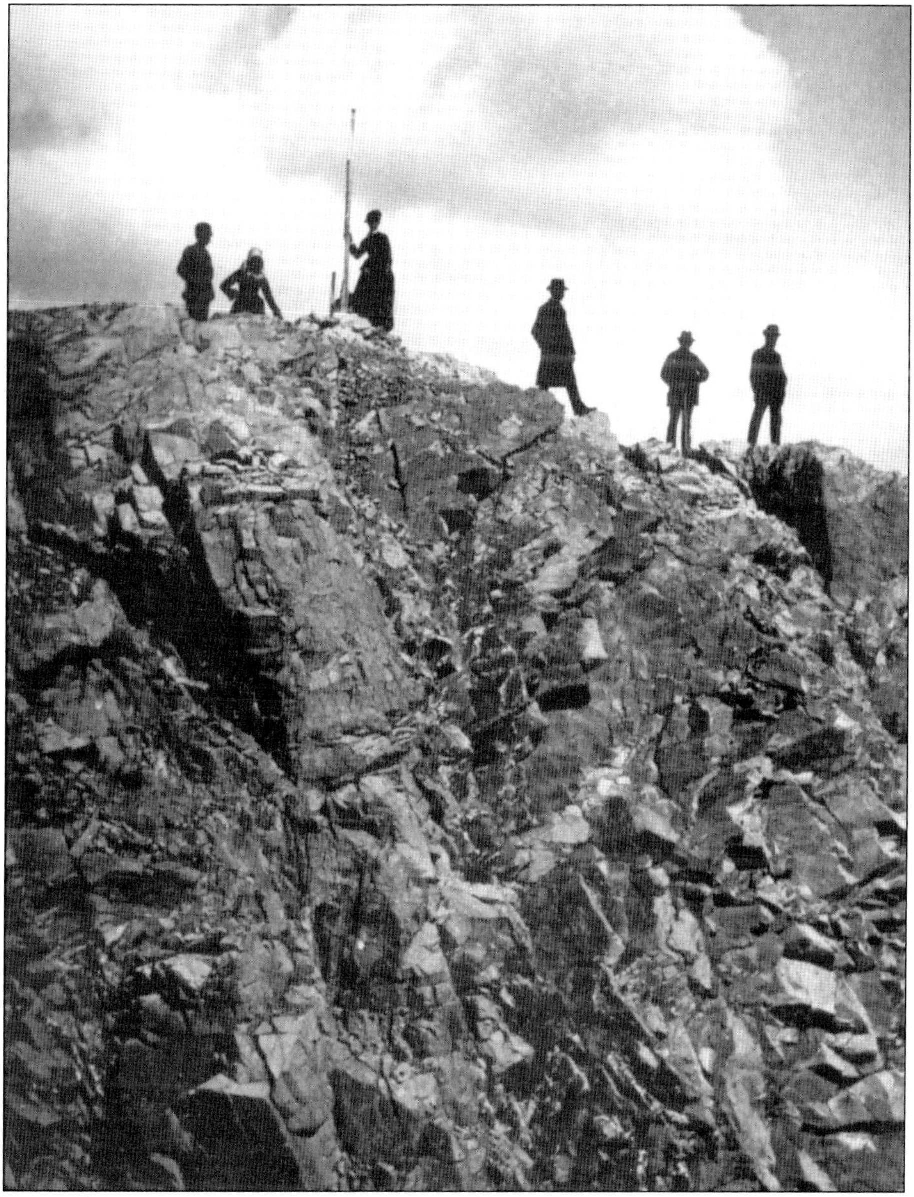

Sophia Hoffman stands at the flagpole on the summit of 14,286-foot Mount Lincoln near the Continental Divide around 1900. One of four fourteeners in Park County, the Mount Lincoln summit has been a popular destination for tourists since the 1860s, when it became fashionable for adventurous Easterners to visit Colorado's raucous mining camps and remote scenic areas. One of the most publicized climbing adventures on Mount Lincoln occurred in 1868, when the Colfax Party summited the lofty peak. The party included vice-presidential candidate Schuyler Colfax; William Bross, editor of the *Chicago Tribune*; and Samuel Bowles, editor of a Springfield, Massachusetts, newspaper. The trip was heavily covered by the press and did much to promote tourism in Park County. Local residents enjoyed climbing as well. Sophia Hoffman's family settled in the nearby mining camp of Dudley in the late 1870s and held interest in several local mines within the Montgomery Mining District. Today, hikers pass the ruins of early mines on their way to the summit, which provides stunning views of Park County's Mosquito Range.

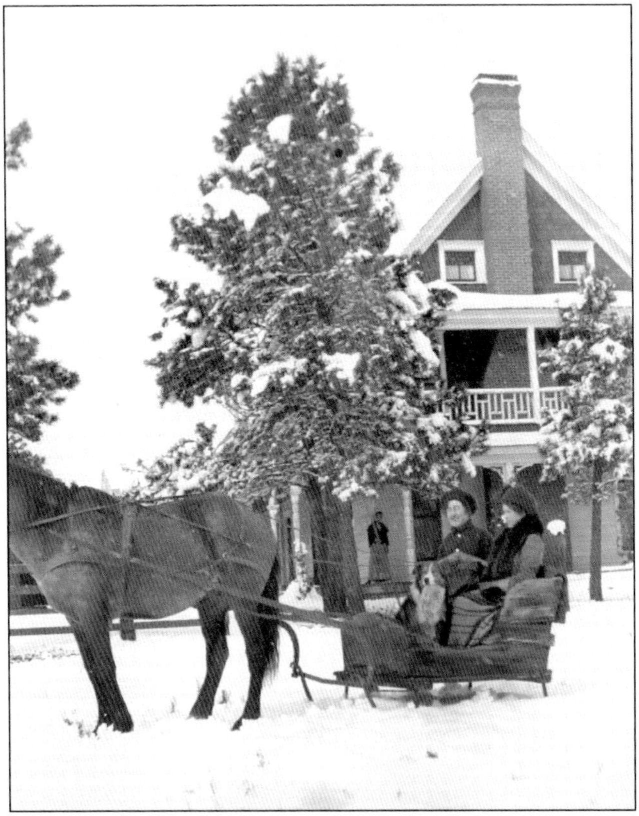

Cold weather didn't stop local residents from enjoying the great outdoors. In Lake George around 1912, two women and their dog enjoy a horse drawn sleigh ride outside the home of Orrin and Ella Battles. Other popular winter activities in Park County included skating, sledding, skiing, and snowshoeing.

Several communities in Park County, including Fairplay, Jefferson, and Como, fielded baseball teams each summer, sparking friendly rivalries between the towns. This is the 1911 team representing Alma.

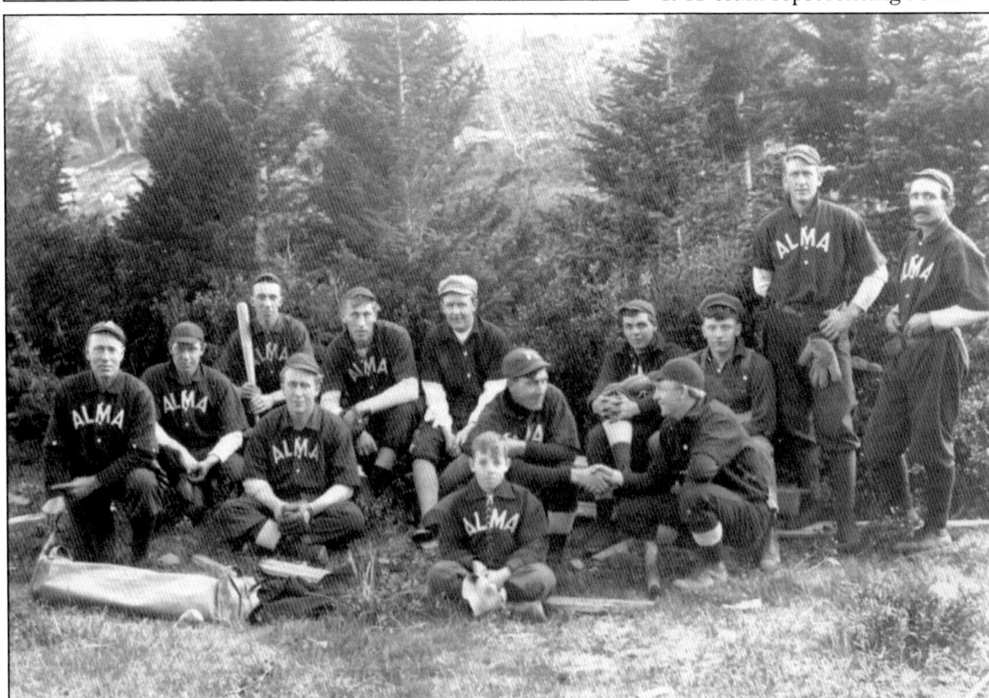

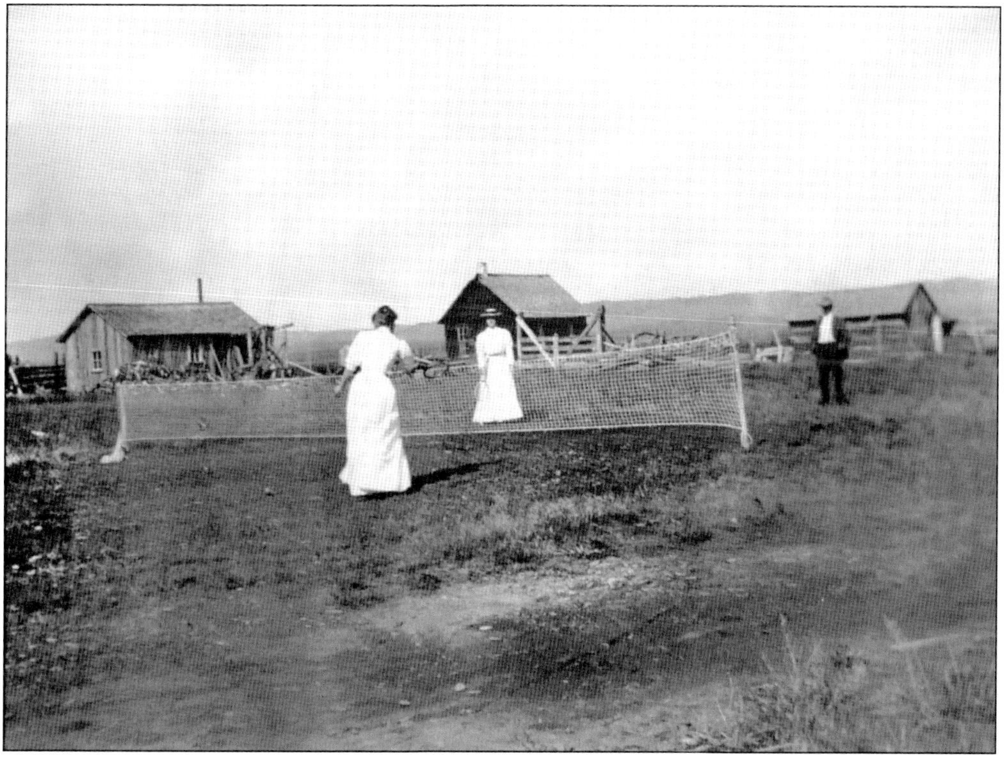

Ranch life had its civilized side, as evidenced by this photograph of Hildur Anderson (far left) and Belle Chalmers playing tennis on the EM Ranch sometime between 1900 and 1910. Belle's father, Harold Chalmers, watches. Located northwest of Hartsel, the EM Ranch was established by Hardy Epperson in 1877 and became part of the Chalmers & Galloway Livestock Company's holdings in 1900. Today, the property is known as the EM Santa Maria Ranch.

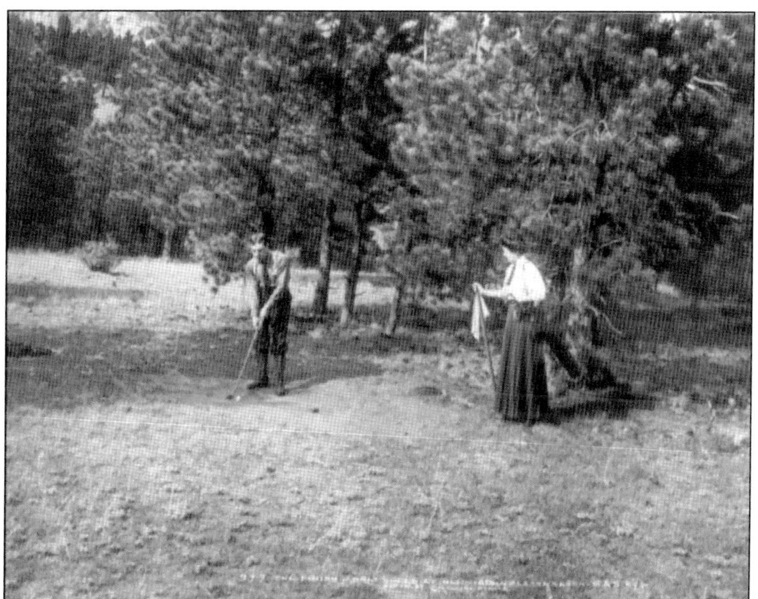

Visitors to the Glen Isle resort lodge play golf in the early 1900s. After the arrival of the railroad in the late 1870s, resorts in the Platte Canyon area offered tourists a relaxing respite from the hot and crowded city.

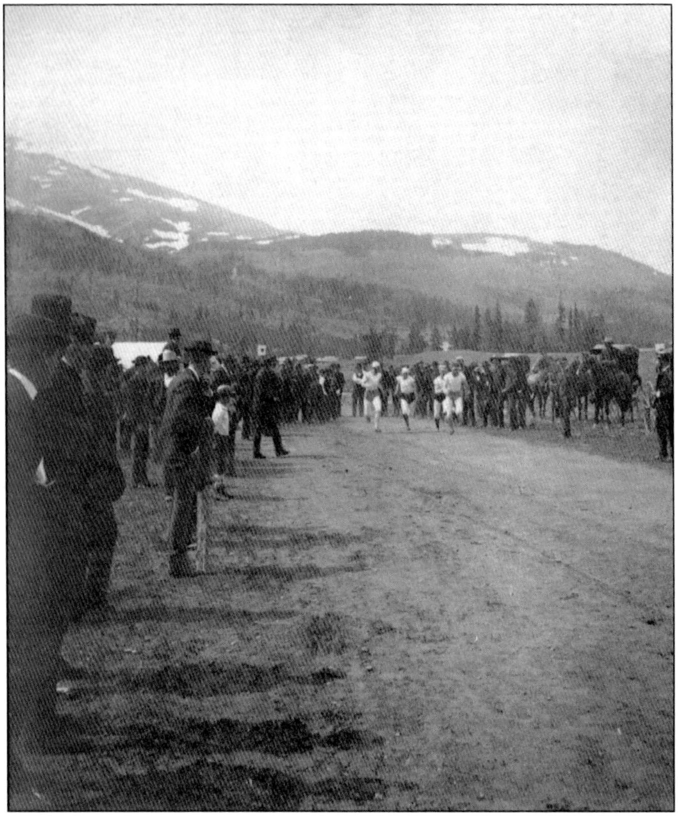

Park County residents enjoyed friendly competitions, like this Fourth of July footrace that took place in Alma in the late 1800s. The tradition lives on in the annual Ed Snell 10K, in which runners and walkers race from Fairplay to Alma for charity.

Ranch hands proved their mettle in local rodeo competitions like this one in Trump, a small South Park ranching community that thrived for a short time in the 1920s and 1930s.

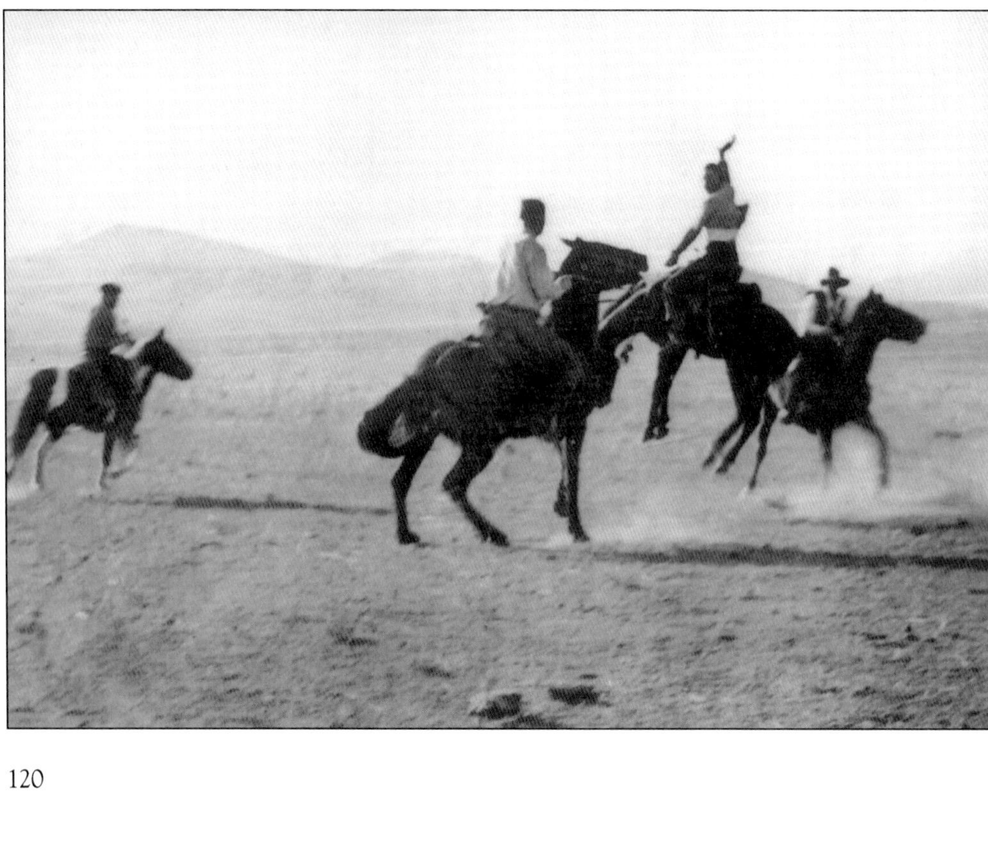

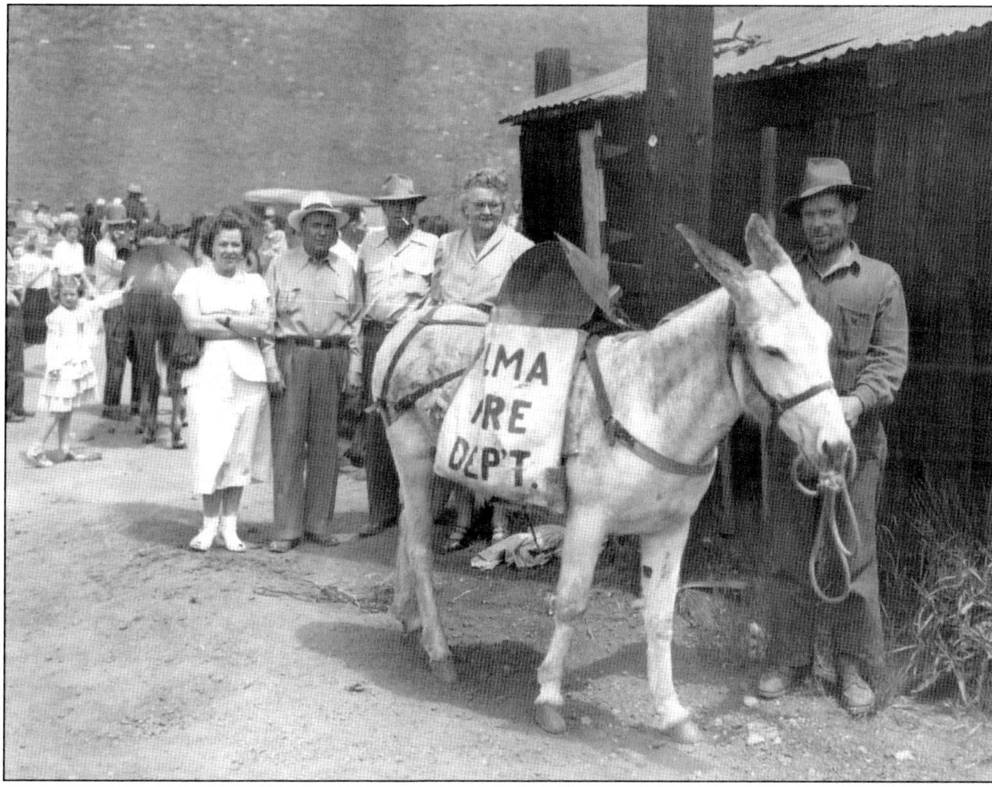

Merchants in Fairplay and Leadville sponsored the first pack burro race on July 30, 1949. For the competition, 21 men and their burros began in Leadville at the Lake County Courthouse and raced across Mosquito Pass to the Prunes Memorial in Fairplay, almost 23 miles away. The race has been held each year since, though the course has changed over the years. In 2012, the Colorado legislature approved a joint resolution designating pack-burro racing as a Colorado summer heritage sport. In the above photograph, spectators at the 1951 race admire the Alma Fire Department's burro. Below, 2014 race participants and their burros run amid the stunning scenery of Mosquito Gulch. (Below, courtesy of Erica Duvic.)

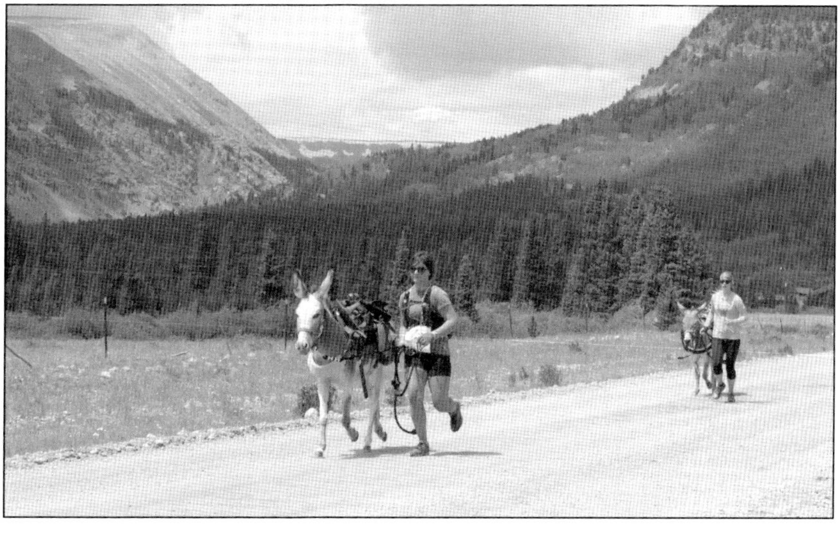

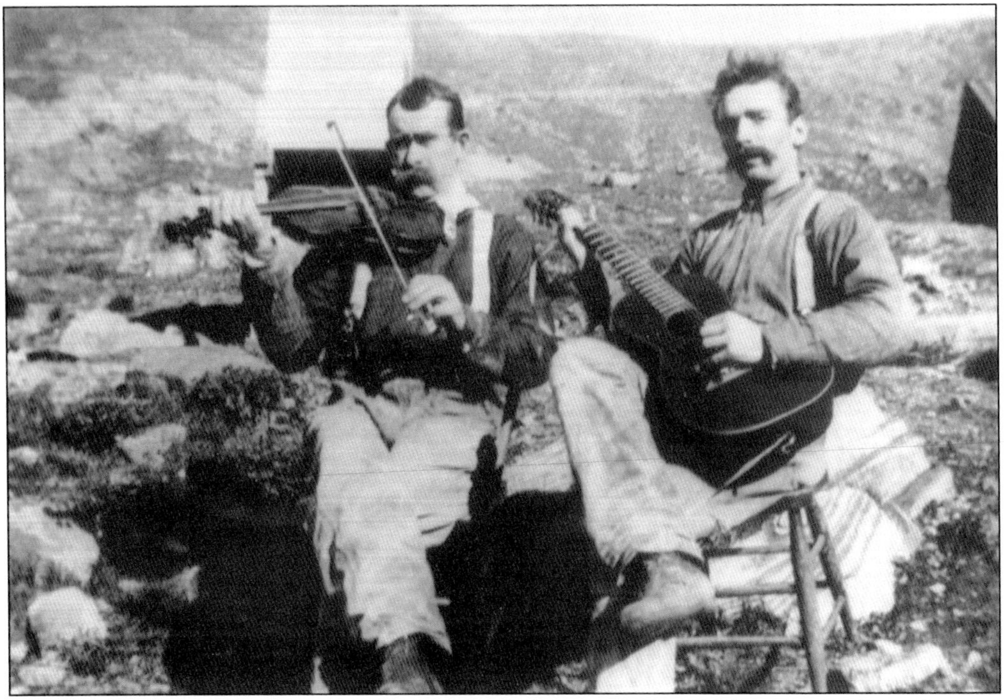

In the early 20th century, two miners at the Whale Mine in Hall Valley play fiddle and guitar. Working the mines, mills, and smelters of Park County was difficult and dangerous work, yet laborers found time to relax and unwind when the day's work was done, often by playing music.

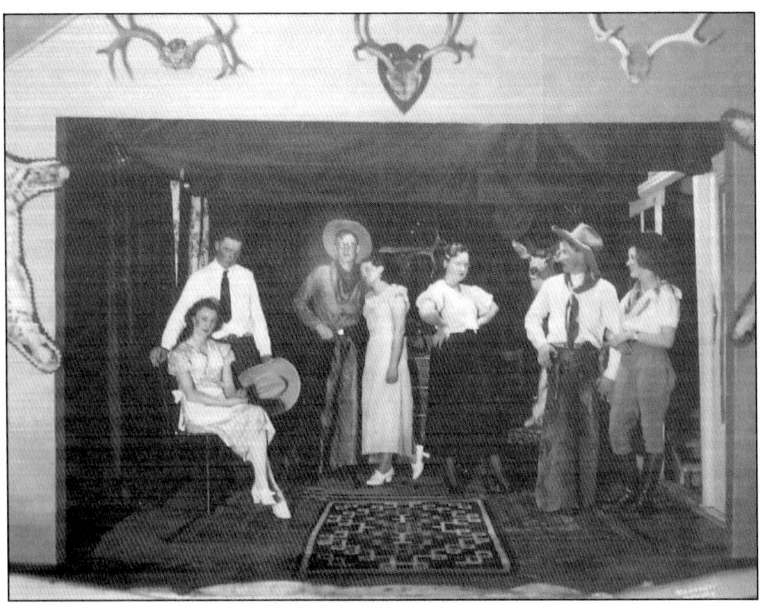

A cast that included locals Fred and Bill Day, Paul Wonder, and Mary Ann Fleming perform a Western-themed play at the Tavern Theater in Bailey in the 1940s. The theater was located on the second floor of the Bailey Country Store, a general store established by Edward and Blanche McGraw in 1878 that still stands today.

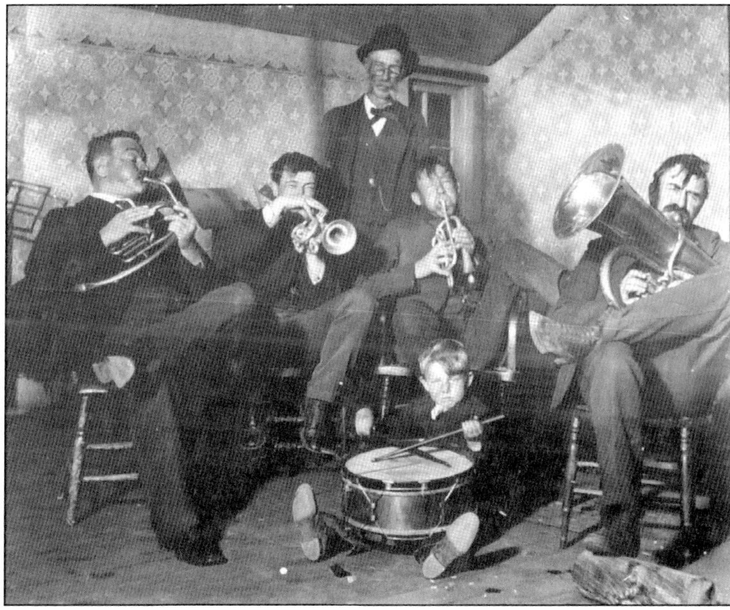

In Fairplay, Gustave Karsch, who also played the violin, plays the tuba with a young Max Heberer on the drum and unidentified bandmates around 1900. Music was an important part of social life in Park County, and many communities supported local bands and orchestras.

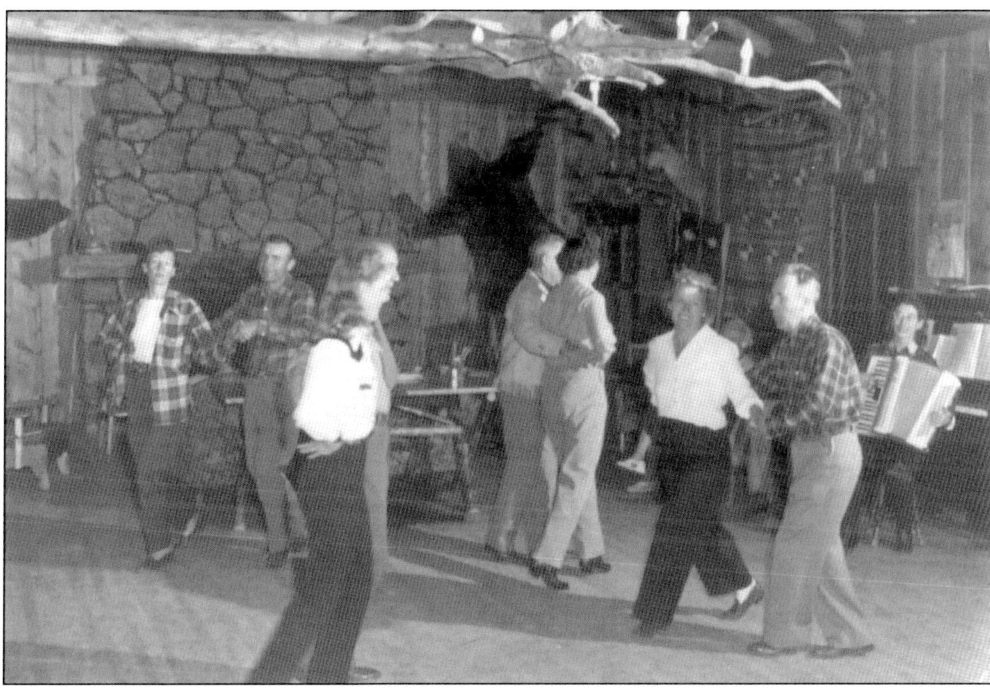

Visitors to the Tarryall River Dude Ranch enjoy a relaxing night of dancing in the ranch's rustic recreation hall in the 1940s.

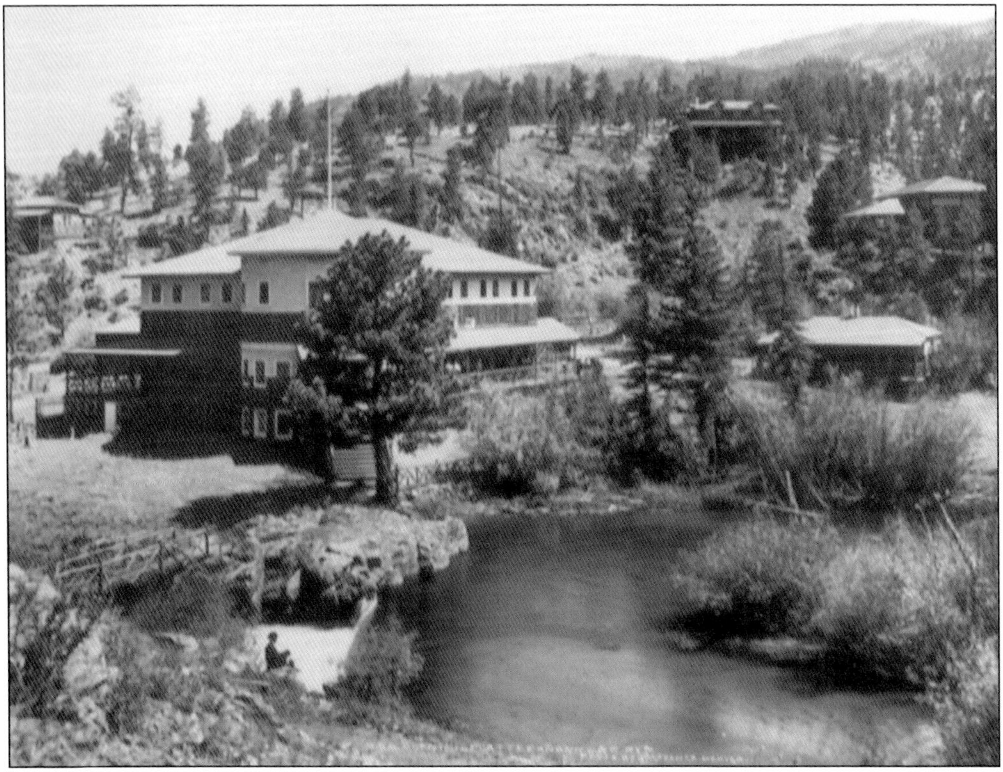

The Glen Isle resort was built near Shawnee in 1901 on a section of the South Platte River known for its exceptional trout fishing. The elegant resort hotel catered to wealthy Denver residents enamored by the rustic mountain lifestyle. The resort was called "one of the most fascinating places in the canyon" and provided a variety of outdoor activities for "people of refinement." Photographed around 1902, the resort included a large rustic-style lodge and 10 summer cottages. Below, two unidentified women relax in one of the cottages on the 160-acre property. After 1924, Arthur and Sarah Belle Baldwin, along with granddaughter Barbara Tripp and her husband, Gordon, operated the Glen Isle as a family-oriented getaway, offering hiking, fishing, riding, square dancing, and chuckwagon dinners, as well as day trips to nearby wilderness areas and historic mining camps.

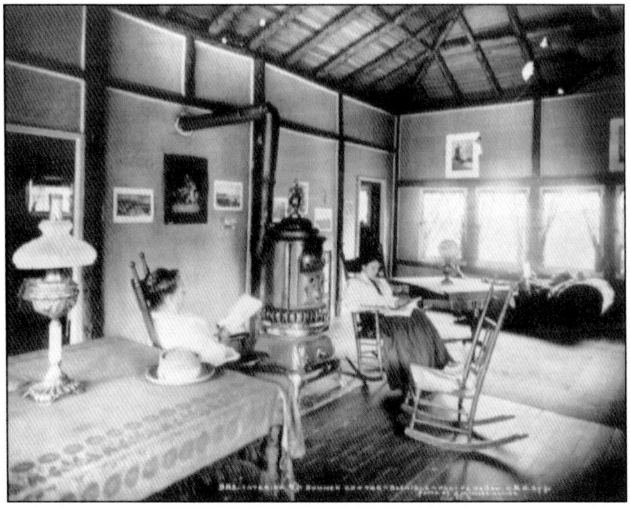

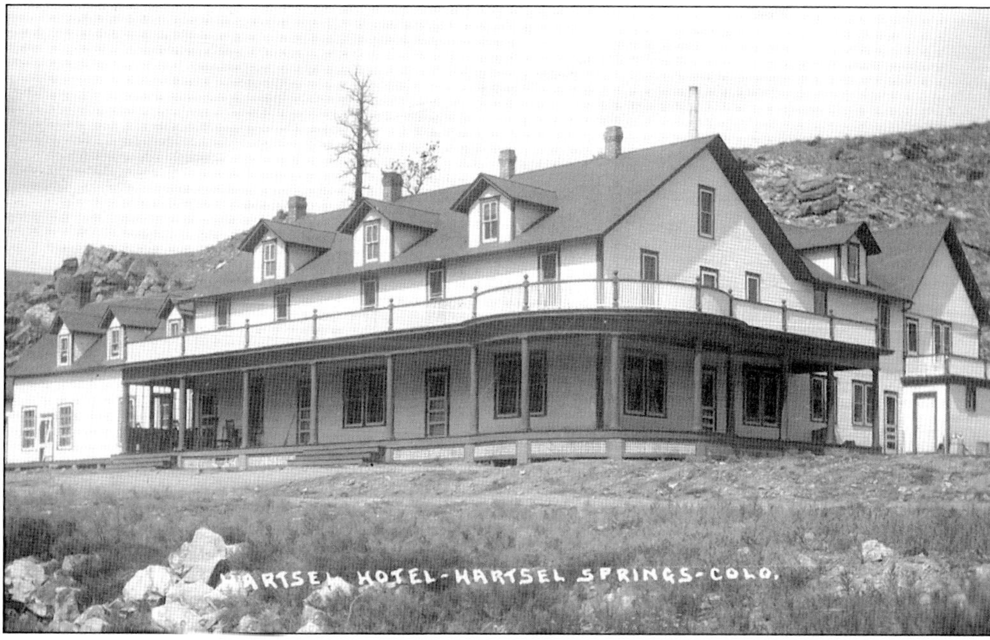

Pioneer rancher Samuel Hartsel established the Hartsel Hotel, pictured here around 1900, in the late 1870s to accommodate tourists seeking the "healing waters" of the nearby natural hot springs. An 1889 Colorado Midland Railway publication touted the beneficial aspects of the springs, stating, "Not a few persons who have come to these springs so badly crippled that they were unable to take a step have gone away walking as straight and firm as an Indian warrior." In 1908, the Hartsel Hot Springs Improvement Company acquired the property and set about expanding the popular hotel. Travelers and locals continued visiting the springs for relaxation and as a curative for health issues well into the mid-20th century. Pictured below visiting the springs in the 1930s are, from left to right, Laura Oakley, Viola Hubler, Victoria Moomey, Vaudeth Weber, Fred Moomey, and Phil Weber.

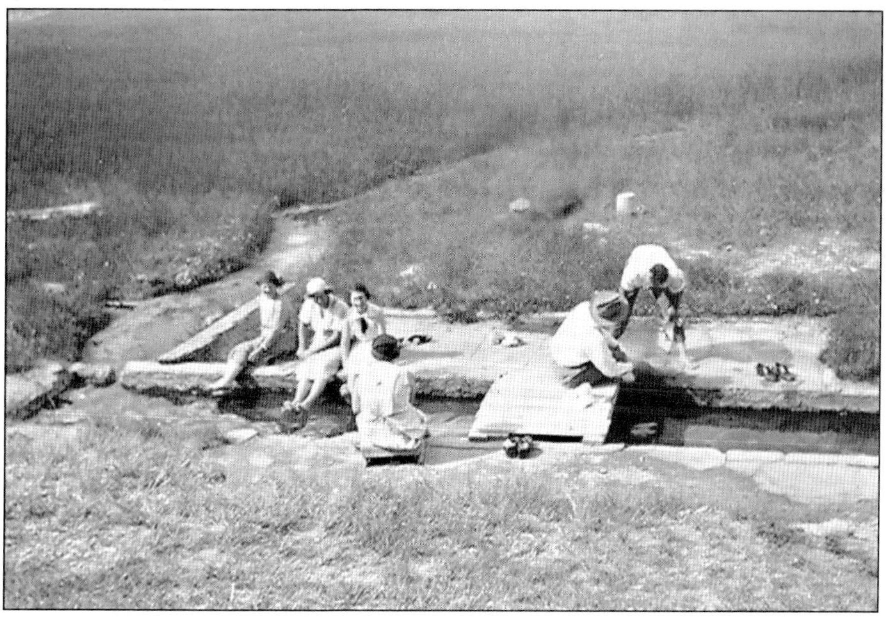

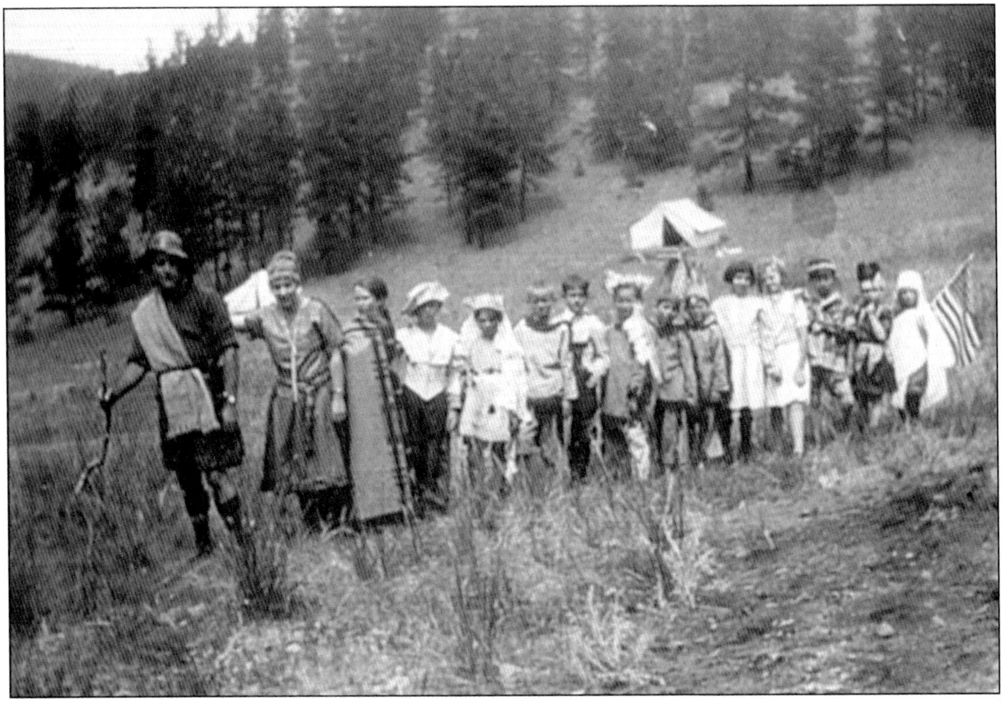

Above, Neighborhood House Camp founders Roy and Marion McGlone pose with costumed campers in the early 1920s. As shown below, the summer camp served underprivileged children and attracted the attention of social workers throughout the country. Roy "Dolly" McGlone, a Denver teacher, and about 10 young boys from west Denver constructed the camp's first cabin in 1920 on 10 acres of land near Bailey, donated by the US Forest Service. The camp consisted of several buildings, including a dining room, recreation hall, and dormitory, 10 cabins, and a laundry, as well as a basketball court, baseball diamond, fishing stream, and hiking trails. The camp later became known as Camp Leslie Deal and continued to operate until the 1960s. The last remaining cabin was moved to McGraw Memorial Park in Bailey in 1992.

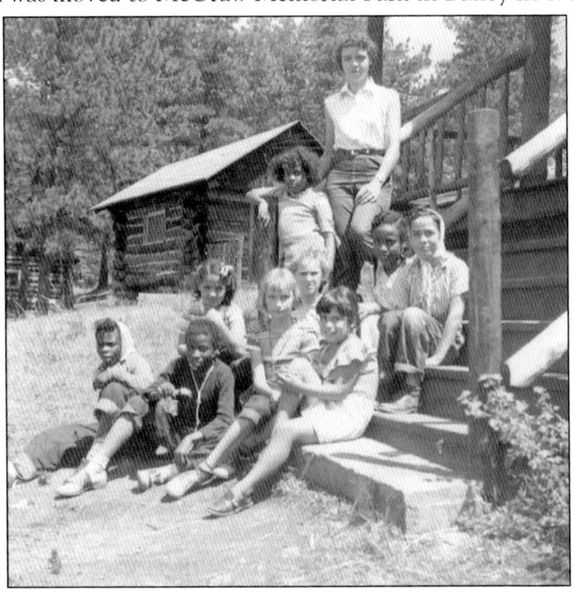

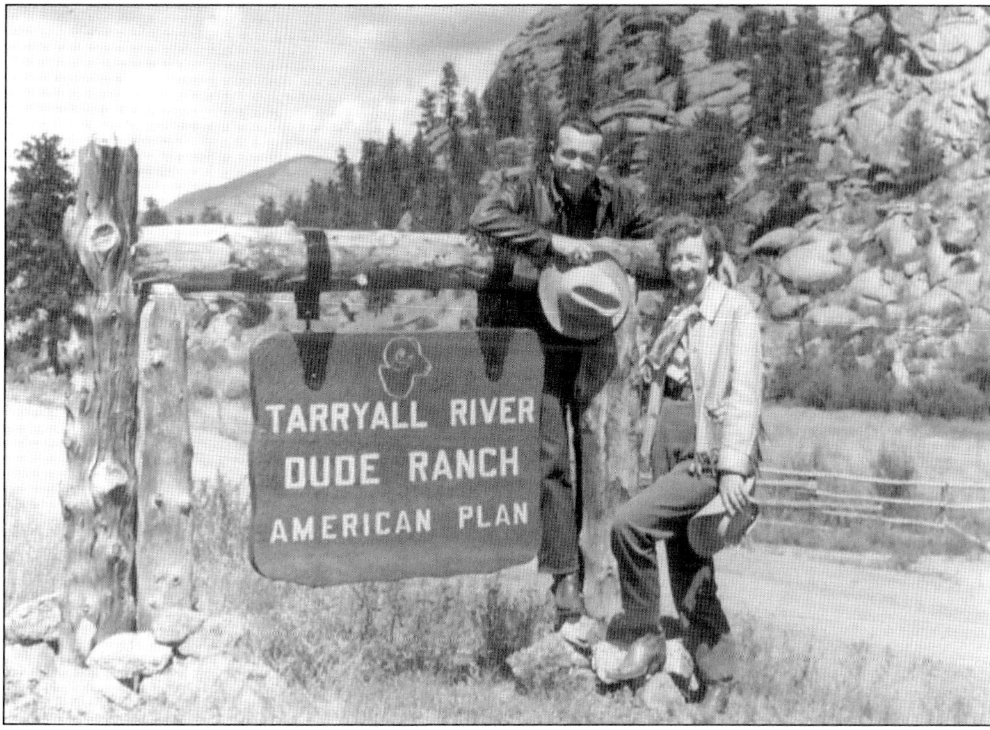

Touted as "one of the most successful dude ranches in the West," the Tarryall River Dude Ranch was established in 1937 by Colorado Springs attorney Leon Snyder. He acquired the former summer retreat from Colorado Springs philanthropist Alice Bemis Taylor and converted it into a dude ranch. Above, an unidentified couple poses at the ranch's entrance sign. The ranch operated under the American Plan, in which per-person rates covered all lodging, meals, and recreational activities, such as horseback riding and fishing. Below, guests at the Tarryall River Dude Ranch enjoy a day of trail riding.

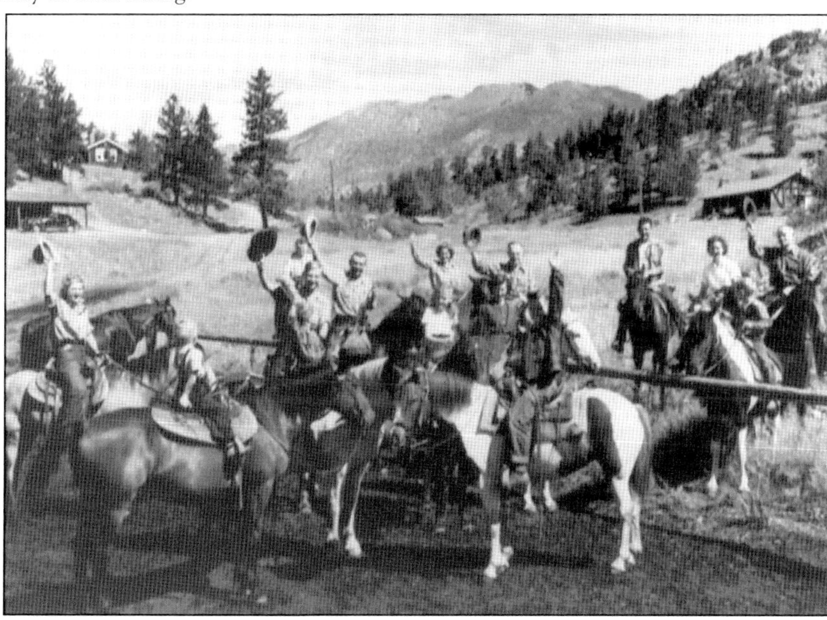

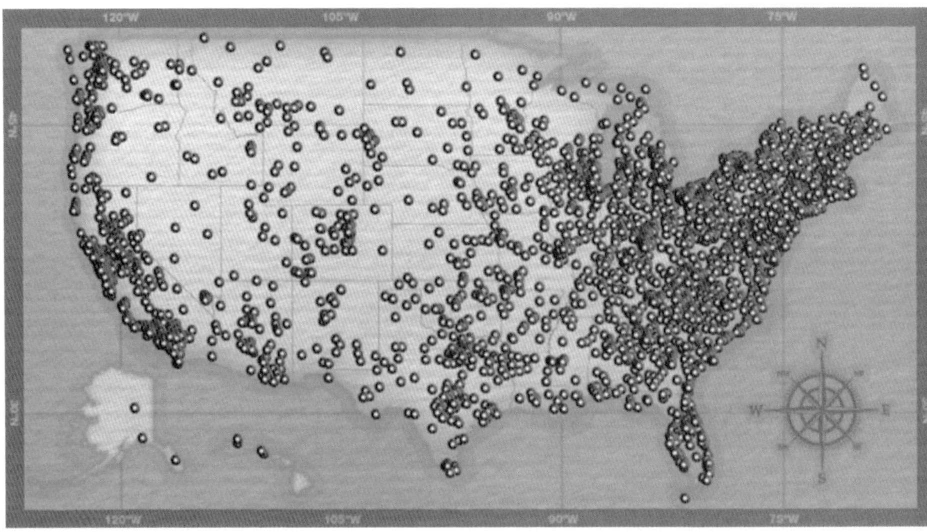